BOOM BOOM

The Life and Times of Bernard Geoffrion

BOOM BOOM

The Life and Times of Bernard Geoffrion

Bernard Geoffrion
Stan Fischler

McGraw-Hill Ryerson Limited

Toronto Montréal New York Auckland Bogotá Caracas Lisbon
London Madrid Mexico Milan New Delhi San Juan
Singapore Sydney Tokyo

Boom Boom: The Life and Times of Bernard Geoffrion

McGray-Hill Ryerson Limited
300 Water Street
Whitby, Ontario L1N 9B6
Canada

1 2 3 4 5 6 7 8 9 0 BBM 6 5 4 3 2 1 0 9 8 7

Canadian Cataloguing in Publication Data
Geoffrion, Bernard
    Boom Boom: the life and times of Bernard Geoffrion

Includes index.
ISBN 0-07-552715-4

1. Geoffrion, Bernard.   2. Hockey players — Canada — Biography.
I. Fischler, Stan. 1932-   . II. Title.

GV848.5.G46A3 1996   796.962'092   C96-931309-8

Publisher: **Joan Homewood**
Editor: **Erin Moore**
Production Coordinator: **Sharon Hudson**
Cover Design: **Dave Hader/Studio Conceptions**
Interior Design/Composition: **Bookman**
Editorial Services: **Ron Edwards**

This book was composed in Impact, Palatino, Giovanni Book using QuarkXPress 3.32

Printed and bound in Canada by Best Book Manufacturers using acid-free and recycled paper.

Front cover photo courtesy of Imperial Oil-Turofsky/Hockey Hall of Fame. Back cover photo courtesy of Bob Fisher © CHC.

Dedication

This book is dedicated to Marlene, my loving wife and best friend.

To our children, Linda, Bob and Danny; and our grandkids, Shane, Mechelle, Joey, Brittney, Nicholas, Blake, Sebastian and Brice. You are so special to us.

Special thanks to Stan and Shirley, who did such a great job of researching and writing the book.

I also wish to thank my editor, Erin Moore, and my copy editor, Ron Edwards, for all their patience. You two are the best.

Special mention to my friend, James Bates, who encouraged me to write my life story.

Boom Boom Geoffrion
Atlanta, Georgia
September 1996

Co-author's Dedication

In 1951, while attending Brooklyn College, I spent many hours at Madison Square Gardens watching New York Rangers home games. I could no more miss an NHL match there than stop breathing. Having realized that I could not be a professional hockey player, I chose to study The Game and write about it for a living. So from opening face-off to the final buzzer I analyzed every nuance of hockey.

One night in 1951 Montreal's glorious Canadiens came to town. The Habs featured a young, crew-cut right winger named Bernard Geoffrion. He wore number five, had a herky-jerky style of skating, and had a weapon the likes of which I had never seen. It was of course the slapshot. Standing at the right point of the Montreal power play, Geoffrion was revolutionizing the sport. While others strained to score with wrist shots and backhanders that reached 40 mph, Bernie was terrorizing goalies with a blast that started with a golf-style backswing and ended with a missile that sometimes cleared 90 mph. I got one look at it and thoroughly understood why they had nicknamed him Boom Boom.

From that point on I became a Boom Boom watcher and fan. But it wasn't until 1995, when Geoffrion and I worked together on SportsChannel's Devils broadcasts, that I got the notion that Boom Boom should do a book. The man could captivate a press room with his vibrant personality: his stories were priceless, and his delivery inimitable. When I suggested that we collaborate, Boom was ambivalent. It wasn't until our mutual pal, James Bates, interceded that Boomer realized it was worth a try.

James deserves a large measure of thanks, along with good friend Allan Turowetz — co-author of *The Lions in Winter* and Jean Béliveau's autobiography — who lent considerable encouragement and helped secure a French-language publisher. And, of course, my wife Shirley, who spent considerable time interviewing the Geoffrions in Georgia and who provided big time editorial help.

Geoffrion plunged into this book with the same enthusiasm as if he was involved in the seventh game of The Stanley Cup finals. His wife, Marlene, and children, Linda, Bob, and Danny, all provided splendid support and contributions to the manuscript.

As both journalist and fan, I still shake my head in giddy wonderment that I was able to collaborate with one of my heroes, who also happens to be a great Hall-of-Famer. Talk about getting the breaks of the game. This was one of the best I ever had. To Boomer and Marlene and their family, I say thanks.

Stan Fischler
New York City
September 1996

A Special Prayer

This prayer has been an inspiration to me throughout my hockey career. I dedicate it to my grandchildren, my treasures, with love from their grandfather.

Dear God,

Help me be a good sport in the game of life. I don't ask for an easy place in the line up. Put me anywhere You need me. I only ask that I can give You 100% of all I have. If all the hard drives seem to come my way, I thank You for the compliment.

Help me remember that You never send a player more trouble than he can handle. Help me, oh Lord, to accept the bad breaks as part of the game and may I always play on the square, no matter what the others do. Help me study the Book so I'll know the rules.

Finally God, if the natural turn of events goes against me and I am benched for sickness or old age, please help me to accept that as part of the game too. Keep me from whimpering or squealing that I was framed or that I got a raw deal. And when I finish the final period, I ask for no laurels. All I want is to believe in my heart that I played as well as I could and that I didn't let You down.

Amen

Contents

Acknowledgements

First and foremost the authors wish to express their heartfelt thanks to their respective wives, Marlene Geoffrion and Shirley Fischler, for their extraordinary help in producing this book.

Marlene was not only an invaluable aide when it came to remembering incidents from yesteryear, but also providing meaningful insights that greatly enhanced the book. She was always helpful and gracious throughout the research, and provided us with an invaluable collection of photos.

Without Shirley there would not have been this book. She worked closely with the authors, did significant interviewing with Boom and Marlene in Marietta, Georgia, and spent endless hours helping to put the manuscript in readable form.

To both spouses we offer a bilingual thanks.

This book never would have materialized without the faith and support of our publisher, Joan Homewood, our splendid editor, Erin Moore, and our meticulous copy editor, Ron Edwards. We are indebted to each of them.

Since Boomer's career spanned generations, across borders, considerable research was necessary. The Fischler Hockey Service team of fact finders did their job admirably pouring through decades of *Hockey News*, magazines and newspaper clippings. Thus a deep bow of thanks goes to head researchers Kerry Gwydir and Ken Lucente, as well as those who uncomplainingly transcribed hours of tapes. These include indefatigable Danny Kasdan, Gary Mignone and Nick Budabin.

Boom Boom and Stan
September 1996

Special People in Our Lives

Marlene and I are lucky enough to have wonderful friends who have enriched our lives together. They will always have a very special place in our hearts.

Dr. Harold Addair, James and Sue Bates, Gerry and Donna Blackmanship, Larry and Rena Boucher, Ernie and Dee Carradori, Ronald and Danièle Correy, Tom and Ann Cousins, Cliff and Boots Fletcher, Emile and Emma Francis, Dr. Robert and Thérèse Gareau, Jean-Paul and Lucette Hamelin, Butch and Mary Ann Hansen, John and Caroline LaBruzzo, Dr. Scott Lampert, James and Betty LaPorte, Jiggs and Marilyn MacDonald, Jim and Penny Nossette, Panos and Paul (our favorite restaurateurs), Dr. René and Pauline Poirier, Dr. Roger and Claire Pontbriand, William and José Putnam, Dr. Marcel and Eileen Remy, Jean and Paula Roy, Dr. Allan Taranto, Dr. Ken Thomas, Allan Turowetz, Ben and Chris Voyles, Bill Voyles, Pastors Dr. Paul Walker and Mark Walker (Mt. Paran Church), Cliff and Sylvia Worsham.

CHAPTER 1

They Love Me; They Hate Me!

It was March 20, 1955. I had just won the National Hockey League scoring championship playing for the Montreal Canadiens and in only my fifth NHL season I had my sights set on my second Stanley Cup. I should have been on top of the world.

But I was returning home from our last regular season road game to face a city full of angry hometown fans. They wanted a Montreal Canadien to win the Art Ross Trophy for most points but they didn't want that player to be Boom Boom Geoffrion. Not by a long shot, a slap shot or even a wrist shot.

The man they wanted to win was my buddy Maurice "The Rocket" Richard.

Richard was also a Canadiens' right winger and the most beloved hockey player in the entire French-speaking province of Quebec. Yet as great a scorer as he was The Rocket had never finished first overall in points. It bothered him that guys like Gordie Howe of Detroit and Buddy O'Connor of New York had won the Art Ross but never Maurice Richard.

A week earlier — leading up to St. Patrick's Day, 1955 — it looked like The Rocket finally would get his wish. We were in Boston to play the Bruins on the next-to-last Sunday of the season and Maurice was sitting right on top of the scoring list with me just behind. On March 13, 1955, Rocket had 38 goals and 36 assists for 74 points and I had 37 goals and 35 assists for 72 points. Jean Béliveau, yet another Canadien, was right behind me with 71.

Like everyone else on our team and many fans even outside Montreal I was pulling for The Rocket to win. He was 33 and didn't figure to have many big years left. *This* was his chance!

But there were a few problems. First of all I wasn't going to go into the tank nohow. Much as I loved The Rocket I also loved scoring goals and setting them up. Second there was the opposition. They may have respected Rocket but they certainly didn't love him. He was too good and too tough.

Cheap shot artists on the other teams were always taking runs at him and many times Rocket went back after them. That season he had already had a run-in with Bob Bailey, a third line forward on the Toronto Maple Leafs, which got Maurice into big trouble with NHL President Clarence Campbell. Plus there were plenty of guys on the Bruins who weren't crazy about him especially after our win against them the previous Saturday night at The Montreal Forum. We had come from behind to beat them 2-1 and Rocket helped set up the winner with 45 seconds left.

Saturday-Sunday home-and-home series could get ugly because grudges developed in the first game and were often settled in the second. We knew we were in for a hard game at Boston Garden but we didn't know it would be *that* hard.

Dickie Moore opened the scoring for us but the Bruins bounced back quickly. By the end of the second period they led 4-1 and had really banged us around. Our coach Dick Irvin was ready to hit the ceiling when we got back into our dressing room. Dick gave us a real pep talk and Rocket got the message maybe a little too well. He couldn't wait to get back on the ice and at those Bruins.

When people ask me what play led to the single greatest riot in hockey history I say it was Rocket trying to score against Boston goalie John Henderson on March 12, 1955.

It all started with a typical Richard rush. He barreled down the right side with the puck and was preparing for his patent left turn swerve toward the Boston net. There was only one player in his way. Boston defenseman Hal Laycoe was tall, wore glasses and had once played with us on Montreal.

As Rocket went around him, Laycoe grabbed him by the waist and held on. Rocket carried him all the way to the corner where Laycoe gave him an elbow to the back of the neck and threw him into the chicken wire at the end of the rink.

Rocket was fuming. He turned around and swung his stick just missing Laycoe. A second later Laycoe swung his stick and hit

Rocket for eight stitches in his scalp. The Rocket swung again and all of a sudden both benches emptied and every player from both teams was on the ice.

Laycoe had stunned Rocket who by now was furious. He went after the defenseman breaking his stick across Laycoe's back. At that point a linesman, Cliff Thompson, who once had been a Boston defenseman, tried to restrain Rocket but wound up on the ice. Rocket was later accused of socking Thompson although I personally didn't see it because I was in the middle of the wild melee that was underway. Richard and Laycoe got thrown out of the game but that was only the start of the troubles.

Naturally the Boston media wanted Rocket's scalp. Some demanded that he be banned for life. Dave Egan of the *Record* was the one exception. He said Laycoe was as much at fault as Rocket and wrote a column headlined, "Ask only justice for Richard vs. NHL."

Richard has still not learned to like or accept defeat. He is still ready to fight the world and I tell you that both for the good of hockey and the good of all sports that this man should be eligible for the play-offs.

Clarence Campbell was president of the NHL at the time and to put it mildly the fans were not fond of him nor was Rocket. He had been on Campbell's carpet many times and earlier in the season Toronto's Conn Smythe had urged Campbell to suspend Richard after the Bailey episode.

On the train ride back home from Boston we all talked about the incident. I liked defenseman Doug Harvey's line: "If I was bleeding from the head like Rocket was and somebody jumped on me like that I would have hit him too."

We all knew that Campbell was going to review the case and that Rocket would be in hot water again although no one realized how hot that water would be.

It turned out to be scalding. Campbell ordered a hearing at his Montreal office. Rocket was there represented by Dick Irvin and Canadiens' vice president Ken Reardon and Laycoe showed up with a contingent from Boston. Everybody said his piece.

Campbell then produced a long report which each of us read avidly. It was a shock:

The facts of the incidents as disclosed by the officials' reports and the witnesses heard indicate that around the 14-minute mark of the third period when Boston were a man short and Canadiens had removed their goalkeeper for a sixth forward, Richard was proceeding just over the Boston blue line. There is some doubt as to who actually had the puck but it was either Laycoe or Richard, and as Richard skated past Laycoe the latter high-sticked Richard on the side of the head. The referee promptly and visibly signaled a penalty to Laycoe but permitted the play to continue as Canadiens were still in possession of the puck.

Richard skated around the back of the Boston goal and back almost to the blue line when the whistle blew. Richard rubbed his hand on his head and indicated to the referee that he had been injured. Suddenly he skated toward Laycoe, who was a short distance away and swinging his stick over his head with both hands he struck Laycoe on the shoulder and face. At the time Laycoe was struck he had dropped his stick and his gloves.

The linesman grabbed the two players and Richard's stick was taken away from him. However, he was able to break away from Linesman Thompson and picking up a loose stick again attacked Laycoe with two one-handed swings striking him over the back and breaking the stick. Again Linesman Thompson got hold of Richard but Richard was able to get away and got another stick and struck Laycoe a third time across the back as he ducked to avoid the blow.

Linesman Thompson again got a hold of Richard and this time forced him to the ice and held him there until a Canadien player pushed him away and Richard gained his feet. When he did so he punched Linesman Thompson two hard blows to the face.

Thompson finally got Richard under control and signaled for the Canadiens' trainer to come and take Richard to the first-aid room where he received four or five stitches on the left side of his head.

The referee reported the penalties to the penalty timekeeper awarding a match penalty to Richard for deliberately injuring Laycoe and a five-minute penalty to Laycoe for high-sticking causing an injury to the head. While at the penalty bench the referee ordered Laycoe to take his place on the penalty bench and when he failed to do so he imposed a further ten-minute misconduct penalty. As he entered the penalty box, Laycoe threw a towel he was using to wipe his face in Udvari's direction striking him on the leg.

Laycoe gave evidence to the effect that in the original contact between him and Richard near the blue line, when the game was in progress, he had been struck a terrific blow on his glasses by Richard's stick to which he immediately and instinctively hit back.

The officials made no reference to this earlier blow and Richard did not know whether he had struck him or not.

It was not denied that all of the blows were struck by Richard and reported by the officials but it was contended that he did not know what he was doing because of the blow he received on the head.

It was contended that when he struck the linesman in the face with his fists he mistook him for one of the Boston players who were milling around the area. This mistake was attributed to the blow and the blood which was coming from his head wound.

Making every allowance for the possible effect which the blow on the head may have caused to Richard for which he might react unconsciously in an effort to strike the person who had injured him, it is conceivable that that might be an immediate and instinctive reaction, but it cannot account for his conduct in persisting in breaking away from the officials, finding other sticks, and renewing the attack twice more.

It is possible that in some cases in a melee at close quarters a player could accidently or mistakenly strike an official who got in the way, but the only person Richard had to contend with when trying to get at Laycoe was the linesman. He had no difficulty locating Laycoe when he was making his attacks. Furthermore, the base color of the Boston uniform is white and the officials' sweaters are a deep orange color.

I have no hesitation in coming to the conclusion on all of the evidence that the attack on Laycoe was not only deliberate but persistent in the face of all authority and that the referee acted with proper judgment in accordance with the rules in awarding the match penalty.

I am also satisfied that Richard did not strike Linesman Thompson as a result of mistake or accident as suggested.

Determining the appropriate penalty to apply in cases of this kind is always difficult. But in this case there has been singularly little conflict in the evidence as to the important relevant facts. Assistance can also be obtained from an incident which occurred less than three months ago in which the pattern of conduct of Richard was almost identical, including his constant resort to the recovery of a stick to pursue his opponent, as well as his flouting of the authority of the officials.

On the previous occasion he was fortunate that the officials and his teammates were more effective in preventing him from doing any injury to anyone and the penalty was more lenient in consequence.

At that time he was warned that there must be no further incidents of that kind and he gave solemn assurance to that effect.

It is very regrettable that in this case the officials and his teammates had not been as successful as in the earlier episode and it is even more regrettable that his teammates did not assist the official instead of interfering with him.

Consequently, the time for probation or leniency is past. Whether this type of conduct is the product of temperamental instability or willful defiance of the authority in the game does not matter. It is a type of conduct which cannot be tolerated in any player, star or otherwise.

Campbell ended with these words:

In the result, Richard will be suspended from all games, both league and play-off, for the balance of the current season.

Elmer Lach, who was Rocket's center for many years on The Punch Line, had the best crack of all. "They always tried to get The Rocket and now they finally have."

I can't begin to tell you how shocked we were. Not just the Canadiens players but the entire City of Montreal was stunned that Campbell would come down so hard on Maurice. We figured he would be suspended for the three remaining games on the schedule. That we could understand and even accept. But to take Rocket away from us for the rest of the season *and* the play-offs was terrible. Before the suspension we had been in first place and had a good chance to win the Stanley Cup. Without Rocket we wouldn't be in such good shape to go all the way.

You should have seen and heard the reaction. It made headlines in every paper and all the radio stations were talking about it. Almost everyone had taken Rocket's side and the more people discussed the suspension the angrier they became, especially French Canadians.

We had never been particularly fond of Campbell and this decision was like a slap in the face not just to hockey fans and Montrealers but to all French Canada. Whether Campbell meant it or not really isn't the point. What mattered was how a lot of people felt. That feeling grew more intense as the St. Patrick's Day game with Detroit approached.

Since we were in a neck and neck homestretch battle with the Red Wings for first place the St. Patrick's Day game would be the most important one of the season. We didn't know what would happen at The Forum once the game started. When I arrived at the rink late that afternoon there were already hints that trouble was brewing. You could smell it in the air and with all the stories in the media the anger kept growing. The big question on everyone's mind was whether Clarence Campbell would show up for the game as he usually did.

Although he had been suspended Rocket was there. He had grabbed a chair from one of our trainers and sat next to the goal judge at the end of the rink. Maurice tried to remain calm and he did until Campbell arrived. Because his office was in Montreal the president had season tickets at The Forum and attended most games usually with his secretary Phyllis King. But this was a different situation and what with all the threats and anger a lot of people, myself included, thought that Campbell would stay away.

He wasn't there when the game started and even though Dick Irvin said we would play our greatest game of the year we were flat. Detroit had us all over the place. Around the middle of the first period Campbell walked in. It seemed that everyone in the building was waiting for this. Pretty soon fans were throwing eggs and tomatoes at the president. He didn't move even when one of them came right up and squeezed a tomato on his head. Others tried to punch and slap him.

The scene was getting out of hand. Police finally arrived to escort Campbell to safety when suddenly a tear gas bomb was tossed in the air. It was intended for Campbell but landed right in front of our manager Frank Selke's box. Then there was pandemonium.

The smoke from that bomb rose all over The Forum and those of us who were on the ice had to stop playing. Over the public address system the fire chief announced that everyone had to leave the arena. The game ended then and there forfeited to Detroit who were leading 4-1 at the time.

The smoke was so thick that I couldn't see across the rink. All the players were worried about our wives. I went looking for Marlene and couldn't see anything. As it happened she and the other Canadiens' wives were taken to the ladies' room.

Dick Irvin took us back to the dressing room while The Forum was being evacuated. There could easily have been a panic and a stampede: more than 13,000 people had to be taken out of the arena. A lot of them were coughing and crying from the tear gas. France O'Brien, the wife of sportswriter Andy O'Brien, was temporarily blinded. Some fans pulled out handkerchiefs and covered their faces. For the most part the crowd was pretty well behaved until they got outside.

A large, angry crowd had gathered outside The Forum and before long were rampaging up and down St. Catherine Street breaking store windows, turning over cars and throwing things at the trams. The police estimated that more than 50 stores were looted. The rioting went on for four hours.

Somebody had brought the burned out shell of the tear gas bomb to the dressing room and showed it to Dick Irvin. He took one look at it and said, "I've often seen The Rocket fill The Forum but this is the first time I've ever seen him empty it!"

Marlene and I escaped through a back door at The Forum, crossed the street and looked for our car. It was scary seeing the mob starting fires and I looked at them and said to myself, "This isn't right."

To this day I lay the blame on Clarence Campbell because under the circumstances he should never have come to the game. He should have waited a few days until the fans had calmed down. But he said, "I am the president of the league and I am going to show that you don't do these things." If he had stayed home nothing would have happened.

Rocket was shaken by the rioting and the next day he went on radio and television pleading for calm. He said, "Listen, stop doing this!" Richard had spoken and they stopped. "I will take my punishment," he added, "and come back next year to help the club and the younger players win the Cup. I want to do what is good for the people of Montreal and my team. So that no further harm will be done I would like to ask everyone to get behind the team and help the boys to win from the Rangers and Detroit."

But the damage had been done to our city and our hockey team. We were in first place before the riot and by the time it was over we were in second. We still had a chance. There were a couple of games left: on Saturday we faced the fifth-place Rangers who we should have been able to beat and on Sunday we would be at Detroit; that would be tough.

This put me and the team in a bind. We had to win the remaining two games to finish first which meant that I had to play my best and try to score goals and set them up for my teammates. On the other hand everyone wanted Rocket to win the scoring title especially now that he had been suspended for the rest of the season. But if I let Maurice win it that meant that I wasn't trying my best for my team.

Marlene said to me, "Boom, that's the first time I've heard you question whether or not to try and score goals." She knew how everyone felt about Rocket. Then she said, "When you get an opportunity you have to take it even though it might mean The Rocket won't win the scoring title."

My teammates knew exactly how I felt. Doug Harvey, who was one of the wisest players in the NHL, pulled me aside before the Rangers game. "Listen," he said to me as serious as I've ever seen Doug. "If you have a chance to score and you deliberately miss the net you and I are going to have a little talk."

Dick Irvin straightened me out once and for all when he said, "Boom, this is a hockey team here. We're going for first place and if you happen to get an assist or two and a goal, well, that's too bad for Rocket."

Maurice didn't say a word to me before the game. He wasn't like that. Rocket knew I had a chance to pass him when he got suspended. Meanwhile there was talk that the Saturday night game might also be canceled. Instead the Fire Department announced that it would man hoses to disperse the crowds if there was a repeat of St. Patrick's night.

Saturday March 19, 1955 was a night I'll never forget. As I took the ice against the Rangers I was still torn between my team and my buddy Rocket. But when the referee dropped the puck at center ice instinct took over and I was the real Boom Boom. Just 68 seconds into the game I set up Floyd Curry who beat Gump Worsley. Less than two minutes later I fed Baldy Mackay and we were up 2-0. In less than two and a half minutes I had two assists and was tied with Rocket.

At 11:34 my center Jean Béliveau slid a pass over to me and I quickly shot the puck toward Worsley. The red light flashed and I was ahead of Rocket. We beat the Rangers 4-2 and headed for Detroit to play our final game. Unfortunately they killed us 6-0 but the good news was that I had won the scoring championship.

Well, it *should* have been my finest hour.

It wasn't.

When we returned home from Detroit by train I wanted to go into hiding. The Montreal fans — my fans — were mad at me because I beat Rocket for the Art Ross Trophy. I heard it in the streets and on radio and television. My sons were harassed by schoolmates and there were threatening phone calls. I had to hire a bodyguard to protect my family until the furor calmed down!

After a while the fans got distracted by the play-offs. After all we were still shooting for the Stanley Cup and beat Boston four games to one in the semifinals. In the finals against Detroit we rallied with a 6-3 win to tie the series at three games each. I scored the winner for my eighth goal of the play-offs. However in the final game at Olympia Stadium we lost 3-1.

Still without Rocket we had done a lot better than expected and by the middle of April when the play-offs ended the anti-Geoffrion feeling had died down quite a bit. I could now do without a bodyguard for my kids but there was nothing I could do about the reputation I had developed as the man who "stole" the scoring championship from Rocket Richard.

Rocket never did win an Art Ross. I wound up winning it twice. But I can assure you that I had more heartbreak in taking the trophies than Richard had in missing them. But that's the story of my life. Every bit of good news seemed to be counterbalanced by something bad.

CHAPTER 2

From the Sidewalks of Montreal to The Forum

I was a Depression baby born February 16, 1931 right in the middle of the hard times and unemployment when everyone was wondering where the next dollar was coming from. I was born in Montreal but it was a different, smaller Montreal. St. Catherine Street, the main downtown thoroughfare, was filled with streetcars which are long gone. The Forum on St. Catherine at the corner of Atwater seemed far from downtown. It was seven years older than me and had only 9,000 seats.

We had two NHL teams in my city at that time. Les Canadiens were largely French Canadians and the Maroons mainly English. I was five the year the Maroons went to the play-offs against the Detroit Red Wings in the opening round.

The first game was the talk of the town and for good reason. It was the longest hockey game ever played starting on the night of March 24, 1936 and ending about 2:30 the following morning. Normie Smith, the Detroit goalie, and Lorne Chabot, in the nets for Montreal, had shutouts going into overtime. They played one, two, three sudden-death periods and still no score.

Wouldn't you know it a third-stringer, a complete unknown named Modere Bruneteau from St. Boniface, Manitoba, won the game for the Red Wings. Jack Adams, the Detroit coach, wanted some speed so he looked down the bench at his exhausted team and realized that "Mud" Bruneteau was fresh; he hadn't played all night. Adams gambled and put him on the ice at the 12-minute mark of the ninth period. Bruneteau got the puck in his zone, passed to Hec Kilrea, took a return pass and shot it past Maroon goalie Chabot. After 116 minutes and 30 seconds of overtime the Red Wings had defeated the Maroons 1-0.

My father told me about it the next morning; I was only five and not allowed to stay up that late listening to the game on the radio. Kids lived a much stricter life during the 1930s but nobody complained about it. My father Jean-Baptiste was a big man — about six foot two and 225 pounds. A great athlete, he would have been a professional baseball player had it not been for a leg injury. Instead he went into the restaurant business and even though the country was in the midst of The Great Depression we made do with what we had. We weren't rich but life was so good we didn't know it.

Our apartment was on the second floor of a house in Drolet east of Montreal. There were three bedrooms, a dining room, a nice kitchen and a parlor. Our house was filled with warmth because my mother Florina and Dad were both good people, very giving, very family oriented. When they celebrated their sixtieth anniversary they were as much in love as they were on their honeymoon.

As far as I was concerned my parents were the best. Whenever I think of my mother special pictures come to mind. When I was a youngster I remember watching her do the washing in winter. The temperature was about twenty below zero and she had to hang the clothes on a line in back of our house. After an hour Mom would walk outside, take all the frozen clothes off the line and bring them in so that she could iron them for us to wear to school the next day. My mother always seemed to be sitting in the parlor sewing somebody's pair of pants.

We were Roman Catholics and my mother would pray for us every day; she wanted us to be something in life. No matter what I did my mother was behind me. If I made a mistake she would correct it but in a nice way. My father and mother were my two best friends.

Our family, like many French Canadian families of that era, was very tightly knit. My father was the patriarch, the monarch, the absolute boss of the household, no questions asked. Each of the kids understood it and respected him as "The Boss."

There were five Geoffrion children altogether and I was the fourth in line with my sister Lucille the "baby" of the entourage. Jean-Paul was the oldest brother and like myself a very funny guy.

Next was my sister Marguerite who we preferred calling Margo. She had the vim, vigor and vitality of the Geoffrion clan, maybe a little more so than the others. Margo was a big help to me in a lot of ways. When I was very young and my parents were busy with other things or other kids Margo would take me down to the local skating rink and babysit me while I took my early strides on the ice. Later on she encouraged me to develop my singing career. That was very nice of her except that the voice teacher and I didn't get along. The voice teacher wanted me to learn how to read notes and all I wanted to do was fake it. Nice try, Margo!

Roland, the third oldest of my siblings, was more of the quiet type. He was an excellent defenseman and could have been a top hockey player on the senior level à la Montreal Royals. Unfortunately his career never developed because he quit hockey in order to help my father with his business.

Lucille was the youngest of our troop and very much like Roland in that she was a bit less vocal but an awfully sweet person.

While some kids in my shoes might have had favorites it wasn't that way with me. I loved every one of my brothers and sisters equally although I didn't see them all that much. After school I'd head out to the rink and skate and shoot and skate and shoot. When I came home Margo and Lucille had their own work to do. But on Friday, Saturday and Sunday all the family would get together.

On Sunday morning we would go to church and then in the afternoon my mother would make the great meal. Her roast beef with sauce, mashed potatoes and vegetable was a work of art. She handled that carving knife the way a surgeon handles a scalpel. The way she sliced it we always had leftovers for Monday and Tuesday.

We said a prayer before every meal to thank the Lord for the food He gave us. As you can imagine the Catholic religion was very big in our house. My mother went to church every morning and from the age of seven to 13 I would leave with her at 6:30 in the morning because I was an altar boy. And since my father was up early every morning to go to work and didn't return home until midnight I naturally was closer to my mom.

My brothers and I got along famously compared to brothers in other families. We might have an argument over something from time to time but never ever did we have a fist fight. Not once.

Pop could have been tougher if he wanted to be. But despite his size he was very soft spoken. He never talked about the bad things, only the good things in life. Being in the restaurant business he was around people all the time and had lots of friends. He loved all people especially children.

One reason I turned out to be the fun-loving person that I am is my roots. Time and again our family would get together and sing and dance. If it wasn't at our house it was at my uncle Maxim's. He was my father's brother and he married my mother's sister Regina. He was my uncle twice over!

Hockey was very important in my house as far back as I could remember. My career began with a pair of double-runner skates when I was four. I call them skates but they really were more like extensions of my shoes and not much help in learning to get around on the ice. For Christmas when I was six there was a brightly colored box sitting under the tree. I had no idea what was in it until I finally opened it. My eyes popped. It was a brand-new pair of Daoust skates.

I wouldn't have been more dazzled by them if they had been the crown jewels. They never left my sight; I even took them to bed with me. They were golden — the greatest gift I ever received. After every skate I would wipe them clean to be sure that not a speck of rust would blemish the shiny silver blades.

Oddly enough skating did not come easy to me, not in the NHL and not when I was a kid. I constantly tell kids not to get discouraged if they don't do well with their first pair of skates. I know. My first time out I fell — a lot. I was horizontal more than I was vertical. But I stuck to it and after a while I got used to the skates and got pretty good.

In those days Montreal had natural ice rinks in every neighborhood. I would play for hours and hours and when I finally got home I would put the skates under the wood stove until they thawed out.

Hockey for kids was a lot different 60 years ago. There were few rinks with artificial ice; the winters were colder and you could depend on natural ice from late November until March. It was nothing for me to go out and play when other people were huddled indoors. I'd be out skating when the temperature was down to fifteen or twenty below zero. No problem. I was so crazy about hitting the puck and skating around that I could have done it until my toes were frostbitten which they nearly were many, many times. If it was snowing, we'd get out the shovels and scrape the ice clean so that we could keep playing.

I didn't care how cold it was because I had a dream that warmed me. I just wanted to be a hockey player. Period. And by the time I was nine I was playing on my first organized team for Immaculate Conception Parish in my neighborhood. Even though I wasn't a good skater they opened their arms and gave me a chance. I never could have been a professional hockey player if it hadn't been for Immaculate Conception and especially Father Robitaille, my first coach.

When I joined Immaculate Conception World War II had just begun and The Great Depression was ending. But even during the worst days I never worried. I had everything I needed: a hockey stick, a pair of skates and a puck. Our neighborhood was very close and warm with families always helping others in need. When we were playing on the outdoor rinks our mothers would run a convoy bringing hot chocolate for all the boys who were playing and freezing.

Like any devoted French Canadian kid I rooted for Les Canadiens when I wasn't actually playing hockey. The Maroons had folded in 1938 and the Canadiens were *the* Montreal team. But in the late 1930s the Habs had a poor team and hardly ever filled The Forum. During the 1939-40 season Montreal finished seventh in the seven-team NHL, winning only ten out of 48 games. Some games drew only a couple thousand people and there was even talk that Les Canadiens might follow the Maroons and pack it in altogether. Everything changed when Dick Irvin left Toronto to coach Montreal. In a couple of years he turned Montreal into a powerhouse. One of the main reasons of course was Rocket Richard.

Rocket was called up to the big team in 1942-43 and fans began filling The Forum. The following year the Canadiens finished first and Rocket had become a star. He played right wing with Elmer Lach at center and Toe Blake on the left. The Punch Line led Montreal to the Stanley Cup in 1943-44, its first since 1931.

I was living, breathing and eating hockey 24 hours a day. When the Canadiens games were on the radio I would listen for every mention of The Rocket. For me nobody could be bigger than Maurice Richard and when he scored the roar of the crowd was music to my ears.

Once I was in high school I made up my mind that I wanted to make a career out of hockey although I knew that it wouldn't be easy. There were so many good players everywhere and it was hard to break into the good junior leagues. I had some good luck. But like everything else that seemed to happen to me, that was almost canceled by some bad luck!

When I was only 14 years old I skipped several grades in school and began playing hockey for College Mount St. Louis. One Saturday we were playing at The Forum in a sort of hockey carnival and I was lucky enough to score five or six goals. The legendary former Canadien Sylvio Mantha was in the stands and came around to see me afterward. He offered me the chance to try out at the Concordia Juniors training camp the next fall. I was excited.

Then came the bad luck. When I went into the dressing room for my first tryout a complete stranger came up to me and said, "No, you're never going to make it!" and proceeded to throw my equipment into the corridor outside. That was it! No tryout. I was crushed.

What I didn't know then was that this fellow was Bob Rochon, the president of the club which would later become the Nationale. Rochon obviously had a problem with me; he just didn't think I had it. What he said really hurt but I wasn't going to give up. The following day I headed back to the arena. I arrived there before anybody else, went into the locker room and got dressed. When the rest of the players arrived Rochon didn't even notice I was there. I can't even begin to tell you the extra pleasure I would get a few years later when I was presented the Calder Trophy as NHL Rookie of the Year by none other than Monsieur Robert Rochon!

Rocket used to train by riding his bicycle and his route often took him past my father's restaurant in Bordeaux, a Montreal suburb. He began dropping by the restaurant and I was there one day when The Rocket happened to stop in. My father introduced me and I said to him, "Mr. Richard, you are my idol. I listen to you on the radio all the time. I am going to work hard and I want to be just like you." He responded by saying, "I hope you make it one day, kid."

What The Rocket didn't know, nor did many other people for that matter, was that I had been working on a shot that would revolutionize hockey. It also would give me the nickname that has stayed with me my entire life. The blast became known as The Slap Shot and the nickname was Boom Boom. The shot developed over many years of experimentation; the nickname came in one night.

First the shot. Its roots go back to my first team in organized hockey, Immaculate Conception. Before and after team practice I'd spend hours working on my own. Instead of coming home from school I would go right to the rink and shoot the puck over and over again. At the time, like all the NHL players, I used only the wrist shot and the backhander but one day an accident occurred that changed hockey history.

I had skated in on goal, released a wrist shot but missed the net. It always upset me when that happened but this time I blew up and began wildly slapping my stick at the puck as if to give it a spanking. I connected and the puck moved so fast it went *through* the net. I couldn't believe it! When I saw the puck come out the other side I thought to myself, "This is something that goalies are going to be afraid of for a long, long time."

But would it work on a second or a third shot? I began trying it. Sure enough it worked. I would bring my stick back in an arc and then — POW! — I'd whack it like a golf ball. I could tell immediately that I had a better and harder shot than anyone else.

Once I knew it could work I decided to try it in a game. The first time I let the puck fly at the opposition goalie he nearly dropped dead from shock. Everyone — my coach, my teammates, the other team — was wondering what was going on. No one had ever seen anything like it. This was brand new, an invention.

Naturally there were plenty of skeptics. Coaches tend to be conservative. The slap shot — remember it didn't even have a name then — was radical. "Forget about it," they said. I told them, "When I get this thing perfected every goalie in hockey is gonna be scared of me."

So I worked and worked on it and once I got into juniors and had the backswing down pat I never used the wrist shot again. Meanwhile more and more people were taking notice of me and my shot. One of them was the popular francophone Montreal sports writer Charlie Boire. Charlie happened to drop around when I was all alone working on my shot in an empty arena.

I had a dozen pucks lined up along the blue line. One by one I would smack them at the net. Some went in and others went wide. When I missed the net there would be a crack of the puck hitting my stick blade and another crack when the rubber bounced off the backboards. To Charlie Boire the twin cracks sounded like *boom* and *boom*. "I'm going to nickname you `Boom Boom,'" said Charlie. It sounded good to me.

And so it was. In 1948-49 I had my first really big year as an amateur player. At the age of 17 I had become a star in the Quebec Junior Hockey League (QJHL) which was loaded with stars at the time. In addition to my team, the Nationale, there were the Quebec Citadelles, Jean Béliveau's team; Montreal Junior Canadiens, Dickie Moore's team; Three Rivers, Mitch Perreault's team; Montreal Royals, Fred "Skippy" Burchell's team; and Verdun Cyclones, Gump Worsley's team.

That year I won the QJHL scoring championship with 52 goals and 34 assists for 86 points. That put me six points ahead of Big Jean Béliveau. The guy who really helped me was Skippy Burchell, a centerman who had helped the Royals win the Memorial Cup the year before. "Burchell was what The Boomer needed," wrote Boire in the *Montreal Star*, "a good center who could figure out the big fellow's style."

Charlie was right but there is another person who deserves plenty of credit — our coach Mickey Hennessy who had the good sense to put Burchell and me on the same line. What made Burchell so good for me was his shiftiness and the fact that he was such a smooth skater. He was easily the best playmaker in the Quebec League at the time.

The difference between Skippy and me was size. At 17 I was already standing five feet ten inches tall and weighed 160 pounds. By comparison Burchell was a little guy (5'6", 145 pounds) and I always felt that that was the reason he never made it big in the National Hockey League.

In one game I scored seven goals and Skippy, always unselfish, set me up for six of them. Not many centermen can make that statement. Between us we were responsible for more than half of Nationale's goals. Unfortunately I was laid low by an appendix attack just before the 1948-49 play-offs and the team just fell apart. We were knocked out by Quebec in four straight games while I was in the hospital.

Now that I had my new nickname and a scoring title I was determined to make an even bigger name for myself in 1950-51. We had a new coach on Nationale, a terrific former player named Pete Morin, and he kept Burchell and me together as linemates. Here's what *The Hockey News* said about us:

> As a team, Geoffrion and Burchell have no equal in the Quebec
> loop. Skippy knows just where and when to put the puck and Geoffrion

knows just when and where to be. They have worked out a lot of trick plays between them and usually can outguess their opponents.

By now I was actually the "property" of the Montreal Canadiens. Back in the days before expansion and the universal draft the NHL had a system based on what they used to call the Form C. Scouts from the NHL teams would come by the juniors and seeing a kid with promise, would talk him into signing a Form C. Voilà! He was now the property of that NHL club. As I recall when I was playing I think every player in the Quebec Junior League had signed a Form C with the Canadiens. This meant that in theory every kid playing in Quebec juniors was the property of Montreal — if they wanted them, that is.

So I was now the property of the Montreal Canadiens. My only question was how long would it take me to be noticed? I hoped it wouldn't be too long. Les Canadiens were reorganizing — getting rid of some of their older players and looking for younger ones. Frank Selke who ran the team threatened to trade any player on the club with the exception of Rocket. Since I knew that I was in the Canadiens' future I kept an eye on them every day and read all the papers.

Early in December 1950 Selke made one of the most important trades in the team's history. He dealt Leo Gravelle to the Detroit Red Wings for Bert Olmstead. Gravelle was one of the fastest skaters in the league which earned him the nickname "Gravelle The Gazelle." Olmstead was a hard-nosed left winger who loved to dig the puck out of the corners. Of course I didn't know it at the time but "Dirtie Bertie," as the other teams called him, would play a huge part in my career.

"I'll trade anyone for someone I think will strengthen the club," said Selke. "Right now I'm trying to secure a French Canadian right winger."

Hey. I was a right winger and French Canadian. The way the Canadiens were going I figured they would give me a shot any day. Sure enough I got the call on a Saturday morning just before Christmas. It was December 16, 1950 and the Canadiens were playing the Rangers at The Forum.

Montreal was in fourth place at the time while New York was sixth and last but they had some good players including goalie Charlie Rayner. The previous Wednesday in New York the Rangers had beaten the Canadiens 3-2 and Selke was furious; it was his club's fifth straight loss. He promoted me and two other amateurs — Jean Béliveau who was playing for Quebec Citadelles and Dick Gamble who was the top scorer in the Quebec Senior League with Quebec Aces.

It was a real panic in Montreal. Selke also called up Hugh Currie, a defenseman from Buffalo, and signed Tommy Manastersky who was better known as a football player for the Montreal Alouettes. All the focus was on Béliveau, the big, handsome, fair-haired boy of the Quebec Junior League. Big Jean was put at center with Rocket on the right and Norm Dussault on the left. My center was Billy Reay, a seasoned veteran who had been in the NHL since 1943 and knew his way around hockey rinks.

I knew most of the fellows on the team because I was a fan and also because I was always at The Forum. Our junior team had played there so often I even knew many of them personally. But now for the first time I would be walking into the Canadiens' dressing room and sitting there and suiting up with the likes of Rocket Richard and Butch Bouchard!

There were 14,158 people in The Forum when I stepped onto the ice and let me tell you I was scared. Who wouldn't be? This was not only *the* big game for me but it also meant a lot in terms of the future of the team, and everyone knew it.

Even though we were on a five-game losing streak there were still plenty of good players in our lineup. Short, chunky Gerry McNeil, in goal, was one of the best. Doug Harvey, Tom Johnson and Bud McPherson were our best defensemen. McPherson was one of the biggest men in the league at six feet three inches and 205 pounds but he didn't use his size to intimidate players. Harvey and Johnson were young and neither had yet hit his peak.

We had some winners among the forwards. Kenny Mosdell, a big center who had broken in with the old New York Americans at the start of World War II, was one of the most underrated players in the NHL. Elmer Lach, the great center of The Punch Line, was still playing although he was in the twilight of his career. Paul Masnick was a promising young scorer.

Once the puck was dropped the butterflies left my stomach in a hurry. It didn't take long for me to realize that I could keep up with the big leaguers although I knew that Béliveau was outshining me. He had several shots on goal in the first period — nine for the whole game — and seemed to get Rocket to skate even faster. Still, neither team scored in the first period.

Charlie Rayner was playing inspired goal for New York but I studied him carefully every chance I could when I was on the bench. Finally just past the four-minute mark of the second period I got on the ice with Billy Reay. He took a pass from Tom Johnson, fed the puck to me and whoopee, it was in the net at 4:51 of the second. My first game; my first NHL goal.

I skated over to the net and grabbed the puck and as I skated back to our bench all of the guys were slapping my back and congratulating me. My first NHL goal wasn't the game winner; New York scored six minutes later and we ended tied 1-1. For one game at least I proved I belonged. Frank Dean of *The Hockey News* predicted, "Geoffrion will be given further chances to show his wares. Both he and Béliveau have tremendous shots."

Selke sent Béliveau and me back to junior hockey where the two of us were in a neck and neck race for the Quebec League scoring title. Big Jean was ahead of me when we both got the call again from Montreal. This time it was January 27, 1951 at home against the Chicago Blackhawks. Montreal was in third place at the time; Chicago was sixth. In goal they had Harry Lumley who had won The Stanley Cup for Detroit in 1950 and up front were some future Hall of Famers such as Bill Mosienko and Doug Bentley. But Chicago didn't have much of a defense and that made things easier for me and Big Jean.

Selke decided to promote Béliveau and me for the second game of our three-game trial only this time he put us on the same line. Wow! What a treat having "Le Gros Bill" — that was his French nickname, Big Bill — dishing velvet passes to me all night. And I handed off a few good ones myself.

As a matter of fact on our first goal I was the one who sent the puck to Big Jean who put it past Lumley at 9:32 of the first. We went up 2-1 early in the second when Béliveau returned the favor and I fired it in at 4:42. We went on to win 4-2. In my second NHL game I had the game winner. Two games, two goals. Not bad for a 20-year-old!

My first taste of the NHL was unbelievably sweet. I thirsted for more and right away. But right after the Chicago win Selke sent Béliveau and me back to the juniors where we resumed our personal race for the scoring championship. I took over the goal-scoring lead and was over 50 when *it* finally happened.

The date is forever etched in my mind. It was February 14, 1951, St. Valentine's Day, and the trading deadline for the 1950-51 season. Selke still was concerned that his Canadiens might miss the play-offs again. Two straight play-off misses would have been considered sinful in Montreal and Selke knew he was on the hot seat.

Only a couple of hours before the deadline Selke dropped the bomb. He traded defenseman Hal Laycoe, who was later involved in the Richard Riot, to Boston and in a complicated series of moves wound up adding three promising forwards: Bobby Dawes, Paul Meger and me.

I got the call from The Boss before the deadline and went to his office where he laid out the three-year offer. Quite frankly I would have played for nothing. That's how desperate I was to play in the National Hockey League. Who cared about money? Being in the NHL was the greatest thing in the world.

But there was a catch to my contract. I would play the last 18 games of the 1950-51 season and then start as a regular the next year. The reason? The Calder Trophy for rookie of the year was given to players who had skated in 20 or more games. Thus by limiting me to 18 games I would be eligible to win it the following season.

But that was in the future. My main concern now was helping Montreal make the play-offs and playing the best I could alongside my idol The Rocket. In the back of my mind was the thought that maybe sometime down the line I could be as devoutly worshipped by the hometown fans as Richard was by every Montrealer. And if I had any doubts about how intensely the Quebecois cared about Maurice they were resolved less than a week after I had signed my pro contract with Selke.

It was February 17, 1951 and the City of Montreal had declared it Maurice Richard Day. That night between the first and second periods of our game with Detroit, Rocket was honored at center ice before a crowd of 15,780 screaming fans. As I gaped from the sidelines Maurice was showered with gifts including a brand-new DeSoto sedan with license plate number nine, the same number Rocket had on the back of his uniform.

What came through to me was the absolute adulation of the man even from politicians such as Quebec Premier Maurice Duplessis and Montreal Mayor Camillien Houde. The mayor's speech was short, sweet and to the point. "On the ice he is a fine player and off the ice he is a fine family man whom all Canada can be proud of. I can add no more to that."

I was to learn over the years sharing a dressing room with Rocket that the mayor was right on. But what shocked me most of all was what happened as ushers rolled up the mats from the ice. At that point Sid Abel, captain of our hated Detroit enemies, led the Red Wings' starting lineup across the ice. Abel, Ted Lindsay — who Rocket hated most of all — Red Kelly, Leo Reise, Gordie Howe and Terry Sawchuk each in turn shook hands with Maurice.

Rocket tried to make the night a perfect success by scoring the game's first goal. Not to be outdone Howe came up with a beauty of his own which turned out to be the winner in a 2-1 decision for Detroit. Knowing Rocket I am sure he would have traded in all those gifts for a Montreal win.

We were still touch and go for a play-off berth down the home-stretch of 1950-51. By early March the Rangers had surged ahead dropping us into fifth place and out of a playoff spot. Everybody was feeling the pressure, especially Rocket. On Saturday March 3, 1951 we had another bitter game with Detroit at The Forum.

Kenny Mosdell gave us an early one-goal lead but Howe got one right back and Detroit went ahead in the third period. Meanwhile the Red Wings were going out of their way to get Rocket. At one point he swerved in on goal and wound up in a pileup outside the crease. I could see him gritting his teeth with rage as he skated after the referee Hugh McLean.

Rocket was yelling for a Detroit penalty. Sid Abel had grabbed him by the neck and nearly twisted his head off. Instead McLean sent Richard off with a misconduct. Rocket was livid and even more so because he said, "McLean laughed in my face when I asked him why he didn't call a penalty."

As Maurice skated to the penalty box Leo Reise began needling him: "Rocket, you can't take it!" That did it. Richard swung at the Detroit defenseman and this time McLean tacked on a game mis-conduct. Rocket went straight to the Forum clinic where our trainer Bill Head stitched up a cut on the bridge of his nose. When he came back on the ice and skated toward the bench another argument began. This time linesman Ed Mepham grabbed Richard's stick and Rocket let him have two short jabs on the chin before turning around and heading to the dressing room.

As he went past me I could tell that Rocket was so livid he might have put his stick through me if I had said a word. Even worse, we lost the game. On the long train ride to New York for a big game with the Rangers who we still were trying to catch, Rocket didn't sleep a wink.

In Manhattan we headed straight to our New York headquarters, the Picadilly Hotel. Rocket was still complaining about Referee McLean when he walked through the revolving door and saw his nemesis standing in the hotel lobby next to Linesman Jim Primeau. Rocket started complaining about the incident from the night before and then grabbed McLean by the throat while cursing him up, down and sideways. Luckily Paul Raymond, the Canadiens' treasurer, and our publicity man Camil DesRoches were close to the scene. They moved in and separated the two but the damage had been done. NHL President Clarence Campbell ordered a hearing and slapped Rocket with a $500 fine.

We were lucky that Rocket didn't get suspended because we needed every bit of help we could get if we were going to catch the Rangers. Two weeks before the end of the season we were still behind them but two things were happening. New York was starting to lose and we were starting to win — and Boom Boom the rookie was right in the midst of one of the most exciting races for a play-off berth in a long time.

On Saturday March 10 we killed Chicago 12-2 — I got the winning goal — while the Rangers lost a 3-2 heartbreaker to Detroit. The next night we were at Madison Square Garden for what would have to be considered the game of the year for us. If we lost we would have been dead meat as far as a play-off berth was concerned. If we won or even tied we'd stay alive with every possibility that the Rangers would choke in the final week.

Elmer Lach staked us to a one-goal lead in the first but the Rangers answered with four straight. I scored midway through the second to tighten the score at 4-2. Early in the third Don Raleigh made it 5-2 for the Rangers and we seemed out of it. Then a hockey miracle happened. In the middle of the last period Tom Johnson put a shot past second-string Ranger goalie Emile Francis. That made it 5-3 but we still looked like sure losers. There were only about 70 seconds remaining when an absolutely crazy thing happened.

For this game only Irvin had added a guy named Claude Robert to our lineup. Robert never played another NHL game in his life but on this night, in the waning seconds of the game, Glen Harmon fed Robert a pass inside the Rangers' blue line. As he was falling Robert took a desperate swipe at the puck and somehow drove it past Francis.

Now we were only behind by one with a minute left. Off the center ice face-off we sent the puck into their zone and got a face-off there. Irvin pulled the goalie and sent out an extra forward. Rangers tried to clear but Butch Bouchard trapped the puck at the left point.

Butch let one go that flew toward the net. It seemed to me to be one of the easiest shots in the world to stop and Francis saw it all the way. Emile, who one day would hire me to coach the Rangers, was a very good baseball player but he would have earned an error on this play. He reached for the puck only to see it bounce off his glove and into the net.

The game ended in a 5-5 tie but it was like a victory for us. We knew the Rangers were absolutely demoralized after blowing the three-goal third period lead and if there was any doubt it was erased on March 15 at The Forum. That was the night I proved to myself that I could handle pressure even though I was a green rookie.

New York had a two-goal lead twice but I led the comeback and wound up with two goals and an assist. We beat them 5-3 and guaranteed ourselves the play-off berth we once thought was never going to be. We finished third behind Toronto and ahead of Boston which meant that first-place Detroit would be our opponents in the opening play-off round for The Stanley Cup.

What an experience it was for a kid like me. The first game went into four overtimes before Rocket beat Terry Sawchuk and the second game went to three overtimes. Who else but Rocket scored the winner again! I was getting a lesson in clutch playing.

Detroit rebounded to tie the series at two games apiece but in the decisive fifth game at Olympia Stadium we came out on top 5-2. I shot the winning goal late in the second period on a pass from Paul Masnick. That sent us back home where we wrapped up the series 4-2 for one of the biggest upsets in NHL history.

In the other series Toronto whipped Boston which meant that we would meet the Maple Leafs in the finals. I had played less than half a season in the NHL and already I was competing for The Stanley Cup.

This was an interesting series because our coach Irvin had once coached Toronto and had absolutely no love for the Leafs. The more I played for him the more I realized that Dick was a piece of work. He had been a terrific player before suffering a career-ending injury and then became an NHL coach in Chicago. Some people compared him to the legendary Notre Dame football coach Knute Rockne and for good reason. Rockne and Irvin had been close friends. In fact Dick liked to tell us how he met Rockne during the 1929-30 season when he coached Chicago:

> *Tom Shaughnessy was manager of the Blackhawks that year which was a break for me. Tom was a big likeable fellow and a graduate of Notre Dame University. He was also a friend of Knute Rockne, the great football coach, and he arranged with Rockne to let us do our preseason training on the Notre Dame campus at South Bend.*
>
> *We did our calisthenics and running on a corner of the campus before football practice. Then I'd wait around to see the practice which gave me a chance to watch and study Rockne's methods.*
>
> *Rockne was suffering from a leg infection that fall. He was so crippled by phlebitis that he couldn't walk and he sat in a motor car near one of the sidelines directing the practice through a loudspeaker. He had a brusque and commanding voice and was a great believer in discipline. He was also a stickler for perfection and was a man of infinite patience but he could laugh too.*
>
> *I remember one occasion when he was watching the first team in a practice game against the freshman team. At one point he stopped the game and called over Hunk Anderson, his line coach, and told him to give the ball to the first team and run off certain plays. The freshman team stopped the first team cold. At first Rockne was mystified, then worried, and finally he called over both teams and began to bawl out the first team with fine sarcasm. One of the freshman laughed and Rockne broke off and demanded to know what he was laughing about.*
>
> *"You forgot that you were sitting right there before the amplifier when you told Hunk Anderson what plays to use, sir," the freshman explained. "We knew what was coming every time."*
>
> *Rockne himself led the laugh that followed. It was a relief to him to know that the fault wasn't with plays or with the first team, as he must have suspected.*

Rockne made a big impression on Irvin which explains why Dick became the fiery coach that he was with us. He patterned himself after the Notre Dame legend and used the same sarcasm on us in the dressing room that Rockne did with his football team.

Like Rockne Dick had the knack of coming right to the point. He once explained his whole theory on hockey by saying, "As long as they play this game on skates, you have to be able to skate to win." And when he brought up the bunch of young guys like myself and Bob Dawes, he said, "The way they're playing the game today I'll take a young pair of legs over an old head every time."

Irvin used a lot of expressions that nobody had ever heard from any other coach in the NHL or elsewhere. Instead of complaining that "the breaks went against us" after a loss Dick would say, "We were beaten by the unseen hand."

He was very sharp especially when other coaches would needle him. Once the Red Wings manager Jack Adams tried to put him down: "That Irvin has the first nickel he ever made in hockey. He even washes his own socks on the road." Dick wasted no time with the comeback: "At least I wash mine. Adams wears his until they drop off."

Dick was the only coach I ever met whose hobby was raising pigeons. He would tell us that he learned about people by studying his birds. He even used the pigeons to help his coaching. "Every pigeon I own reminds me of a certain hockey player," he said. "One will fly a little way and come back huffing and puffing. Another will fly a long way straight and fast and will arrive without causing a stir. Others you can't even get to move. They're more human than humans."

Dick didn't smoke or drink and didn't eat candy either. But he loved walnuts and would carry bags of them in his overcoat pocket. Whenever we got into pressure situations in games he would reach for his pocket and pop one into his mouth to relieve the tension.

Dick had plenty of tension to cope with once we reached The Stanley Cup finals against Toronto. The Maple Leafs had beaten Boston in a five-game opening round series and still had a nucleus of players who had won three straight Stanley Cups from 1947 through 1949. We knew they were going to be tough and sure enough they won the first game at Maple Leaf Gardens 3-2 when Sid Smith scored early in the first overtime. We came back in the second game and tied the series, also in overtime, and Rocket came through for us again. He tore down the right side, faked goalie Turk Broda onto his stomach and backhanded the puck into the empty net.

Incredibly every single one of the games went into sudden-death overtime and that killed us. The Leafs bounced back in Game Three when Ted Kennedy beat Gerry McNeil early in the first overtime and then Harry Watson killed us in the next game. We thought we had them in Game Five. Paul Meger had given us a 3-2 lead early in the third period and we held them off until the final minute. With 32 seconds left Toronto tied it and won in sudden-death on a shot by defenseman Bill Barilko.

The guy I felt sorry for was the fellow he beat, Gerry McNeil. He had done a terrific job in goal for us. In 11 play-off games he didn't have a bad one. Even in the last one that we lost to Toronto he was outstanding and the fans at Maple Leaf Gardens knew it because they gave him many ovations. In the dressing room after we were beaten Gerry sat in front of his stall crying.

I was just as sad because I didn't do more to help our club. I finished the play-offs with only one goal and one assist. Other than that I had nothing to complain about. I had made the big team and had nothing but great days ahead of me. Meanwhile my junior competitor Jean Béliveau was still in Quebec City, a long way from the National Hockey League.

He had a good deal there making a ton of money on the side working as a public relations man for a local dairy and other things. The Montreal Canadiens badly wanted Big Jean to turn pro with them and I knew that if he did we would play on the same line together which would be great for both of us. I knew that if he got a fair chance at training camp in September 1951 we could make some beautiful music together.

CHAPTER 3

The Calder Trophy and the Girl of My Dreams

During the summer of 1951 a little thing happened which would affect the rest of my life although I had no idea at the time. The *Montreal Standard* magazine had sent a reporter to Lake Placid that summer to cover the Junior Championships of Montreal. While there this reporter found a group of figure skaters also down there training and wrote an article about them.

I noticed the piece for two reasons: for one thing one of the young women featured in the article was a real beauty; for another she was the daughter of one of the Canadiens' legendary superstars Howie Morenz. This girl, whose name was Marlene, had been only three when her father died and I don't think she had even been to an NHL game. But somehow she had taken up skating and had even won a silver medal from the Canadian Figure Skating Association.

I was so struck by her that I asked whether anybody knew this lovely *jeune fille* named Marlene. It didn't seem that we'd ever meet though. I was off to training camp and it appeared that she was destined to become a star of the Ice Follies or maybe the Ice Capades. It turned out though that we would meet before hockey season began.

Right at the corner of St. Catherine and Atwater Streets there used to be a coffee shop and I would go there nearly every day after practice. One day there were two young women standing at the counter when I went to pay for my coffee. One of them was blond and beautiful — the girl I had seen in the *Montreal Standard* article. As she went to settle her bill I tried in my terrible English to say that I would pay. "Thank you very much; I can pay my own way!" she said firmly.

It wasn't long after that I happened to be at The Forum but not to play a game. But I'll let Marlene tell you that part of our story:

> *I was taking part in a Catholic High School ice carnival at The Forum in September 1951 when just before I was to begin my routine, they introduced some of the young, about-to-become-star players of the Montreal Canadiens hockey team.*
>
> *I looked over at these fellows and one of them, with the most blazing blue eyes I had ever seen, was staring right at me. The whole time they were making the announcements I could feel him looking at me. I thought he was pretty arrogant and had no recollection of ever having seen him before.*
>
> *Then they announced my routine and I skated out. I have to admit that I skated deliberately in front of this cheeky guy who had been staring at me. I was going to show him some real skating!*
>
> *Unfortunately during the announcements some of the audience had thrown things on the ice including lids to those little ice cream cups they sold at The Forum and as I got to about the halfway point in my routine, I skated over one of the lids and wham! I fell flat on my derriere and skidded to a stop right in front of him. When I could stand to open my eyes after this humiliation I looked up and he was laughing.*
>
> *I was furious. But they cleaned the ice and then I did my routine perfectly. I was still fuming later when my brother Howie Morenz Jr. came up to me in the hallway outside the dressing room and said, "Sis, I'd like you to meet a buddy of mine. This is Boom Boom Geoffrion and he's going to be a big star someday." I was still miffed so I snapped right back, "Boo Boo Who?"*
>
> *He hardly spoke a word of English although he could understand it fine but he tried to make amends and apologized for laughing at me and within minutes we were all laughing together.*
>
> *Boom asked through my brother the interpreter if he could call me and I said okay. It was only a few nights later when he called and asked me out to an event at The Forum the next Monday night. Imagine my shock when it turned out that he was taking me to a boxing match! I started to have serious second thoughts about going out with this fellow again but on the way home he was so sweet and so*

*charming that he won me over. We began seeing each other steadily
— as steadily as you could when your beau was playing big league
hockey which wasn't much. . . .*

When I arrived at training camp in September 1951 I still could-
n't believe I was a member of the Montreal Canadiens and playing
alongside The Rocket. Even though we hadn't won The Stanley Cup
I could tell that we had a good team that was only going to get better because good kids were being added to the lineup.

But what was so terrific for me was the manner in which I was
welcomed by the veterans. On some teams the rookies were given
a hard time but that never happened to me. Guys like Butch
Bouchard, Elmer Lach and Rocket were a big help even in those
pressure-packed nights of the homestretch when we beat New
York out for a play-off berth.

I got to see firsthand what makes a team tick and it isn't just superstars like Richard. The foot soldiers are just as important and we had
one who was an example to everyone. Like myself Floyd Curry was
a right winger but unlike me he had been around for a while and
played an entirely different game. Curry was a first-class digger.

Frank Selke was right on when he said:

*Players like Curry never attain stardom and don't get the pub-
licity but they are essential to us. They're the workhorses and it's a
nice feeling for Dick Irvin to look down the bench and know that a
guy like Floyd is there to check and kill penalties.*

Curry did have one thing in common with Bouchard, Richard
and myself — he had a neat nickname. Everyone called him
"Busher" and it was a nickname that stuck throughout his career.
Lloyd McGowan, who covered hockey for the *Montreal Star*, said
Curry reminded him of Hall of Famer Busher Jackson who starred
for the Maple Leafs during the 1930s. "Floyd skated fast, just like
Jackson," said McGowan, "and his shoulders moved in the same
fashion as Jackson, so I called him Busher."

Busher played on a line with Ken Mosdell and Cal MacKay who
also had a wonderful nickname — "Baldy" — even though he had
a full head of hair!

When training camp began in Montreal that September Dick
Irvin was telling the sportwriters not to pick us to finish high.
"Last year you picked us to finish in the cellar" said Dick "and we

made the finals. The lower you pick us the harder my guys play. Just don't have us finishing first."

Nobody dared pick us first because we were not the strongest team down the middle. Jean Béliveau wouldn't be with us — he had decided to sign with Quebec Aces in the Quebec Senior Hockey League — so we were left with four centers. Billy Reay, Elmer Lach and Kenny Mosdell were nearing the end of their careers and young Paul Masnick hadn't really proven himself. Before Béliveau opted for Quebec Irvin hoped to put him between Rocket and Bert Olmstead. Lach would work between Paul Meger and me.

I didn't care who I played with as long as I got to take a regular turn. I knew I had a lot of hockey to learn but I also had a natural confidence and there was that goal of winning the Calder Trophy that I had set after I signed my pro contract with the Canadiens.

That was not going to be a cinch. On my own team Paul Meger was a terrific prospect as well. He was one of the best skating left wingers I had ever seen and a hard worker too. Plus there was a prize crop of rookies around the league so it meant that I would really have to work for the trophy.

We also had other new faces. One of them was a real character. His name was Johnny McCormack but everyone called him "Goose." But the funny thing about us getting McCormack is that he became a Canadien because of his marriage. I'm serious!

He was playing for Toronto the previous year and was a real good prospect: a big, smart, defensive center who could score the odd goal. But he made one mistake. In the middle of the 1950-51 season he got married. Normally that wouldn't have been such a big deal but it was a *big* deal to Conn Smythe who ran the Leafs. He figured none of his players should be distracted in midseason by marriage. The minute Smythe found out about McCormack's wedding Goose was sent down to the minors and never played for Toronto again!

We were lucky to get him because McCormack was a first-rate forward and would help us. So would Dick Gamble who had been one of the best scorers in the Quebec Senior League and who signed a two-year deal with us.

As soon as camp opened Irvin put me on right wing with Meger and Lach. I thought I was having a good camp but not everyone agreed. Len Bramson, who covered us for *The Hockey News*, came down a little hard on me:

Boom Boom's potential is a 25-goal season because of his blister-ing shot but he has shown himself to be a little lackadaisical. He is not the hard worker that Meger is but his main fault is not taking advantage of his chances or his blistering shot.

I noticed as the season progressed and I had gotten about 20 goals that the puck didn't seem to be coming to my side as much as it had been at first. So after two or three games without a goal I decided to get the puck myself. I started to just take the puck and shoot it. Naturally the coach would say to me afterward, "Boom, there are other players on the ice too." Already I had been accused in print of not taking advantage of my chances but accused by my coach of taking too much advantage! The darned-if-you-do and darned-if-you-don't part of my life was already coming into play.

Still I had plenty of veterans around to give me a hand and one of the best was Butch Bouchard, a defenseman and the team's captain, who had come to his first training camp a dozen years ago. Like me Butch was from Montreal but when he came to try out with the Canadiens he did it a little differently than I did.

"I had my skates tied together and hung them over the handle-bars of my bicycle," said Butch. "I peddled 25 miles to The Forum and when Dick Irvin saw me coming down St. Catherine Street and asked me why I was doing it that way I said, `I gotta keep in shape.'"

Butch had just opened a restaurant and club in Montreal that was one of the most popular hangouts for hockey players. Management wasn't too crazy about that because they figured that Bouchard would be distracted from his hockey playing but at that stage of his career Butch wasn't going to be taking orders from anybody but himself.

I listened carefully to everyone especially the coach. I didn't want to screw things up for anybody especially myself. So when we opened the 1951-52 season at home against Chicago on October 11, I was ready. Irvin put me on a line with Paul Masnick and Paul Meger and we were flying.

So was Rocket. He buried a shot past Blackhawks goalie Harry Lumley in the first period and then Bud MacPherson gave us a 2-0 lead. I finally got on the scoresheet at 3:34 of the third with what proved to be the game winner although I got one more with nine minutes to go. We beat the Hawks 4-2 and everyone was happy.

Our first road game was in Boston and I knew that I was here to stay when I got on our Pullman. Remember in those days of the six-team NHL everyone traveled by train whether it was to Chicago in the west or Boston in the east.

Rookies usually had to defer to the veterans when we took the train. The old-timers all wanted lower berths in the sleeper because they were supposed to be more comfortable. In the upper you could feel the train bounce over every rail gap and when the train hit a curve it felt as if you were going to fall out of bed. Since I was wearing the number five jersey the club cooperated by assigning me to a number five berth on the Pullman and I lucked out — that was nearly always a lower one.

Train rides brought the team together. Win or lose we'd head to the lounge car where the guys would relax, shoot the breeze and go over the game we had just played. It made for terrific camaraderie because there wasn't any place else to go on that train. It made for one big, happy family.

When other teams rode on the same train our rivalry was intense. I can't begin to tell you how much we disliked each other. The Rocket was especially intense. If he so much as saw Ted Lindsay or Gordie Howe he'd turn right around and walk away! He wouldn't talk to the Red Wings and wouldn't even look at them. All of us felt much the same about the opposition. They were the enemy with a capital E and that meant absolutely no fraternization on or off the ice.

I loved traveling in my rookie year because everything was so new to me. On my first trip to New York I was like a perpetual sightseer. As soon as we checked in to the Picadilly Hotel I phoned my mother and told her that I was heading for the Metropolitan Museum of Art and the Metropolitan Opera House. In our family we all loved opera so it was a treat for me to walk out of the hotel on 45th Street near Broadway and stroll through Times Square to the old opera house on 41st Street near Seventh Avenue.

Before we went our separate ways a bunch of us would stand on the corner near the old Hotel Picadilly rubbernecking and gabbing until this one particular visit to the Big Apple. We were standing there on the corner as usual when somebody — I can't remember who — noticed a lot of pigeons perched on the buildings across from the hotel. We all turned simultaneously to see if there were pigeons nesting on the Picadilly's ledges but we didn't catch the fact that there were pouters roosting on the lamppost next to us. All of a sudden, *plop*, one of us got bombarded by a pigeon! We never again hung around on that particular corner!

New York was special to me because it had a life of its own and was so much bigger than my native Montreal. Right down the block from our hotel were dozens of nightclubs and legitimate theaters like the Shubert, the Martin Beck and the Alvin.

Old Madison Square Garden, where we used to play the Rangers, was located on Eighth Avenue between 49th and 50th Streets, not far from the hotel. To get there we'd often walk north on Broadway past the Astor Theater, Jack Dempsey's Restaurant, McGuinniss' Sea Food Restaurant and then take a left on 49th.

Some guys liked to drop in to St. Malachy's Roman Catholic Church on 49th between Broadway and Eighth because it had a special Actor's Chapel that was also used by the hockey and basketball players who were heading for the Garden. One of my favorite stories was about the time Sugar Jim Henry, the Bruins' goalie, was on his way to a game and stopped at St. Malachy's for a prayer. As he got up to leave he looked down the next aisle and saw Charlie Rayner, the Rangers' goalie, praying as hard as he had been. That night they finished in a 1-1 tie!

The two Gardens, Madison Square and Boston, ranked among my favorite arenas because they both had mezzanines and balconies that overhung the ice. Fans were really into the games in both cities and they seemed to be sitting right on top of us. It was no trouble getting up for a game against either the Rangers or Bruins just because of the fans.

On my first trip to New York a fan, a complete stranger, approached Dick Irvin on the street and peeled off $25 from a large roll. "Here," he said to Irvin, "give it to the guy who scores our first goal."

We weren't too friendly with the Rangers going back to the previous season when we were fighting them for a play-off berth. New York was still one of our main competitors and any win over them was considered a big one for us. On this night they had old Charlie Rayner in goal. He had been around a long time and a lot of people figured that this would be his last season in the NHL because the Rangers had two good young goalies, Emile Francis and Gump Worsley. I had played against Gump in the Quebec Junior League.

Now we're on the ice and I'm remembering the guy who had given Irvin those dollar bills. Billy Reay was my center and Paul Meger was on the left side. My philosophy was simple: shoot the puck and keep shooting the puck. In those days none of the goalies wore masks so they were a little more sensitive about getting hit in the face. And the way I was firing that six ounces of vulcanized rubber a hit in the face could be like an exploding hand grenade.

I know Bobby Hull used to like to take aim at the goalie's head on his first shift but I never deliberately tried to hurt a goaltender. I was aiming for the corner and if the puck happened to rise and go directly for the goalie's head that wasn't my problem. I was trying to put the puck in the net. Beyond that I didn't care where it went. If it hit him in the head and he stopped it, fine. If he didn't then he didn't.

Ten minutes into the game Rayner didn't. I took a pass from Ross Lowe, our new defenseman, and blasted it past old Charlie. We were up 1-0 and then Rocket got one three minutes later. We beat the Rangers 3-2 and Irvin peeled off a five and two ten-dollar bills. I gave one to Lowe for setting up the goal for me.

My point total was pretty good for openers but it couldn't compare with my penalty time. After three games I was leading the league with 18 minutes. Reporters were saying that I had the same kind of temper that got Rocket in trouble.

In a way they were right. If I went four or five games without scoring I wouldn't talk to anybody. Not the media. Nobody. I brooded just like Maurice but there was one difference between us that nobody knew about. Nobody, that is, except our trainer Bill Head.

He understood my temper because he knew that I had a bleeding ulcer. Sometimes I would get sick every period. When you have a bleeding ulcer your moods go up and down depending on how your stomach is reacting. One day I would be fine; the next day I wouldn't want to talk to anybody.

Why didn't I tell anyone about it?

Simple. When the NHL was a six-team league you fought for your job every single day because you knew there was a dozen guys in the minors just itching for a chance to grab your spot. I didn't tell anybody because I didn't want to lose my job. That's why.

Not that I was afraid to talk. On one trip to New York I was interviewed by Jimmy Powers, sports editor of the *Daily News*. He asked who I thought would win the Calder Trophy. I answered him with one word, "Me." Powers must have been impressed because he wrote a whole column about yours truly.

Still it was Rocket who got most of our headlines. When he wasn't scoring goals he always seemed to be getting into some kind of trouble with the opposition. At the end of October we got beat 1-0 by the Leafs in Toronto and Rocket got into a shouting match with Dr. Jim Murray, the Leafs' doctor. Rocket had been frustrated because he couldn't score his three-hundredth NHL goal and took exception to a remark made by the doctor.

The next night we played the Leafs at The Forum and Rocket got into a fight with Fern Flaman, one of the toughest defensemen in the league. Referee Bill Chadwick sent both of them to the penalty box but before Richard got to his seat Flaman's partner Bill Juzda needled Rocket.

That was a big mistake. Rocket popped him in the left eye and knocked him unconscious for a full minute. It didn't stop Rocket from scoring. As a matter of fact Rocket and I were the most consistent scorers on the club and even the critics started to change their tune about me.

Dink Carroll, who wrote a widely read column in the *Montreal Gazette,* said this about me after my first month and a half as a rookie:

> *It's apparent by now that Canadiens have a pretty good hockey player in Boom Boom Geoffrion, maybe an incipient star. He can drill that puck as hard as most of them and his shots are usually on the net. He's also a better-than-average stickhandler and while he is a jerky skater, he is also decisive; it must be that he gets on the ice with considerable speed because you don't see the backcheckers bothering him too much. What's missing from his line is a good playmaking center.*

That "good playmaking center" was still in Quebec running up big numbers with the Aces — Jean Béliveau. I wasn't against Paul Masnick as a center but it was clear that he just couldn't do the job the way we figured Big Jean could. Béliveau was playing for Punch Imlach in Quebec and filling up Le Colisée. But we all knew that he was a big fish in a little pond. Frank Selke knew it and Dick Irvin knew it. What they didn't know was when Béliveau would sign a Canadiens' contract. Without him we weren't a championship team. After 43 games we were in third place (19-18-6) but 16 points behind the leader — Detroit.

But we did have something nobody else had and that was the best defenseman in the league — Doug Harvey. He was a piece of work: unbelievably cool, smart and tough. He played the same way in practice as he did in a regular game — with control. From one end to another Harvey was in command. He'd lead a rush by skating straight ahead right up to the other blue line and then he'd dish off a pass. And if the other guys went into the corner with him they had to keep their heads up. Doug wasn't a dirty player but he could be mean if you treated him badly.

The Rangers once had a center named Red Sullivan who got a bad reputation for "kicking skates" — coming up to an opponent and when he least suspects it whacking his legs out from under him with a swift kick. Sullivan once did that to Harvey at Madison Square Garden and Doug wheeled around and put the blade of his stick in Red's stomach. They rushed Sullivan to the hospital with a ruptured spleen and a priest gave him the last rites. Sully recovered and played again but Harvey, and I give him credit for this, never denied what he did. Everyone in the NHL knew what he was talking about when Doug gave his simple reason for impaling Sullivan: "I did it because he kicked skates!" No other explanation was necessary.

Not that we played hockey like Snow White. Our club was sprinkled with disturbers. Bert Olmstead was right up there and so was Dickie Moore who was a rookie left winger along with me. We had fought a great deal when he was playing for Junior Canadiens and I was with Nationale. Moore didn't join us until the twenty-seventh game of the season.

Even after he had become a regular Dickie didn't make many headlines because he still hadn't developed a scoring touch. Still I knew from my experience playing against him in juniors that he would be a winner. Even as a kid player Dickie was very intelligent and very tough. I had liked playing against him because when he hit you he hit you fair. But if you hit him dirty he'd hit you right back the same way. Moore could play hockey any way the other team wanted.

Even though we had gone at it pretty hard in juniors Dickie and I became good friends as soon as he joined Canadiens. Frankly I would have loved to have had him on my line — we did work together for a short time later — but I usually played alongside Paul Meger.

By midseason I was leading in the Calder Cup race. People were taking notice of my slap shot and comparing it to the hardest shots they had ever seen. Hap Day, who had coached the Leafs and had played alongside the great Charlie Conacher when Charlie had the hardest shot in hockey, gave me the biggest boost of all:

Boomer's shot is definitely harder than anything Conacher shot. I watched Geoffrion closely on one play. I saw him draw the stick back, but I never saw the puck until it bounced off the goalpost. It's the first time I never saw the shot I was looking at!

It meant a lot to me to get praise from Toronto because the rivalry between Montreal and Toronto was very intense. Even the Toronto writers began saying nice things about me. My favorite was Milt Dunnell who did a column for *The Toronto Star*. After one of our trips to Toronto Dunnell wrote, "A colorful character named Boom Boom Geoffrion has been getting more ink than a printer's shirtsleeve."

I may have been getting ink but Paul Meger was catching up to me in the race for the Calder. Joe Primeau, who coached Toronto to The Stanley Cup in 1951, said he'd vote for Meger over me and added that Paul meant more to Canadiens than I did.

That didn't bother me as much as what my boss Frank Selke said. He told Dunnell that Meger was a better all-round player than I was. But then he added, "But Paul will never rise to the heights as Boom Boom can. Geoffrion will go the length of the ice and score a goal. That's something rare these days." That made me feel a little better.

Over the years I would have a pretty good relationship with the press and the main reason I could be fairly philosophical about the knocks I got was because of a longtime friendship I had already established with one of Montreal's premier sportswriters, Jacques Beauchamps.

Jacques was like a second father to me. When I was in juniors I used to live just 10 or 15 minutes away from him and I would go over to his place occasionally for advice. He was very close to The Rocket and I'd say, "Jacques, do you think I have a chance?" Jacques knew just what I meant. "Boom," he'd reassure me. "You can make the Canadiens. Just keep doing what you have been doing. You aren't the guy who's going to run around and hit everybody but you have the ability to put the puck in the net — which is the raison d'être for the Montreal Canadiens."

Then when I began to play for the Habs he really helped me sort out all the confusion I was feeling when they started on me in the French press. He was always fair; if you played poorly he told you, and if you played well, ditto.

I remember early on when he wrote something I didn't like and I asked him why. He said, "Boom, if you can't take the heat then get out of the kitchen. I cannot always write only about the things you're doing right. Sometimes if you do something bad I have to write about it. I'm a writer."

I know it sounds too simple but Jacques' remarks put the whole thing in perspective for me and I realized that I was just going to have to take my lumps in print just the way I had to take them on the ice. Sure there were reporters who seemed to take a dislike to me or who I felt weren't ever fair but most of the time I think I got more good words than bad from the press.

In the meantime I also had to learn to take some lumps on the romantic front, as Marlene explains:

> *By December Boom and I became engaged. He was wonderful to be with and had a kind of old-fashioned charm that I enjoyed so much.*
>
> *It was really funny when I started going to all his games because I had never seen a pro game before in my life. But I was engaged to Bernie Geoffrion and the daughter of Howie Morenz so fans immediately began asking my opinion on things like disputed offsides and such. I didn't have the heart to tell them that I didn't even know what an offside was!*
>
> *But I did know that I intended to pursue my budding career as a figure skater and not long after Boom and I became engaged I received letters of invitation from both Ice Follies and Ice Capades. I decided on the Ice Follies and was told I would have to report to them sometime late in January.*
>
> *When I told Boom this his answer was fast and pretty furious: "Oh, no, when you marry me you don't go skating."*
>
> *I was stunned but still determined to explore a career so in his car on the way to a game against Boston I — very regretfully, mind you — gave him back his ring. He was furious and we hardly spoke the rest of the way. This was going to be awful because he was going to have to drive me back home again too. I was only 17 years old and as a properly brought up young Catholic girl there was no way I could go home alone!*
>
> *I'll never forget that night. Bernie skated out and glared up at me. He began taking his anger and frustration out on the Bruins and got six penalties banging the penalty box door loudly every time he went in.*
>
> *Somehow that night the rumor spread around The Forum and up to the media that I had given the engagement ring to an usher to return to Boom and for years afterward there was no way I could dis-*

pel that tale. I was the evil woman who had been so callous that I ended our engagement by handing Bernie's ring to an usher! There is no way I would ever have done that.

We were both miserable but we were both stubborn too. We didn't speak for two months. Of course I only realized what a mistake I had made afterward. I missed him horribly and realized that I truly loved him.

To make matters even worse several of my former skating friends, who had already joined the Ice Follies, came home for brief visits and I was terribly discouraged by the depressing tales they were telling me. The hours were long, the traveling was grueling, the pay wasn't great. In other words there was little of the glamor and excitement I hoped I'd experience. Shortly after the New Year I realized that the last thing I really wanted to do was spend the rest of my youth on the road with the Ice Follies. Needless to say I sent my regrets and never reported to them at the end of January . . .

Then while the team was away on its long road trip at the beginning of February I got a letter from Boom (later he told me it was the first time he had tried to write a letter in English) and then he called me from the road asking me to meet him at the train station when he got back.

This was a pretty brazen thing to do back in the early fifties; a sheltered, convent-raised young woman who wasn't engaged to this guy anymore meeting him at the train station along with all the wives, but I did it. I wanted Boom to know I was going to meet him halfway, that I was committed.

I remembered that his birthday was near Valentine's Day so I made him a really fancy cake with a big heart on it and made sure he got it at The Forum! By mid-February we were engaged again.

Even better than that was Valentine's Day 1952. We played Toronto at The Forum and it was two days before my twenty-first birthday. Marlene's surprise birthday/Valentine cake appeared with the Canadiens' crest in the middle — a chocolate puck in the upper left corner and a heart in the upper right corner. On the bottom it said, "Happy Birthday, Boom Boom."

It was a bloody game. The Leafs' tough defenseman Gus Mortson bopped me in the nose during a second period fight. I got gashed on the forehead and slashed all over the place and was still a bloody mess after the game. But the big thing was that I was on a line with Dickie Moore and Elmer Lach and they set me up for what was my twentieth goal of the season.

Still Meger kept up with me; he got his twentieth and so did Rocket. By early March we were in second place behind Detroit. I was leading the Canadiens in scoring and was sixth overall in the league; Meger was fourteenth. "The rookie award looks to be Boom Boom's already," said Len Bramson of *The Hockey News*. "Most fans and experts cannot understand how it could possibly go to anyone else."

It didn't.

I finished the season with 30 goals, wound up sixth in scoring — behind Gordie Howe, Ted Lindsay, Elmer Lach, Don Raleigh and Sid Smith — and won the Calder. It worked out exactly as Frank Selke and I had planned the previous year and I couldn't have been happier. The only thing that could have been better was winning The Stanley Cup. That was next on our agenda.

Boston was our first-round opponent. The Bruins were solid and tough with a smart, veteran goalie named Sugar Jim Henry. It didn't stop us. Rocket got two in the opener which we won 5-1. In the second game I got my first play-off hat trick. On the third goal I went around my old teammate Hal Laycoe and just froze Henry with the shot. He looked like the Statue of Liberty when the puck went past him.

Up two games to none we got cocky. We thought the series was in the bag but we learned an important lesson that you can't let up even a little bit in the play-offs. We did and the Bruins jumped all over us. They swept the next three games and put us on the ropes for Game Six at Boston Garden.

These were desperate times and management was close to panic. They figured we needed some new faces. Eddie Mazur, a big guy we nicknamed "Spider," was called up and the night before the big game Paul Masnick arrived in Boston from our Cincinnati farm team in the American League. Masnick had bailed us out with a pair of big goals in the 1951 series with Detroit.

Once the game started it looked like we were dead. Milt Schmidt and Dave Creighton each scored for Boston in the first period. We got nothing. Finally in the second period Selke's moves began to pay off. Mazur scored on relays from Billy Reay and Floyd Curry at 4:35.

We were down 2-1 going into the third and Henry was stopping everything. The time had come for a clutch goal and who do you think got it? Rocket stole the puck from Schmidt, dashed straight down the middle of the ice and beat Henry with a thirty footer.

We were alive but just barely as the game went into sudden death. Gerry McNeil made some big saves for us in the first overtime and kept us alive into the second sudden death. Masnick had hardly played except for a few shifts in the first overtime and Irvin decided to use his fresh legs. Back and forth we went until it got close to the eight-minute mark. Then Doug Harvey took over. He picked up a loose puck in our end and noticing that three Boston players were laying on the ice, out of play, he rushed straight up center. When he crossed the Boston blue line he let a high shot go that rolled off Henry's pads. Mazur rushed in and took a swipe at the loose puck. He missed but Masnick followed up and tossed it into the open net over the sprawling goalie.

That sent us home tied at three games apiece with Game Seven on April 8, 1952. I can tell you right now that it was one of the greatest hockey games that I ever had the good fortune to be associated with even though I didn't score a goal.

Good old Spider Mazur gave us a one-goal lead early in the first but Eddie Sandford tied it up before the period had ended. In the second period Rocket's career was almost ended. Maurice was knifing through the Boston defense when he was blindsided by Leo Labine, a very rugged forward, a split second after Rocket had tripped and fallen to his knees. It looked like a high stick had torn away the outer skin from Maurice's face. He fell to the ice unconscious and for a minute we thought he was dead.

Rocket's legs were spread out in an inverted V as our trainer Hector Dubois and physiotherapist Bill Head worked over him. On the bench I was praying. Rocket finally responded to smelling salts and eventually they took him to The Forum medical room. Rocket told me later, "I didn't remember anything after I got hit. They told me it was Labine. I don't know. The next thing I knew I woke up in the medical room."

He passed out again in the medical room and was completely unconscious when the doctor put six stitches in his forehead. After a while he came to his senses and returned to the bench. We didn't expect Rocket to play again because he still seemed out of it. One Montreal reporter said that Rocket "was in a partial coma." On the bench Rocket said his legs were all right but his head was "all foggy."

It was still 1-1 in the third and with every minute that passed we sensed that the next goal would be the one to win the game and the series. Rocket insisted on playing and Irvin, who knew him better than anyone, was willing to gamble on his favorite player. Late in the third period he put Richard on the ice.

Woody Dumart was carrying the puck toward our zone when Butch Bouchard intercepted it and sent a pass to Rocket who was right near center ice. My eyes were glued to him as he started toward the Boston zone. He was going in a straight line until he approached their blue line where he momentarily bobbled the puck.

Bruins' defenseman Bill Quackenbush was waiting for him and drove Rocket into the right hand corner by the red line. It looked as if Rocket had been boxed out of any kind of play. We thought so. So did the Bruins. "I thought I had him carried wide," Quackenbush later said, "but he got around."

At the red goal line Rocket swerved sharply to the left leaving Quackenbush flat-footed. Then he headed straight for the net and as Henry tried to come out and intercept him Maurice shot the puck into the far left corner.

When the red light went on the sound in The Forum was like nothing I ever heard before or since. Even the Bruins were amazed. Later their coach Lynn Patrick said, "I have never seen a better goal. When he saw his chance and cut for the net he looked like only one thing, a rocket. That's how he got the name and it fits."

Jim Henry couldn't believe it. "He came by me so fast I could hardly see him."

Almost as amazing was the reaction of my teammates. Elmer Lach was following looking for a rebound but when the red light flashed he skated over to the boards and fainted. Literally!

"It was the excitement — the strain," Lach told us later. "When I saw that light go on I just draped myself over the fence and quietly passed out. It was the greatest goal I ever saw."

I couldn't agree more.

Billy Reay got an insurance goal with 34 seconds left but that was it. We had been saved by The Rocket.

The dressing room scene was wild. Over and over again reporters asked Maurice how he possibly could have done what he had done. "What is it that they say about boxers who get hit on the chin early but fight on and around the seventh round ask if it's the second? Instinct. I had a hazy idea of what I should do and I did it."

Elmer quipped, "You play better when you're unconscious."

Rocket's father Onesime, beaming with pride, put his arm around his son's shoulder and hugged him for all he was worth.

Maurice, the toughest competitor I have ever had the pleasure to play with or against, broke down and cried.

That win drained us emotionally and we never recovered. Detroit swept us in four straight although there were some complaints about the officiating especially in our camp. Foremost among them was Irvin who took all defeats harder than any coach I have ever met. When he heard that Conn Smythe said the Wings could put the best seven men on the ice of any team in the league Dick shot back, "And the referee must be one of them!"

Dick was bitter. He refused to congratulate the Detroit players or their coach Tommy Ivan and would not talk to the Detroit reporters. To prove he was serious he slammed the dressing room door in their faces.

I was upset too but not to that extent. Even though we lost I had a lot to be thankful for starting with the Calder. After all I beat out some good competition. Wally Hergesheimer, the Ranger right wing, was right behind me with 42 points to my 58. Dickie Moore was third with 36 and Paul Meger, who I once thought might beat me out, wound up with 17.

I know compared to today's numbers those point totals don't look so impressive. But remember this was 1952 and my 58 points were right up there. If you think those numbers were small you should have seen the ones we so-called stars took to the bank! Just to give you an example, to get a $2,000 bonus from management back in the early fifties you had to finish the regular season in first place, win the play-offs *and* get The Stanley Cup. For winning the Calder Trophy I probably got something along the line of $500.

You have to put the times in perspective. In the early 1950s there were only six teams, less than 500 guys — on the whole planet — playing in the NHL and it was definitely an owners' market. For the privilege of playing on an NHL team — and especially for the Canadiens, one of the greatest winning teams in the history of the league — most of us would have played for nothing.

Still I had made enough that Marlene and I felt we could afford to get married right away. There were so many reasons for me to be happy. Not only did I win the Calder but I was about to win the most wonderful woman as my bride — and inspiration — for the rest of my life.

Life is funny. On the same day that my fiercest enemy — the hardest checking left wing I ever met — Ted Lindsay married Patricia Snell I walked down the aisle with Marlene Morenz.

Lindsay had Pat and The Stanley Cup and I had Marlene and the Calder. I felt like the real winner.

Our wedding was the Montreal event of the year. We had invited about 250 people but ended up with about 3,000 crowding around the doors of St. Raphael of Outremont, a big church in the affluent west end of Montreal. The whole team showed up as did all my old buddies from "down east," the blue-collar neighborhood I was from.

There was no question about my best man — my Dad was the greatest guy on earth. Marlene and I were married under an arch of flowers. She was so beautiful — this was better than winning The Stanley Cup! Marlene and I were preparing to go off on our honeymoon and were heading toward my yellow Mercury convertible parked outside the Canadien Private club where we had our reception. There in the backseat were Billy Reay, Rocket, Harvey and Bouchard! Marlene and I got in the front seat ready to leave but the guys refused to get out. "We want to go with you!" they chimed.

A couple thousand people were waiting for us to leave so with four Canadiens sitting in the backseat I turned the key and the car wouldn't start! Pretty soon everyone was laughing, clapping and chanting: "Boom Boom needs a new car. Get a new car!"

After about five minutes of this Harvey finally relented, got out of the car, stuck his head under the hood and said, "Hmmmmmm, I think I can fix this . . ." and reattached the battery he had unhooked!

My new bride and I were so happy to be on our way and so intrigued with the new convertible that we spent three days driving to Miami, Florida with the top down. When we arrived we were so sunburned we couldn't touch each other and spent our first couple of nights of our Miami honeymoon fighting over who would get to sleep next to the air conditioner!

CHAPTER 4

Tasting My First Cup of Champagne

Before the first puck was dropped for the 1952-53 season Frank Selke was asked about our chances for the new hockey year. "If we get Dickie Moore back," said Selke, "and sign Jean Béliveau we'll probably win The Stanley Cup." Dickie had suffered knee injuries that nearly ended his career. Big Jean was still in Quebec with the minor league Aces. Moore would come back but Béliveau would keep us waiting.

What Selke had said sounded good but after Detroit had swept through the 1952 play-offs with eight straight wins — four over Toronto and four over us — the hockey writers predicted that the Red Wings would go on winning Stanley Cups forever or at least for the next couple of years.

Let's face it; they had one heck of a team. Terry Sawchuk was one of the best goalies I ever faced. At a time when more and more teams were trying to "screen" the goalies Sawchuk had developed a new crouching style that allowed him to see the puck through the players' legs — and it worked. In the 1952 play-offs he had four shutouts and a 0.62 goals-against average. It doesn't get much better than that.

Red Kelly, Marcel Pronovost and Bob Goldham were three of the NHL's best defensemen. Kelly could rush the puck like Doug Harvey; Pronovost was a good all-around player and Goldham was one of the first defensemen to block shots by throwing himself in front of them.

Up front they had The Production Line with Sid Abel centering for Ted Lindsay and Gordie Howe. That Howe was something! He could shoot the puck, stickhandle with the best, throw beautiful passes and play tough. Some thought he played too tough, even rough. He wasn't a dirty player but if you did something to him he wouldn't forget. And since teams were matched 14 times a season there was plenty of time to get you back. I had great respect for Gordie Howe as a player and a person.

I remember the night they honored Rocket at The Forum. As the presentation was ending Maurice was headed for the sideboards. All of a sudden Howe called out, "Hey, Rocket!" As Richard turned Howe pulled off his glove and extended his hand. For a second the entire Forum was silent as the two supposed archenemies shook hands at center ice.

The crowd was taken completely by surprise but then a second later everyone stood up and it was like thunder. They were applauding for Rocket of course but also for Howe because he was a gentleman.

Something happened in the 1952-53 season that would change things forever for Howe and the Red Wings. Sid Abel left the team to become player-coach of the Chicago Blackhawks. It was a shock. Sid had been with the Red Wings for a long, long time. He was captain and leader of the team and he was the only centerman Gordie had ever had. Without Abel they wouldn't be the same.

Meanwhile we were getting better. Dickie Moore, Paul Meger, Dollard St. Laurent, Tom Johnson and myself were all young guys who were getting better. Meger, Moore and I were doing fine, our points at the top of the league, and I knew that with Béliveau we could be a Stanley Cup team for certain. He had as much talent as each of us — possibly more.

He had led the Quebec Senior Hockey League in scoring and had been voted rookie of the year. Everyone who saw him play said that he belonged in the NHL. But I knew that the Aces would do everything they could to keep Big Jean.

"I'd love to have him," said Dick Irvin, "because he's the greatest prospect I've ever seen and I'm sure he'll be a star. But I'm not counting on him and we won't stop functioning if he decides to stay in Quebec."

I returned to Montreal with my new bride and while I was ready for a big season to follow my Calder Trophy I was also adapting to being a newlywed. Marlene and I had moved into our first home together and Marlene recalls how she tried her best to be as good a new wife as she had been a figure skater:

I'll never forget the first time I cooked a chicken for Boom. We had only been married for about 40 days when Boom had a good friend paint our apartment for us. On this particular day he asked the friend to stay for dinner saying, "Why don't you stay for supper; my wife is cooking up a great meal. . . ."

I had been in convent school most of my life and didn't have the faintest idea of how to cook . . . anything. Here I was now in a totally French Canadian environment and all of the women were great cooks. Both of Boom's older brothers, Jean-Paul and Roland (Rolie), had married women who were superb cooks and his mom Florina was the best. Anything she made was always wonderful.

But I was nothing if not determined; if I wasn't going to be a skater I was going to be a gourmet cook. So I stood there looking at my first chicken. I had been told to clean it well but was entirely unsure what that meant. Back in those days you still got your chickens from the market with little bits of pinfeathers sticking out of them.

So I cleaned it. Meaning that I took the Dutch Cleanser and scrubbed all those pinfeather things out of the skin. In fact it didn't have much skin left by the time I got through cleaning it. Of course I didn't look inside it; I just poured a ton of butter on it and stuck it in the oven. When I took it out it looked absolutely gorgeous.

I put out all these little plates with peas and carrots and things and brought out the chicken. Everything was going fine until I put the chicken on the table and told Boom he could do the carving.

Well Boom had never carved a chicken in his life so he just started in the middle. All of a sudden from the middle of the chicken came all of this disgusting goo — eggs, insides and all!

While Boom and his friend just sat there in some kind of shock watching the guck ooze out of this chicken I suddenly felt really, really sick and promptly went into the bathroom and practically threw my own innards out. While I was in the bathroom being horribly sick I heard Boom say to his friend, "Listen, when she comes out make sure you say it doesn't bother you."

"But Boomer, I'm not going to eat that stuff!" he cried.

"I know," said Boom. "We will take her out to the barbecue."

Now that was adding insult to injury. I was in tears and couldn't believe that now I had to go to a restaurant. We ended up at the St. Hubert Barbecue and I looked at the barbecued chicken and thought to myself, "I am never going to cook chicken again." I would eat those words later and now I make the best chicken in the world!

Two days later I found out I was pregnant which explained why I got so sick. But somehow that made the whole experience all the more embarrassing. Here I was about to be a mother and I couldn't even cook a chicken. I went right over to my mother-in-law's and she told me how to do this and how to do that.

One of her masterpieces that I could never grasp was strawberry pie; hers was the best in the world I think. She showed me how to do it by taking a sliver of this and a handful of that and throwing it all together and rolling it out and voilà! It was wonderful. Then I'd go home and try to repeat exactly what she did; I'd roll it out and it would stick to the rolling pin so I'd throw it out!

She said, "Marlene, don't worry about it. Every Friday I make the pies and you can come over to pick them up and that will be his pies for the week." And that's what I did. When Boom would look at me and say, "Your meal is good, my dear," I knew in my heart that I had a long way to go and in time I did learn. And except for that chicken Boom ate everything I ever cooked for him without a word of complaint.

I was looking forward to another season playing for Dick Irvin because he had the same passion for winning as The Rocket and I had. Months after we were beaten by Detroit fans were still writing letters to *The Hockey News* complaining about Dick not shaking hands with the Red Wings after they beat us. Irvin had a good answer:

I don't know why everyone is mad at me. I didn't say anything about the Wings. They beat us; that's all. What did everybody want me to do: stand up and scream, "That was the best team I ever saw?"

It wasn't. And even if it was I wouldn't have said that. They beat the Leafs in four straight but Conn Smythe didn't scream that it was the best team he ever saw. All he said was the Wings could ice the best seven-man team in hockey.

Everybody jumped on me when I refused to go into the Detroit room and shake hands. I'm still waiting for them to come to me after we beat them the year before. They didn't come around. As a matter of fact, I didn't see them again until we were back in Detroit the following season. So what are they yelling at?

Dick was right. In that six-team league the competition was intense and none was hotter than the feud between Irvin and Jack

Adams of Detroit. Once the puck was dropped the other team became your sworn enemy and every game a war. As Dick said, "This business is murder. Everybody is out to get the other guy. Why should I go up and shake hands with them, pat them on the back and then turn around and try and run them down next time. I don't think it's right."

Irvin's concerns went beyond shaking hands with the Red Wings. Our two leading centers Billy Reay and Elmer Lach had slowed up considerably. Without Béliveau he was missing a key center. He even tried moving Dickie Moore from left wing thinking him a natural center but that hadn't worked out. A bright spot on the team was that Rocket looked better than ever and Irvin predicted he would score 55 goals!

Unfortunately Rocket didn't get off to a great start and neither did I. Then came the fourth game of the season against the Rangers at The Forum. Going into the game neither Rocket nor I had a single goal. Neither team scored in the first period and for most of the second. Then a strange thing happened.

At the 17-minute mark Busher Curry picked up a loose puck at our blue line and shot down the middle with their defenseman Allan Stanley, hooking him all the way in so he couldn't get off his shot. Honestly it didn't look that serious to me because Curry really wasn't that much in the clear. But I wasn't about to argue when referee Bill Chadwick blew his whistle and pointed to center ice calling for a penalty shot.

Dick Irvin had to decide who would take the shot. Most people assumed he'd pick Rocket especially since he'd scored our last penalty shot the previous New Year's Day against Chicago (we won 3-0). But when Irvin looked down the bench Rocket immediately shook his head no. For some reason — maybe his slump — he didn't want any part of this. "You take it, Boom!" Irvin yelled at me and although I had never taken a penalty shot before I jumped over the boards and approached the puck on the blue line. Fourteen thousand fans started to cheer. I coasted into the Rangers' zone. I knew Worsley well enough from our days in junior to figure out this equation. I faked a shot freezing him solid and let a knee-high shot go into the short corner before Worsley could move. I had my first goal of the season and we won 3-1.

By the end of October we were in a groove. On October 25 even with the great Terry Sawchuk in goal we beat Detroit 9-0. For me the most meaningful part of the game was my goal in the dying minutes of the second period. It didn't play an important role in the game but it did for me. It was the first time in over two seasons that I had ever scored against Sawchuk.

Before the season had started Irvin had predicted that I would score 40 goals, ten more than in my rookie year. Maybe Dick had put too much pressure on me and maybe I wasn't ready for another big season but this much I can tell you. I flopped. I wasn't even matching what I had done the year before. I know I started to put too much pressure on myself, started to worry a bit and push myself.

Butch Bouchard used to warn the rookies, "It's a very short trip from a hero to a bum." I found that out on the night of November 30, 1952 and it was at home. We played Chicago to a one-all tie that night and I didn't do very much to help the team. In the third period they began booing me and yelling, "Go home, ya bum!" That was tough to take.

All of a sudden the media began analyzing me, trying to figure what had gone wrong. Everyone had an opinion and thankfully Frank Selke stuck up for me:

> We're being a little hard on the kid. To run him down may do a lot of harm. Boom has always been a star ever since he's played hockey and has always been in the headlines. When the goals didn't come so easily this year he began to worry. He's a little befuddled but I have not lost faith in him.

Jean Béliveau finally agreed to come up to us on a three-game trial and Dick Irvin stuck him in the lineup with Rocket and Bert Olmstead for a home game against the Rangers on December 18, 1952. I remember saying to Marlene at the time, "Whatever Jean's going to do I'll do it too." And I did.

Big Jean scored a hat trick in that game and so did I! In fact between us Béliveau and I accounted for all the goals in the 6-2 win. Big Jean got a total of five goals during the three-game trial. He was named "Player of the Week" but after the three games he went back to Quebec and nobody had a clue when he would play with us again or *if* he would.

I finally got out of my slump in the second half of the season. Maybe it had something to do with the fact that our daughter Linda was born on February 8, 1953! By the start of March I had become the sixth player in the league to hit the 20-goal circle, roughly equivalent to hitting .300 in baseball. On top of that my shot was clocked as the fastest and hardest in hockey, faster even than Rocket's.

The club stayed close behind first-place Detroit. We never did catch the Red Wings but we did prevent them from being too happy about the finish. Gordie Howe was hell-bent for a new scoring record (he got it — 91 points!) as well as the first 50-goal season since Rocket's in 1943-44.

With seven games left in the season Gordie had climbed to 46 goals and looked like he would break Rocket's record. When he came to The Forum Howe was booed every time he touched the puck. "You know," said Howe,

> *it would be a funny thing if I had 49 goals going into the last game of the schedule and that game was in Montreal. Imagine what would happen if I broke away with Ted Lindsay in the last minute of play with nobody back, pulled (goalie) Gerry McNeil out of his nets and passed to Ted. Can you see that Montreal crowd?*

To us it was no joking matter. We didn't want anyone to beat Rocket's record, least of all Howe. With two games remaining Howe needed only a single goal to tie Rocket. He failed to score against Chicago and we were in Detroit for the last game of the season. It was up to us to finish the job and save Rocket's record. Dick Irvin, who worshipped Rocket, wasn't going to take any chances. We had already clinched second place so our focus was strictly on Howe. Dick put two and sometimes three checkers on Gordie.

I scored in the first period putting us up by one. Howe got nowhere. We suffocated him on every shift although Detroit managed to tie the score early in the third. We played the rest as if it was the seventh game of The Stanley Cup finals. Bud MacPherson wound up with a concussion and I had an 11-stitch cut in my head but Howe got nothing!

At the final buzzer Irvin leaped out on to the ice, grabbed Rocket and raised his hand like that of a boxer and pranced around to show that here was "the winner and still champion."

Stopping Howe one short of Rocket's record felt great but it was soon overshadowed by the reality of the play-offs. Having finished second we lined up against fourth place Chicago.

The Blackhawks had not made the play-offs for seven years but once Sid Abel became coach they were a completely different team. Al Rollins gave them really good goaltending and the defense of Bill Gadsby and Gus Mortson was as good as any in the league. Players like Jimmy McFadden, Jimmy Peters and George Gee, who had bounced around the league, played extremely well for Chicago.

Before the series started a reporter asked me how I expected to do against Chicago. "I'll get all the tying goals," I said, "so long as somebody else takes care of the winners." I was right on! In Game One at The Forum Doc Couture opened the scoring for Chicago and I evened it up. We went on to win 3-1. In Game Two we were behind 3-2 when I scored the tying goal. In Game Three at Chicago Stadium I beat Al Rollins for the first goal of the game and it held up until two minutes before the end. Al Dewsbury beat Gerry McNeil and Chicago went on to win in sudden death. Still you could call my goal the tying one.

At first no one thought much of the Chicago victory. After all we were up two games to one and seemed to have a much stronger lineup than the Blackhawks. But hockey is unpredictable. The Hawks were filled with the energy that comes from a team that hadn't made the play-offs for so long. Whatever got them going Chicago won the next three games and there was panic on St. Catherine Street after we dropped Game Five at home. First of all our goalie was feeling the crunch. Goalies do that you know. For example in the 1950 Ranger-Canadiens play-off the great Bill Durnan pulled himself out of the series and let young Gerry McNeil take over. This time it was McNeil who got the jitters. After we got down three games to two McNeil approached Dick Irvin and told the coach that he had to pull him out of the series. "If we lost," said McNeil, "I'd feel personally responsible."

That didn't leave Dick with much room to maneuver. He had only one goalie in the minors who was up to replacing McNeil. Jacques Plante had played for our farm team in Buffalo and had filled in with us for three games earlier in the season when McNeil was hurt.

You couldn't argue with his record. He won two and tied the third. His goals-against average was 1.33 but those were regular season games and this was the play-offs. Besides, Plante was eccentric. In his spare time he had a hobby of knitting *toques*, the wool caps popular in Quebec. He also was eccentric on the ice. Instead of staying in the crease the way every goalie did Plante got this brilliant idea of drifting behind the net for the pucks. This enabled him to control the puck and pass it off to a teammate, a revolutionary concept at the time.

But that wasn't the half of it. In addition to McNeil Irvin benched three other regulars: Paul Meger, Paul Masnick and Dick Gamble. He called up Lorne Davis and Baldy MacKay from Buffalo and

Spider Mazur from the Victoria Cougars. It was a whopper of a gamble because all four replacements had played for last-place clubs.

"A desperate situation calls for desperate measures," said Dick.

If I take a chance and lose I'm going to be second-guessed to death, but what of it? It's now or never. I've had a feeling ever since the 1952 (Brooklyn Dodgers-New York Yankees) World Series that the Dodgers would have won if (manager) Charlie Dressen had benched (first baseman) Gil Hodges. What was the point in keeping Hodges in the lineup? He was in a slump and everyone knew it. He wasn't doing the team any good. (Yankees manager) Casey Stengel didn't hesitate to make changes. He wouldn't hesitate if he was in my position right now.

Irvin's gamble was tested almost immediately. Jimmy McFadden, who was one of Chicago's leading scorers, got a clean breakaway. We all held our breaths as he went right in on goal and Jacques, one of the cockiest, most confident goaltenders I ever met, stoned him cleanly.

That was one of the biggest play-off saves I can remember because it gave us life and a comeback. Just before the six-minute mark I beat Al Rollins on a pass from Dickie Moore. Rocket and Kenny Mosdell scored in the second and Plante turned away the best shots Chicago could throw at him. The 3-0 win tied the series 3-3 and sent us back to Montreal for the deciding game.

It wasn't easy even though I put us ahead at 1:38 of the first. Bill Mosienko got Chicago right back in the game late in the second which is when Dick Irvin's genius came through again. He tossed Spider Mazur on the ice right after the tying goal and he scored less than a minute and a half later. Rocket netted another early in the third and Mazur closed it out late in the third. Final score: Habs 4 Chicago 1. On to the finals!

Remember at the start of the season everyone assumed that Detroit would win another Stanley Cup because of Howe, Lindsay, Sawchuk and Kelly. And they finished the regular season in first, 15 points ahead of us. However the play-offs are another story. Whoever coined the expression that the play-offs "are a whole new season" must have had the 1953 Bruins in mind. They had just an average team that finished 21 points behind Detroit during the regular season. In the first play-off game the Red Wings killed them 7-0.

But a team should never take a series for granted and the Red Wings did. They thought they had the Bruins over a barrel but Boston came back and tied the series in Detroit and then went ahead when a third-liner named Jack McIntyre scored the winning overtime goal in Game Three. The Red Wings never recovered and in one of the biggest upsets in NHL play-off history were eliminated in six games.

That suited us just fine. We had played Boston a lot and even though we respected guys like Milt Schmidt, Jim Henry and Woody Dumart we weren't afraid of them. I was thrilled because for the first time I could see a Stanley Cup within my grasp. This was only my second full season in the league and I was in the finals twice!

We opened at home on April 9, 1953 and you wouldn't believe what our coach did. Dick Irvin gathered the reporters together and without a hint of a smile baldfacedly said that the Bruins would win the series in four straight games! Of course we didn't believe him and neither did the Bruins, especially Hal Laycoe who had played defense for us before we sent him to Boston.

"I know Irvin," said Laycoe. "He always used to tell us never to read the newspapers or believe anything he was quoted as saying. It was his way to fire up a team and he usually succeeded in doing just that."

Laycoe was right. Dick's prediction that we wouldn't win a game was tongue-in-cheek and we all knew it. There was method to his madness. Dick's antics helped pump up the older players like Kenny Mosdell, Elmer Lach, Billy Reay and Butch Bouchard. Elmer had been threatening retirement every year since I came to the Canadiens. Reay and Mosdell also were close to the end of their careers but they all had that winning spirit that inspired young fellows like myself. Butch had become the take-charge guy from the moment Plante replaced McNeil against Chicago. His bodychecking and driving play would be awesome.

In a sense Irvin was right about the Bruins. They gave us a real run just as they had done against the Red Wings. Even after we won Game One Irvin insisted that it would be a long, tough series. Sure enough Boston bounced right back beating us at The Forum in Game Two. That sent the series to Boston for the next pair of games.

We could have been in big trouble. Boston Garden was always a difficult place to play in because of the smaller rink size and the fact that the fans were practically on top of you. If we weren't on top of our game they could have killed us. That's when Irvin pulled another one out of his hat. Jacques Plante had been weak in Game Two. We lost 4-1 and Dick felt that McNeil would have stopped at least two of those goals so he yanked Jacques and put Gerry McNeil back in the net for Game Three in Boston.

To a man we all loved McNeil. What we didn't know was whether or not he was over the nervousness that made him pull himself out of the last game against Chicago. He had also suffered a foot injury and the doctor had to shoot him full of painkiller if he wanted to go between the pipes. Still Irvin was willing to take the chance and McNeil had the bad foot frozen.

If Gerry had butterflies you would never have known it by the way he played. Gerry was reassured by Tommy Johnson's goal in the first period and that's all he needed. He gave Boston nothing and Paul Masnick got two more goals in the second and third periods. We played our butts off for McNeil. It looked as if we had booby-trapped all the lanes going toward our goal. If we had done that all winter McNeil probably wouldn't have had any problem with his nerves. It was as pretty a 3-0 shutout as I've ever been associated with even though I didn't get a single point.

That win gave us tremendous confidence enabling us to take Game Four with a 7-3 win. Rocket came through with a hat trick but I got the winner with the second period's only goal. Even though he gave up three McNeil was solid for us and now we were only one win away from The Stanley Cup!

We had one day off before Game Five on April 16, 1953 at The Forum. In that 24-hour period I couldn't keep my mind off the Cup. I kept imagining what the scene would be like if we actually beat Boston on our home rink. All of my young life I dreamed about playing for a Stanley Cup winner and now at age 22 I was one victory away from turning it into reality.

We got back from Boston at seven on the morning of Game Five. At the rink my old buddy Elmer Lach told me that he was in the doghouse. He had forgotten his house key and had to wake his wife out of a sound sleep. It was so chilly at home Elmer couldn't wait to get to The Forum and some sympathy. Little did he know that he would get himself out of the doghouse, big time, in a dozen hours.

Just about everyone in the City of Montreal was talking about the series and believe me there was plenty to talk about. All the goaltenders were limping. Boston had started the series with Sugar Jim Henry in the nets but he had hurt his ankle in the second game and was replaced in the next two. But for the fifth game the Bruins couldn't take any chances. Even though Sugar Jim had a puffed, painful ankle and limped badly he put himself back in the lineup. His coach Lynn Patrick refused to let the doctor freeze Henry's ankle on the grounds that he might be risking permanent injury. His manager Art Ross agreed. "I'm running a hockey team not a racing stable," said Ross. On the other hand McNeil *wanted* his injured leg frozen and all the arguing in the world wouldn't have changed his mind.

The game was one I'll never forget. No score in the first period; no score in the second period; and no score in the third. Only one penalty was called — against Dickie Moore in the middle of the second — and we managed to stop their power play. Irvin's plan was to use as many fresh legs as possible up front. By the second half of the third period he was rotating four lines and we began to take the play away from them. With a few minutes left Henry made a fantastic save on Lorne Davis from ten feet out that looked like the winner. If the two injured goalies were hurting you couldn't tell by the way they played. Henry had 24 saves and McNeil four less heading into the first overtime.

As I sat in our dressing room I was shaking with emotion. Montreal hadn't won a Stanley Cup since 1946. I knew it might be the last chance for Butch, Rocket, Elmer, Kenny and maybe even for Dick Irvin. I can't begin to tell you how much I was hoping that we'd put it past Henry as quickly as possible.

Irvin opened the overtime with Rocket's line. They were on for more than a minute when Rocket sent the puck in behind the Bruins' net and defenseman Bill Quackenbush went after it. The puck bounced away from him to Elmer. Rocket was in front of the net so Lach, who set up many of Rocket's goals, was expected to pass it to him for the big shot.

Instead Elmer took the puck on his backhand and faked a pass to Rocket to throw Jim Henry off guard. Lach wheeled, stopped then wheeled a little more and let it fly, a waist-high shot that went past Henry on the far side of the cage. A split second after the red light flashed Rocket flew from the crease area and leaped into Elmer's arms. Their four skates were off the ice as they embraced. "I didn't know I scored," said Elmer, "until Rocket let out a yell and came charging over." By the time I got on to the ice blood was dripping slowly down Lach's nose as we hoisted him high on our shoulders. Later I asked Elmer why his nose was bleeding. "After

I scored," said Elmer, "Rocket came charging at me and when he whirled in his elbow hit me on the nose and we went down in a heap. But to win the Cup the price is cheap."

Then we dragged Irvin off the bench and lifted him on our shoulders. And well he deserved it. Dick had done a masterful job juggling lines and playing the psychology game to the hilt. Afterward he admitted that he had predicted a four-game Boston sweep for a reason:

> *Bruins thought pretty well of themselves after they knocked off Detroit. I figured I could inflate their ego still more by buttering them up. It succeeded and our own players set out to show me how wrong I could be. So it worked both ways.*

It was everything that I had dreamed of from the moment Elmer beat Sugar Jim to the presentation of the Cup by NHL President Clarence Campbell. The Forum was shaking for a long time after the red light flashed on and in seconds fans tumbled over the boards to embrace us. Kenny Mosdell skated around the ice carrying his four-year-old daughter Bonny. In the dressing room Toe Blake, who had been left wing on Rocket's Punch Line with Lach, embraced Irvin. Toe was wearing a cowboy hat and patting everybody he could find.

Our share of the play-off bonus was $45,000 which was split among the players. The Bruins drew $31,500 and nobody complained. The celebration lasted for three days going to parties with our wives. After that the guys were so tired of partying half of them disappeared. Some of us continued on to Florida. Mosdell, Rocket and a few other fellows went to a hotel called Blue Horizon near Miami and enjoyed their championship.

In the quiet moments we wondered whether we could repeat the win and we wondered who would be back. Plus there was that one question that always seemed to be asked — when will Jean Béliveau become a Canadien? When he had come up for the three-game trial earlier in the season I had sworn to do whatever he did. He got three goals and so did I. I knew Jean was going to be a great player and I wanted him on Les Canadiens. I knew he would be great for the team and for me.

CHAPTER 5

Getting into Trouble

I must have come of age as a Canadien. When we sat down for our official Stanley Cup championship photo a few days later they put me right in the middle of the front row right next to The Boss Frank Selke. Nobody was closer to the Cup than I was, not even Rocket. Afterward we went to a banquet honoring the team. It was there that Selke said, "I'm not going to preside over the disintegration of a Stanley Cup team."

He felt we could repeat as champs if he could sign Jean Béliveau and spent the entire off-season pursuing that goal.

Béliveau didn't sign anything but I could sense that they were getting close. Already the sportswriters were speculating about who Béliveau would center for when he came to Montreal. One of them suggested that the line would be Béliveau, Spider Mazur and me. That sounded good to me especially since I was coming into the 1953-54 season with a brand-new contract.

Selke was pleased with the way I came through during the play-offs and gave me what was for those days a decent raise. This was long before the players' association had been formed and legitimized and salaries were never made public. We were all, from stars to journeymen, just tickled to be in the National Hockey League and I was particularly pleased that Selke had recognized my accomplishment of scoring more than 20 goals in two straight seasons.

The Béliveau negotiations dragged all through the summer with all kinds of crazy rumors circulating. We finally got him in

September 1953. It was funny because the same day that Béliveau agreed to his deal Detroit's general manager Jack Adams announced that he had signed *all* his players in six hours! Which told you how much control NHL executives had in those days. That's why Béliveau's negotiations were so special and why so many of the players were interested in his independence. At one point Big Jean came to Selke's office with an accountant named Roland Mercier which was unheard of at that time.

Béliveau made his debut with us in the 1953 All-Star Game at The Forum. On one side were the All-Stars and on the other was our club, The Stanley Cup champs. We lost 3-1 but Big Jean helped set up Rocket for our only goal in the third period. The line was Béliveau, Richard and Mazur.

In a *Hockey News* poll the experts picked us over the Red Wings. We opened the season at home beating Chicago 3-0 and then clobbering Detroit 4-1 at The Forum. Dick Irvin had juggled the lines to work Béliveau into the rotation. He took Elmer Lach away from Rocket and put him on a line with me and Mazur.

Naturally all eyes were on Le Gros Bill, particularly mine. After all I had played against him in juniors before I had made the jump to the NHL. I was proud of that and knew that Jean would be great when he arrived.

On October 15, 1953 we returned home to play the Rangers. My line with Lach and Mazur really clicked. I scored twice — including the game winner — as we hammered New York 6-1 and Béliveau got his first two goals of the season. As the writers had predicted we moved up to the top of the league battling Detroit neck and neck for first place.

Now in my third full season I had become a confident performer but continued using Rocket as my role model. We had become good friends as had our wives Marlene and Lucille. Playing alongside Maurice I noticed how he held his temper while the opposition hooked him, held him, tripped him or butt ended him. Then after it became unbearable Rocket would explode. I was the same way except that I managed to stay out of trouble. As it happened 1953-54 was another story.

The first incident that got me on the wrong side of NHL President Clarence Campbell occurred at home on the night of November 12. We were leading Chicago 4-1 late in the third period and the game was in the bag. Frank Udvari, a referee I never was too fond of, gave me a two-minute hooking penalty which I didn't think I deserved.

In retrospect I would have been better off if I had kept my mouth shut but I flew into a tantrum and charged Udvari. The referee got away from me and headed for the penalty timekeeper but I had lost it and skated after him again and this time shoved him. Udvari gave me a match penalty and threw me out of the game. Campbell hit me with a $250 fine.

Instead of moping about it I came back playing harder than ever. I moved ahead of Rocket and Howe to lead the league in scoring and had more winning goals than anybody. Everything seemed hunky-dory until just before Christmas in New York. There was no Christmas spirit around Madison Square Garden on that night. We had been feuding on and off with the Rangers ever since I started playing for the Canadiens and tempers seemed to be building as this season progressed.

Not surprisingly this was a mean game and growing meaner in the second period as the Rangers took a 2-0 lead. There was a scramble along the right boards that seemed like an ordinary high-sticking duel. Ranger defenseman Bob Crystal and Paul Masnick, who was playing on my line that night, began the scuffle. Another New York defenseman big Leo Reise moved in to help and then I came to help Paul.

The fuss would have ended right then and there except that Ron Murphy, a 21-year-old Ranger right winger, butted in and began massaging my head with his stick. I dropped my stick figuring he wanted to fight with his fists. Instead he speared me. My blood was boiling. I roared at him, "If you want to fight drop your stick!" Instead he whacked me on the head and I could feel the blood running down my face.

That's when I flipped out. I picked up my stick and fenced for a minute. Murphy backtracked to center ice and now I was even madder. I lost it. I drew my stick back like a baseball bat and swung at his head. He ducked just in time and I missed but Murphy was frozen with fear. When I swung the second time just as hard as the first I connected. My stick caught him flush on the jaw and he went down like he had been shot. A pool of blood surrounded his head and the entire rink went silent. I thought I had killed the guy!

Once I saw Murphy on the ice I began to feel a little guilty. After all I could have killed him. But I was bleeding as well — I had a four-inch gash on the side of my head — but stood my ground in case any of the Rangers went after me. Meantime the Rangers trainer Frank Paice and the club doctor Vincent Nardiello came out to take care of Murphy. They eventually got him back to consciousness and carried him off to the hospital.

The referee Red Storey gave us both match penalties and as I moved toward our dressing room a fan tossed a bottle at me. Now it was getting hairy. At the old Madison Square Garden the visiting benches were surrounded by fans with no protection. When I started off the ice a spectator took a punch at me and others charged our bench. My teammates raised their sticks like fixed bayonets and kept them at bay until I could get to the passageway that led to our dressing room. Meanwhile the public address announcer kept blaring that Murphy was in critical condition.

He was. He had a fractured jaw and a concussion. I had two headaches: one from the bop I had taken on my head and the other from thinking about what Clarence Campbell would do to me now.

We lost the game 3-1 and took the train back home. Campbell took his time conducting the investigation. He talked to Red Storey and the linesmen. He talked to eyewitnesses and he watched movies of the game. His decision was that I was suspended for eight games involving the Canadiens and Rangers. Murphy was given a five-game suspension beginning from the date of the incident, December 20. My suspension was to officially begin with the December 27 game between our clubs in Montreal.

Campbell claimed that he was worried that too many players were using their sticks as "lethal weapons" and wanted to put an end to the stick swinging. But I didn't agree with his decision or his explanation.

Campbell gathered the media together in his office and released a detailed statement. I read and reread it over and over:

> The game was played against a background of ill-considered publicity suggesting the renewal of an earlier "feud" between several players on both teams and the players and the fans followed that cue.
>
> Murphy made the error of retaining his stick and striking his opponent who had no stick at the time. This is a cardinal sin in hockey. Players do not always drop their sticks in their tussles with one another and high-sticking by two players occurs frequently but it is contrary to every tradition of the game to hit another player with a stick when he has none. In failing to drop his stick even when warned to do so by the referee he was to that extent the author of his own misfortune.
>
> So far as Geoffrion is concerned it is clear that he challenged Murphy to put down his stick and fight and he was only prevented

from getting at Murphy by the intervention of the linesmen. He was undoubtedly very incensed when he received the blow on the side of the head from Murphy's stick but the injury he sustained was not serious and no such provocation could possibly justify the vicious retaliation Geoffrion made.

Furthermore it is not sufficient to consider only the comparative results for the principals. What is much more important is the possible effect of the entire episode on the game as a whole including other players and the clubs and the public. Stick swinging is the greatest single risk to the careers of the players and jeopardizes the entire conduct of the sport. If players cannot control themselves to refrain from doing it or the club managements cannot train and discipline players not to do it then the only alternative is to bar such players from participating temporarily or even permanently. They are not worth the risk they involve.

Following the episode there were some expressions of approbation of the conduct of these players in this incident. It is to be hoped that these were only expressions of loyalty from a club official because no right thinking person could condone much less approve of what happened in this instance.

I knew what I had done and was willing to suffer the consequences. But at the same time Campbell's decision was hard to swallow. There are certain rules of hockey that professionals accept as a matter of course. One of them is that a player with a stick doesn't whack another in the head if the other one doesn't have a stick. Murphy was dead wrong not to drop his stick and fight me with his fists and that's what got me going.

Rocket I'm sure would have done the same thing and I knew he felt for me. That season Maurice and I were both "writing" sports columns for local papers. I was appearing in *Parlons Sport* while Rocket was in the French-language weekly *Samedi-Dimanche* which was very popular in those days. Rocket's column was called "Le Tour du Chapeau" — "Hat Trick" in English.

Although Richard had someone polish up the stories for him the ideas were his and Rocket wouldn't sidestep a tough issue. The previous season he called Quebec City fans "bandits" for their treatment of his son Normand in a peewee tournament in Quebec. That caused quite a furor but not as much as his comments about Campbell suspending me for eight games.

Rocket's column charged that I had suffered "extraordinary punishment" as well as "humiliation." According to Rocket my punishment was the result of the president's favoring Canadiens' opponents. This is what Rocket wrote:

"According to friends who watch President Campbell during games at The Forum he shows evident partiality in his reactions to the play. He smiles and openly shows pleasure when an opposing club scores against us and it is known that on several occasions he has given his decision against Canadien players."

Then Rocket mentioned how Jean Béliveau was "deliberately" injured by Bill Mosienko of Chicago and Jack Evans of the Rangers.

"No penalty, no fine, no suspension. Did he suspend Gordie Howe when he almost knocked out Dollar St. Laurent's eye two years ago? No!

"It is strange that only Dick Irvin and I have the courage to risk our livelihood by defending our rights against such a dictator."

Rocket didn't stop there. He also criticized Campbell for allowing Detroit papers to get "paper assists" at Olympia Stadium. "It is not surprising that Howe, Lindsay and Reibel are among the top point scorers in the league although I admit Howe and Lindsay are good players.

"Let Campbell get busy with the other little goings-on known about players of the National Hockey League and not try to create publicity for himself at the expense of a good fellow like Boom Boom Geoffrion just because he is a French Canadian."

This was a very courageous but dangerous move by Rocket. I loved him for it although I knew he was heading straight for Campbell's doghouse. Richard was ready for the punishment; it was almost as if he was daring the president to take him on:

"This is my frank opinion and if I am to be punished for it well that's that. I will leave hockey and I have an idea that several other Canadien players who share my opinion will do the same."

He didn't have to guess. We were behind Rocket all the way right up and down the line. Campbell was on the spot. His strategy was to go to the top. He called Selke and our vice president Ken Reardon to his office for a meeting. He put the ball in their court and demanded that they should make the right moves.

"If the club refuses to take action," said Campbell, "it can have no objection to any action I might take."

Selke and Reardon got the message. They told me and Rocket to give up our sportswriting careers. We agreed. Rocket wrote a farewell piece and summed it up bluntly when he said, "Freedom of speech has been taken away from me. I have to obey my employers. I am not judging them but will leave this matter in the hands of my friends."

Two days later I announced that I would quit "writing" my column in *Parlons Sport*. I thanked Rocket publicly and concluded, "Maurice is always on my side when I am right."

The words came from the heart. I loved Maurice like an older brother. I loved the way he played, his integrity as a man who said what he believed and a superstar who had time to help youngsters like me.

I was angry with Campbell. Not just for the way he handled the Murphy affair but also for what happened next. A day after Rocket said he'd drop his newspaper column Campbell's office made a shocking announcement. He said that Maurice had "humbly and sincerely" apologized to the president for the statement he had made. Furthermore Rocket had to deposit a $1,000 check with Campbell!

It was pretty obvious that Selke, Reardon and Campbell had influenced Rocket and forced him into this "apology." The *Montreal Star* columnist Andy O'Brien wrote that "It saddened fans that after almost a dozen rip-roarin' seasons Richard the Lion-Hearted had become a lamb."

Well not quite.

Rocket played as hard as ever and was neck and neck with Gordie Howe in the scoring race. And I was right behind both of them. In mid-March we had the best goals-scored record in the league when Dick Irvin had a brilliant idea. He placed Béliveau between Dickie Moore and me and the "Kid Line" was born. I knew that Big Jean would be a superstar and the best center I ever had.

When the play-offs started Big Jean was in the spot that Elmer Lach had previously occupied on our line. Elmer, whose career was nearly over, didn't even dress for our opener against Boston. We beat Boston 2-0 — I got the second goal. In the second game we flattened the Bruins 8-1. Dickie scored ten seconds after the first face-off and finished the night with six points. Big Jean and I had five apiece.

We stayed hot in Boston where I got one and Dickie got the winner with a little more than a minute left in the third period. Everyone was raving about our line especially our boss. Selke said:

> *If three players can think alike they have a chance of being out-standing. There must be instinctive thinking among the players on any great line. They must know what the other fellow is going to do*

before he does it himself. Generally the most important player is the
center. The whole success of the line depends upon him. He must be
able to lead his wings like Elmer Lach did in his heyday with Rocket
and Toe. He must know when to bore in and when to pass. If he goes
in too often he'll get caught. If he doesn't go in often enough he won't
score.

I figured we might someday become as good as The Punch Line.
When I mentioned it to the Montreal hockey writer Vince Lunny he
called me naive. But I wasn't dreaming; I knew talent when I saw
it and I could see it with Big Jean's artistry and Dickie's grit. In the
fourth and final game we took Boston out 2-0 and prepared to
defend our Stanley Cup against Gordie Howe and the Red Wings.

It was quite a series and one that I believe we should have won
if the breaks had gone our way. But nobody ever said that the best
team always wins in hockey and nobody ever said that there's
logic to the way the puck bounces.

It started with Detroit beating us at Olympia and then we came
back and tied the series in their rink. Home ice proved to be no
advantage to us. We lost the next two at The Forum and it looked
as if we had had it. All of a sudden Dick Irvin pulled one of his
famous gambles. Jacques Plante had been our goalie for the first
four games and faltered in the fourth.

Irvin gave him the hook and stuck old Gerry McNeil between
the pipes although he had been out of action for two months. All
Gerry did was shut out the Red Wings 1-0 at Detroit and then we
beat them 4-1 at home. That set up the seventh game for all the
marbles back at Olympia.

Busher Curry got one for us in the first and Red Kelly tied it for
them early in the second. It remained 1-1 through the third period.
Our two teams were so evenly matched I wouldn't have been surprised if the game had gone into several sudden-death periods.
That is why the quick ending left us all in a state of shock.

Just past the four-minute mark Doug Harvey picked out the
puck from a Detroit attack and cleared it behind our net. It made
a complete circle and slid out swiftly on the opposite side to Glen
Skov of Detroit. He passed it over to Tony Leswick, one of the Red
Wings' defensive specialists.

Leswick was on his way back to his bench for a line change and
shot the puck at our goal to kill time. He whipped a waist-high
drive toward the net. Harvey was standing in front of McNeil and

normally would have reached out and caught it. Doug was an excellent ball player but this time the puck was curving in flight just a bit. It hit Harvey's outstretched hand, took a sharp switch and tore into the high, left-hand corner of the net past McNeil.

"I was checking Skov in front of the net," Harvey later recalled, "and I saw the shot coming. Instinctively I put up my hand and I got a piece of it. But it bounced off behind Gerry who had been prepared to take it on his chest. He had no chance."

It was a crusher no question but as Irvin said, "We played well but the other team won."

That's hockey.

Unfortunately it didn't end the controversy.

As soon as Leswick popped the winner fans swarmed onto the ice and Detroit players were knocked off their feet in the mad rush. Even Tony was buried by the crowd. While all this went on we skated quietly off the ice without shaking hands with the winners.

We had lost the Cup and now had to prepare to regain it for Dick. What we could never have realized as we broke for vacation in the summer of 1954 was that this would be Irvin's last season behind the Montreal bench — and the most tumultuous of all.

CHAPTER 6

The Riotous End of Dick Irvin's Coaching Career

I looked at our club after we were beaten in that seventh game at Detroit and liked what I saw. Apart from that one flukey goal by Tony Leswick we played the Red Wings even. Plus we had a terrific collection of young guys on our roster. Dickie Moore and I were getting better by the year. Doug Harvey was the best defenseman in the league and Jacques Plante looked good enough to replace Gerry McNeil in the nets any time. On top of that we had Jean Béliveau. When he played with Dickie and me during the play-offs, we knew that he had all the goods.

In the meantime strange things were happening around the league. Owners had come to realize that there was an imbalance between "Have" teams like ourselves and Detroit and "Have Not" teams like Chicago and the Rangers.

Chicago was the worst except for that one season when Sid Abel got them into the play-offs. Usually they were on the bottom of the six-team league and the Blackhawks' owners Jim Norris and Arthur Wirtz had spent nearly two million dollars — huge money in those days — in four seasons. It was almost impossible for teams to buy players so the league decided to create a draft. Each NHL club could protect only 18 players. All others over junior age could be drafted by rival clubs for $15,000.

Those of us in Montreal realized that the rule was aimed at the Canadiens' huge and very successful farm system for developing players. Selke opposed the move. "Nobody has the right to deprive us of the results of our sacrifice and hard work in developing amateur hockey," he said.

Selke had no choice. He was voted down but eventually sold a promising forward named Eddie Litzenberger to the Blackhawks to help them improve. As good as Litzenberger was as a prospect we were so loaded down with talent it didn't matter that we let him go. The Hawks didn't stop there. Just before the season started their vice president Bill Tobin said he would pay $100,000 or more for any one of five NHL players: Gordie Howe, Red Kelly, Jean Béliveau, Maurice Richard and myself. Nobody bit because nobody wanted mere cash for star players. Besides, Selke was convinced that he had the personnel for another run at The Stanley Cup.

Even Rocket at the ripe old age of 33 was pumped. He had gotten over the latest run-in with Campbell and was dedicated to having a good season. Rocket also was excited about his kid brother Henri who had become a junior hockey star in Montreal. Maurice was hoping that he could hang around long enough for Henri to get a tryout with Canadiens. Two Richards on one team seemed too good to be true.

Elmer Lach had retired but we had a good kid named Donnie Marshall coming up and he could make it at center for us along with Béliveau, Mosdell and Paul Masnick. In addition to Plante in the net another newcomer was center Jackie Leclair, a 25-year-old rookie with smooth moves.

The big surprise of training camp in September 1954 was the man who wasn't there — Gerry McNeil. One of the best I ever had the pleasure of playing with, Gerry stunned everyone by announcing his retirement at the age of only 28! "I'm through with hockey," McNeil said. "And I don't intend to change my decision." He went on to explain, "I have a nervous temperament and I want to do something that involves less worry. I want to be able to spend more time with my family."

What shocked me was that Gerry was doing this when he was right at the top of his game in his goaltending prime. But goaltending had become more dangerous than ever. Shots were harder — although none were as hard as mine because nobody else was slapping the puck — and the goalies were not yet wearing masks.

No problem. We had faith in Plante in the net — although Jacques was really different out of the net. For one thing he was a genuine loner. He was not a mixer at all and would never hang out with the guys except when Butch Bouchard or whoever was captain would say, "Tonight after the game all the guys have to be there (some club we used to meet in); if you're not you better have a good excuse." Well Jacques would go but he'd never stay more than a few minutes.

Jacques used to annoy management by complaining about some of the hotels we stayed in while on the road. He would say things like the carpet in the hotel set off his asthma. I have already mentioned Jacques' eccentric hobby of knitting. While the rest of us would be gabbing or playing cards in the club car Jacques would sit and knit. And he was always trying to get the coach to let him wear one of the wool hats he had knitted; they wouldn't let him.

We used to make him so angry in practice: five or six of us would get in front of him, each with a puck, and instead of firing them in succession, which was normal, we'd all do it at the same time. He'd get enraged. Once he even skated right out of practice saying to Coach Toe Blake, "If they're going to shoot the pucks like that I don't want to be in the net."

Blake said, "Get back in the net; that was a joke!"

But Plante was one heck of a goaltender when he was "on."

The experts picked us to finish second behind the Red Wings which made sense although Irvin thought that when we were right we had championship written all over us. It bothered Dick when a couple of players came to camp overweight and whenever a newspaperman would discuss out of shape hockey players Dick would refer to his chicken farm. "People tell me that nothing looks quite as bad as a chicken in the rain," said Irvin. "That's true; nothing except a fat hockey player!"

Dick said that he expected Rocket, Big Jean and me to produce a total of 100 goals or more this season. "If they do," he predicted, "we're in because we have enough other fellows on the team to account for the other 100 we'll need to win the championship."

I was in great shape and it showed in the stats. After the first six games I was second in scoring right behind Rocket and we were in first place. Jacques Plante had a 1.60 goals-against average and a shutout. Even my temper was under control although it was severely tested late in October at a game in Madison Square Garden.

It would be the first time I would face Ron Murphy since I clobbered him the previous December. The press speculated that the Rangers' forward might go after me seeking revenge. Murphy threw cold water on that potential fire. "My trouble with Geoffrion was just part of the game as far as I'm concerned," he said.

That was fine with me. I was willing to let bygones be bygones especially since I was off to my best NHL season ever. Early in November 1954 *The Hockey News* voted me its Player Of The Week and called me "The brightest star to come up on the horizon of the Canadiens since Rocket Richard." I had moved into the scoring lead ahead of Rocket.

I became the first NHL shooter to hit double figures when I scored twice against Detroit early in November. I got two more the next night against Boston giving me 13 goals in 13 games. The one I got against Terry Sawchuk (of the Red Wings) was my one-hundredth NHL goal. When the light went on I jumped for joy and dived into the net to get the puck as a souvenir.

But it was a pregame incident that was to have a tremendous impact on the game of hockey. On November 11, 1954 we were scheduled to play the Blackhawks at The Forum. During the warmups before our opening face-off Bert Olmstead took a shot that rose sharply and hit Plante right in the head. The goalie went down covered by blood and was taken to the hospital.

Plante had a fractured cheekbone but more than that he began thinking about the hazards of goaltending. He concluded that something should be done to better protect the goalie. Plante decided that the best protection would be a mask not unlike the kind used by baseball catchers. Eventually Jacques would design a mask that he would use in practice and after yet another accident would introduce in a game.

High shots to the head drove goaltenders crazy. They were a shooter's way of intimidating the puckstopper and I used that technique from time to time. Early in every game I would let one high shot go that was not far from the goalie's head. That made him think that all the rest of them were going to be high and it made it easier for me to score.

Now that I was leading the NHL scoring race for the first time people were speculating about how I had gotten so good. Frank Selke Junior, The Boss' son who was doing publicity for Canadiens at the time, said that since I was older I had gotten smarter. Also that I was working harder. Camil DesRoches, who worked with Selke in the press department, had been around a long time. He said that I had matured. He could have added that Big Jean was helping with his passes but I also knew that I was doing little things better than I ever had before. I was working in closer before I shot the puck and not giving the goalies enough time to prepare for my drives.

But while most of the people were raving about me my coach was still qualifying his statements. Irvin said that I still could hand out a better pass and do more backchecking. The Rangers were in town when he said that so one of the columnists, Dink Carroll of *The Gazette,* ran over to New York's general manager Frank Boucher and told him what Irvin had said.

"If Boomer could do those things too," said Boucher, "he'd be in a league of his own!"

As much as I liked Dick and appreciated his abrasiveness he rubbed The Boss, Frank Selke Senior, the wrong way. He did it once too often during the 1954-55 season and where once the pair had been really good friends a rift began to open between them.

Selke didn't know it at the time — nor did any of us players — but Dick was tiring of Montreal and began to quietly search for another coaching job. The most obvious choice was Chicago where he had once been a star player and where he had launched his coaching career.

As I mentioned earlier the Blackhawks were in such bad shape that the league was trying everything to prop up the franchise and get it competitive again. One way was to sell players like Ed Litzenberger to Chicago but Dick had another idea.

When we were in Toronto late in December 1954 Irvin sat down with Conn Smythe, his old boss when he coached the Maple Leafs, and shocked the old man. "You know," said Irvin, "you fellows are going at that Chicago thing in the wrong way. It isn't enough to just donate players to them. What Chicago needs now is a first-rate coach. You tell Jim Norris if he'll pay enough I'll go to Chicago and put that team in the play-offs for him."

What Irvin didn't realize was that Smythe and Selke although they were adversaries, were very close friends. As soon as Irvin left the meeting Smythe phoned Selke.

"What's wrong between you and your buddy Irvin?" Smythe asked.

Selke replied that he had no idea that anything was wrong.

"Well," Smythe continued, "how come he wants to go to Chicago then?"

Selke was surprised but told Smythe that if Dick thought he could better himself in Chicago, well that was okay with him. Selke said nothing but watched Irvin even more closely than before. "Dick became more and more unsettled as the season progressed," said Selke. "He even engaged in a few sharp clashes with friends he had known for many years. But I blamed his short temper on the tense battle for leadership constantly being waged between ourselves and the Red Wings."

We were alternating between first and second with Detroit through the new year (1955) but I stayed on top of the scoring list. After 44 games I had 50 points (27-23), Big Jean had 47 (24-23) and Rocket had 41 (23-18). We were one-two-three in the race. Gordie Howe was fourth with our Bert Olmstead and Ken Mosdell in fifth and sixth places respectively.

Our power play was the league's best by far. Big Jean would center for Rocket on the right and Bert on the left. Olmstead was easily the best corner man in the league. I was on the points with Doug Harvey, as good a defensive point man as the NHL ever saw.

We may not have invented the modern power play — Toronto led by Max Bentley was ahead of us by a few years — but we refined it to a science. In those days power plays lasted a full two minutes no matter how many goals were scored. There were nights when we scored two and three goals on a two-minute power play.

I'll never forget one night at Madison Square Garden when the Rangers took a two-minute penalty in the first period. The face-off was in their end and Big Jean moved the puck right back to me. I wound up and took the big slap shot but their penalty killer Aldo Guidolin stepped in front of me. The puck ricocheted off his shins and out to center ice. Before I could move, Guidolin raced past me with a breakaway on Jacques Plante. He cut from right to left and stuffed the puck past Jacques to give them a 1-0 lead.

The Garden went wild but we just returned to center, won the face-off and resumed the power play. Within a minute we had two goals on that same power play and won the game 7-1!

If our club had any "weakness" it was in the area of rough play. It wasn't that we didn't have our share of tough players — nobody was tougher than Rocket or Doug Harvey — but we didn't play a dirty game. We didn't have to because our lineup was filled with aces right down to our fourth center Donnie Marshall who would have been a starting center on just about any other team.

In other words we didn't have anyone even closely resembling a goon, policeman or intimidator; call them what you want, but they're troublemakers. Some of them were legitimate players, sort of. For example the Rangers had a big defenseman named Lou Fontinato who had come out of their Guelph, Ontario junior club with Andy Bathgate, Dean Prentice and Harry Howell.

Fontinato wasn't smooth but he could hit and he could fight. Like myself he was very emotional and every once in a while he would leap at a player. Naturally the Rangers' press agent nicknamed him "Louie The Leaper" or "Leapin' Louie." In a sense Fontinato was a bully and in another sense he wasn't. A bully is a big, tough guy who picks on someone who he knows doesn't fight. Fontinato liked to do that. He would constantly run Big Jean although well aware that Béliveau was not a fighter. He did that with some of our smaller players as well. But to give Fontinato credit he'd fight with tough guys too.

One night at the Garden he and Rocket went at it. Rocket was one of the best fighters in NHL history but on this night he had a cut on his head that had been stitched up from a game the night before. Fontinato punched Maurice right on his cut, the stitches came open and Rocket bled like a stuck pig although he really hadn't been hurt. But it sure looked good for the Ranger fans and they figured Louie had destroyed Richard. That hardly was the case.

Rocket's problem was that he never had anyone fight his battles for him. Maurice fought anyone who gave him trouble whether it was Tony Leswick, Eddie Kullman or Fontinato. In those days we never even expected anyone to fight for us because we were our own men.

That made it difficult for Rocket because on the one hand he was the Babe Ruth of his time but on the other hand he also had to be the Rocky Marciano as well. This was an unnecessary distraction especially when Dick Irvin egged him on.

The 1954-55 season was tougher than most on Rocket even though he was playing some of the best hockey of his life. His intensity was close to the breaking point yet it was made even more pressured by the harassment he received from thugs on the opposition.

One of them was Bob Bailey, a part-time Toronto forward who had battled with Rocket several times in a relatively short NHL career. On this particular night at Maple Leaf Gardens right around Christmas 1954 Bailey board checked Maurice but the referee Red Storey didn't call a penalty.

As I watched Rocket react I couldn't help but think of myself flipping out after Ron Murphy had high-sticked me a year earlier in New York. After Bailey had knocked him down Richard went bananas. He straightened up and skated across the rink, caught up with Bailey and knocked out one of his teeth with his stick.

They fell to the ice together and according to Rocket, Bailey tried to gouge his eyes while Maurice fought back. One of the linesman, big George Hayes, tried to separate them and Storey helped out trying to get Rocket to drop his stick. But every time they got the stick away from Maurice he would get another one.

Once when the normally amiable Hayes tried to stop Rocket Maurice slapped him and he shoved his glove in Storey's face as well. In other words my hero had gone as berserk as I had with Murphy.

The pair finally were separated and both were thrown out of the game. In his report to President Campbell Storey was very easy on Rocket and Campbell wound up fining him $250 in addition to the automatic $50 fines for two misconducts.

The incident should have ended there but it didn't. It didn't because of the anti-Canadien feeling among the NHL leaders, especially Conn Smythe in Toronto.

There was a certain irony here because Smythe hated us with a passion yet he had tried to buy Rocket from the Canadiens a few years earlier. Naturally he was told to go jump! Richard would *never* be traded by the Habs. If Smythe couldn't have the NHL's best scorer he would then try to make life as miserable as possible for him.

And he did.

In the days before video replay Smythe would film every game as if it were a feature-length movie. His coaches would analyze the films and occasionally show them to the players. This time Smythe took the motion pictures to New York where the NHL governors were meeting. Among those attending were Clarence Campbell, John Reed Kilpatrick (president of the Rangers), Walter Brown (president of the Bruins) and Jim Norris of the Blackhawks.

None of them liked the Canadiens. Selke, who was always front and center when it came time to defend his best player, said all there was to say on his behalf: "All of the gentlemen demanded that something be done to curb Maurice Richard whose greatest fault was defeating their teams and filling their arenas to capacity."

But Smythe had influenced the owners and Campbell. The president ordered Rocket and Selke to his office and laid down the law. Rocket had better watch himself or else!

Meanwhile Chicago got more and more interested in Irvin and finally in February Norris asked Selke for permission to negotiate with Dick for the following season. It was then that The Boss confronted the coach on the matter. Irvin denied that he was interested and went back to the business of getting us into first place. Nevertheless the damage had been done. Dick didn't know it at the time but his days as Canadiens' coach were numbered.

In the meantime we had a race to win and I had a lesson to learn — from Dick. Despite the fact that I had remained one of the top three scorers with Rocket and Big Jean my play began to slip after the new year. Irvin was not impressed even when I was named to the All-Star Team. He shocked me and the rest of the hockey world by scratching me from the lineup.

"I benched Geoffrion because he wasn't working," said Dick. "No matter how big a star he may be any man who doesn't give his best on this club doesn't play."

I got the message and was back in the lineup one game later. In the meantime Big Jean had taken the scoring lead away from me. There was no jealousy between us because I recognized the enormous talent he had and how he was making us a better team. He was such a quiet and unassuming person that it was practically impossible for anyone to have any ill-feeling toward him — unless you were on the other team.

As we entered the homestretch the few problems we had were small. The worst was Dickie Moore's health. He always seemed to be battling some injury and this time it was a shoulder that was bothering him; but after he removed the shoulder harness that hampered his shot Moore became a spark for us again and we took over first place.

The tension that built up on the homestretch was like nothing I ever experienced before or since. I have mentioned how tightly wound Rocket and Dick Irvin were but the pressure also was being felt by Detroit. Terry Sawchuk, who had been so brilliant in goal for the past few years, had to be benched with an attack of nerves for the first time in his NHL career. The Red Wings promoted Glenn Hall from their farm team.

We must have been a major source of Sawchuk's headaches. Our attack had reached such a high level that by February 13, 1955 the five leading scorers in the NHL all wore the *bleu, blanc et rouge*. Big Jean was first, Rocket second, I was third, Olmstead fourth and Mosdell fifth.

Our power play was so effective — we could score two and sometimes three goals on one two-minute penalty — that the opposition was going nuts. Finally Detroit's general manager Jack

Adams led a fight to have the rules changed so that the unfinished portion of a penalty would be canceled as soon as the opposing team scored a goal on a power play.

It may have been Adams who was doing the talking but in Montreal we were convinced that it was a league-wide plot against Les Canadiens because we had developed such an effective power play. "One goal is plenty without still getting a chance for more," said Adams. "Any time the team with an edge in manpower scores a goal the penalty already has become costly enough."

We disagreed. I figured that if we had been smart enough and good enough to make the most out of a power play, why not? But there were politics involved and it was clear that it was a matter of the Canadiens against the other five teams.

After Irvin had benched me I came out of it with my head screwed back on straight and with no hard feelings toward the coach. I proved it at The Forum on February 19, 1955 which just happened to be the night they were honoring Ken Mosdell. Our opponents happened to be the Rangers and my favorite target Gump Worsley was in goal for them.

What a night for Ken — and me. My present for him was a goal in the first, two in the second and two in the third. The five goals were the most scored by any player in a game that season and the most by a Canadien since Rocket did the trick against Detroit in 1944. I was now leading the league in goals with 34.

Still we were unable to pull away from the Red Wings. Sawchuk got over his nervousness and returned to the nets while Detroit found a terrific center, Alex Delvecchio, to replace Sid Abel between Gordie Howe and Ted Lindsay. Writing in *The Hockey News* Vince Lunny summed up the race for first place: "It appears now that the war of attrition — and of nerves, too — will go right down to the last week of the season with no sign of a truce possibly even to the last night."

If that wasn't exciting enough there was the scoring race among Rocket, Jean and me. On March 6 we went to Chicago and beat the Blackhawks 4-2. I didn't get a point and neither did Big Jean. But Rocket set up the winning goal by Dickie Moore late in the third period and then got the insurance goal 36 seconds later. With that Rocket took a two-point lead over Big Jean and it now appeared that he was in good shape to win the first scoring championship of his career.

Our next game was Wednesday March 10 at Toronto. It was a scoreless tie. Rocket still led by two. Three days later we were home against the Bruins. I got two assists, Rocket got one, Big Jean got nothing. In the point race Rocket was ahead with 74, I was second with 72 and Big Jean was one behind me.

Then came the fateful Sunday night — March 13, 1955 at Boston Garden. Whether Hal Laycoe deliberately attempted to cut Rocket with his stick or not is a question that I'll never be able to answer. But there have been a lot of opinions. Frank Selke said that Laycoe hit Maurice "probably by accident." Red Storey, the referee, said he was "clipped" by Laycoe but didn't say whether or not it was deliberate.

But the big problem for Rocket was not whether the hit was deliberate or not but the blood that was dripping off his head. That's when Maurice charged the defenseman and hit him in the face with his stick. Probably the worst part of it from the league viewpoint was what Rocket did to the linesman Cliff Thompson who had once been a Bruins' defenseman.

Thompson was a rookie linesman at the time and we remembered him as a Boston player who now was siding with the Bruins in this brawl. Thompson tackled Rocket after he had attacked Laycoe twice more and Maurice instinctively reacted to the tackle by punching Thompson twice in the face before the brawl was finally broken up. The fact of the matter is that Thompson went too far.

But then again in Clarence Campbell's view so did Rocket and that's why the president suspended him for the rest of the season and the play-offs. That led to the St. Patrick's Day Riot I mentioned earlier and of course the trouble that fell all over me when I beat Rocket out for the scoring title.

I've often wondered what would have happened had the Rocket not knocked over Thompson and whacked Laycoe. For one thing Maurice would have won the Art Ross that he wanted so much. For another we would have finished first and finally we would have beaten Detroit for The Stanley Cup. Maurice was the most dangerous player on the power play and with him out Detroit had more confidence. Now Detroit turned around and said, "Now we only have to worry about the Béliveau-Geoffrion line."

Instead we took them to a seventh game at Detroit before Alex Delvecchio had his greatest game and beat us. After we lost I realized that the Canadiens team that I knew would never be the same. For several months I had heard rumors about Irvin. One was that he would simply retire. There was also a story in a French-language paper saying that Dick should be replaced by Roger Leger who coached the Shawinigan Falls Cataracts of the Quebec League and that the Habs would recruit an entirely French-speaking team!

Irvin continued to dump on Campbell and that was the straw that broke the camel's back as far as Selke was concerned. Irvin and Selke finally had a showdown and The Boss laid it right on the ice. Selke said:

> *Look Dick, you can't coach this team any longer. It's all very well to keep a team full of fight. But there's a limit to that too. And I don't think you know that limit. Now Dick, you can stay with us or you can go to Chicago. That's up to you. But if you stay with us you can't be a coach. There will be another job for you at your full salary as long as you wish.*

Dick quit the Canadiens that spring to take the Blackhawks' coaching job. The Canadiens — and my career — had reached a turning point. Selke would search for a new coach who would be my Montreal leader for the rest of my career at The Forum. But in May 1955 I didn't know whether that would be Leger, Billy Reay or Toe Blake.

CHAPTER 7

A New Coach and Another Cup

The recuperations from the Richard Riot and our loss of The Stanley Cup to Detroit were long and painful ordeals. Fortunately there were events shaping up that kept me from dwelling on the defeat. The biggest of course was the departure of Dick Irvin, the only coach I had ever had in the NHL, and Frank Selke's search for his successor.

But the happiest event was that Marlene and I were going to be parents for the second time. We were now living in St. Laurent, Quebec and life at home was about as good as it got. I'm sure that people outside NHL hockey thought that our lives were filled with constant glamor and privilege but nothing could be further from reality. Life was wonderful but not because of luxury or glamor. It was because we lived in our hometown and we were surrounded by family and good friends.

Marlene can tell you:

I guess because I was English speaking most people would assume that Boom and I socialized with the English-speaking players and wives but in fact my closest friends were Boom's family and a couple of French-speaking players' wives. Butch Bouchard's wife Marie-Claire was wonderful to me that first season Boom and I were married. She simply took me in hand and gave me wonderful advice on how to manage. I was only 18 and I remember thinking that she at 28 years old looked so good for an "older" woman!

Rocket's wife Lucille, was also a good friend to me. One day when I was first setting up house I was unpacking glasses when Lucille knocked on my door, walked in, and proceeded to help me wash dishes! Lucille was such a warm and bubbly person — the perfect contrast to Rocket who was known to brood. I think that she must have helped to lift him from his moods many times. She adored her Maurice.

The only time player-couples really socialized was sometimes after the fellows came back from a road trip or after Thursday night games. Then we might have dinner with Rocket and Lucille or occasionally with Butch and Marie-Claire.

We were friends but not "buddies." We all lived in fairly separate places and had our own families. It was understood that Sundays meant "rendezvous" with the Geoffrions at his mom's and dad's place. My mother-in-law would cook one of her great meals and all the sons and daughter Margo would gather with their families. This went on for all the years Boom played in Montreal.

By this time I was sitting in Box 15 having graduated from the upper blue seats while pregnant with Linda. I had gotten so huge while pregnant that one of the ticket men took pity on me, worried that I might just roll down the aisle one night, and put me into Box 15 and I sort of inherited it.

I was sitting there the night of the Richard Riot and knew as soon as Mr. Campbell walked in that something bad would happen. You'd have thought he'd have enough sense to stay home that night. I had never been so close to violence like that; it was truly shocking even though the ushers came up and took each wife away to a place of safety.

For all the grief Boom took for scoring those 50 goals we gained a new set of friends afterward. Out of a clear blue sky someone named Jean-Paul Hamelin called Boomer and said, "Since you scored your fiftieth on my son's birthday I'd like to make you a full partner in my restaurant Le Beau Cage!" And that is how Jean-Paul and Lucette became our good and long-time friends.

For some reason Boom and I also became close friends with several doctors in Montreal. Dr. Marcel and Eileen Remy, Dr. Roger and Claire Pontbriand, Dr. René and Pauline Poirier and Dr. Robert and Thérèse Gareau. When we were with them no one cared at all whether Boom had scored a goal that night or not. I learned so much from these women about elegant entertaining — setting up, proper dishes, silverware and the like. Boom and I both learned a lot about friendship.

*In the meantime as I sat up in Box 15 waiting for our second child
to be born and our lives to change again there were a lot of changes
taking place on the bleu, blanc et rouge too. Naturally along with
the other wives I worried over what effect these changes would have
on our husbands but I think most of us never said a word to our men.*

When Dick left for the Chicago Blackhawks the media pegged
several people for his job. Some of the French writers wanted team
captain Butch Bouchard but he wasn't interested. And Roger Leger
was soon scratched off the list. That left two — and only two —
front-runners: Billy Reay, my old center, and Toe Blake, who had
played left wing with Rocket and Elmer Lach on The Punch Line.
Reay was a solid guy who probably would have made a good
coach and several of the Canadiens' board of directors favored
him. But the two people who counted most, Selke and Kenny
Reardon, wanted Blake.

They liked Toe for several reasons. First of all he could coach and
had proved it in Houston, Buffalo and Valleyfield. Secondly Selke
wanted a coach who could rein in Rocket. It had to be someone
who Maurice respected a great deal. That's why Blake got the job.
Selke gave him a one-year contract but said, "It will last for a lifetime" and he was never more right about anything in his life.

Selke and Blake immediately worked together in an effort to
calm Rocket. They invited Maurice up to Selke's office and The
Boss put it bluntly:

*You don't have anything to prove either to the players, the fans
or us. You carried the club during the lean years and now it's time
for the younger players to help out especially when it gets rough out
there. Forget about the past. It's the future — and you — I'm concerned about. Your heart is as young as you ever were but your body
is now 35-years-old. Remember that and we don't want you fighting a world of 24-year-old huskies.*

Rocket listened but didn't say a word. When Blake opened training camp and we started playing exhibition games Toe still had to
work on Rocket. After all he wasn't going to mellow out overnight.
"I often had to cool him out — right on the bench," said Blake. "He
glared at me but he took it maybe because I was an old line mate and
he knew we had been through a lot together and most likely because
he didn't want to make my first season as an NHL coach tougher."

Ken Reardon, who had also played alongside Rocket, was just as dedicated to keeping the lid on Rocket. One night after the Rangers' Lou Fontinato bloodied Richard with a high stick Reardon was sitting in his Madison Square Garden seat behind our bench. As soon as the period ended Kenny stormed into our dressing room and walked over to Rocket who was sitting steaming on the bench.

"That was a lucky hit Rocket," said Reardon, "and we don't want you to do anything about it. Everybody here knows we can't risk for the team's sake another serious jam that might lose you for Canadiens."

Once again Rocket glared his eyes like two searchlights but didn't say a word. The room was filled with anxiety when Reardon walked out but in a second the tension was relieved when Doug Harvey cracked a joke that had everyone laughing. Even Toe smiled and didn't bother with his usual pep talk.

That was one of the big differences between Toe and Dick. Blake knew when it was time to get tough and when it was time to have fun. Irvin never smiled and I never knew what you had to do to make him smile. He was a great man and I loved him with all my heart.

I could see it right in training camp. Toe would lace on the skates and after the workout would play games like "puck-take-away" with us. We used to tell him, "Hey Toe, you're over the hill. You're finished. What are you trying to do taking the puck away from us?" Then we'd all laugh. We could never have done that kind of stuff with Irvin.

Dick didn't make life easier for Toe. After moving to Chicago Irvin predicted that we would finish first by ten games and win The Stanley Cup. "The Canadiens will be as good as last year," said Irvin, "and Detroit won't be so good." In a way he was right. The Red Wings had made a number of deals including one which sent Terry Sawchuk to the Bruins. They lost Tony Leswick, Benny Woit, Glen Skov and Johnny Wilson. Their loss was our gain but still Blake was cautious.

"I am not going to promise a Stanley Cup," said Toe, "but we will continue as a great fighting club."

There was plenty of fight in us when training camp opened in September 1955. Our lineup was loaded with stars and terrific backup players like Busher Curry, Claude Provost, Phil Goyette and Donnie Marshall. Two good young defensemen Jean-Guy

Talbot and Bob Turner were knocking on the door but the biggest noise of all was being made by the smallest guy.

The Rocket's kid brother Henri Richard had already made a name for himself in junior hockey but he was tiny compared to the other forwards and only 19-years-old. Every time he was on the ice he made the scouts do a double take.

When they saw Henri play they knew right away that he was as strong as his brother even if he wasn't as big. He was a good skater and stickhandler and most important he wasn't afraid of anything even though he stood only five feet seven.

But with all the talent he had Blake felt he was too young and wanted to send Henri down to the minors for a year or two. "Another year might help him to develop his blazing shot," said *The Hockey News* writer Vince Lunny. "It also might enable him to add some more pounds to the 157 he carries on a well-muscled frame."

Rocket was smart enough not to try to influence any decision made by the front office but he couldn't help but marvel at his kid brother. "It's not easy keeping up with him," was all Maurice would say. Henri said even less; in fact he was the quietest kid I have ever met at a training camp bar none! He was so shy you felt you were alone in the room when he was there. He seldom said a word but when he stepped on the ice he was talking with his stick. He was so great.

Somebody had nicknamed Henri "Flash" in juniors but now a reporter gave him a better nickname — "Pocket Rocket" — and it stuck. A couple of days before training camp broke Blake made the final decision and Henri stayed with the big club.

Toe put The Pocket on a line with Dickie Moore and Rocket. Right off the bat it was as good a combination as Big Jean, Bert Olmstead and me. Blake only worried that Rocket would go out of his way to protect the kid if any of the big guys on the opposition went after him. "We figured," said Toe, "that if they were together they'd always be looking out for each other or if The Pocket got into a scrape The Rocket would be over in a second and explode."

This is exactly what happened at the beginning but after a while Rocket realized that Pocket could fight his own battles and even though Henri was small he knew how to use his dukes. Once at Boston Garden Pocket leveled two of the Bruins' toughest players, Fernie Flaman and Jack Bionda. After that word spread around the league that Pocket didn't need Rocket to protect him.

In a preseason poll *The Hockey News* picked us to finish first ahead of Detroit. I agreed with that because we were better than the Red Wings at every position — on the power play and with penalty killing. The only advantage they had over us was Gordie Howe but we still had Rocket and even in his mid-thirties he was full of pepper and vinegar.

"If we finish anywhere but first I'll feel I've done a very bad job," said Blake. "If things go right we should win by ten games. But any hockey man will tell you that things don't always go right."

He was right. In our opening game against Toronto I was crashed into the boards by Maple Leafs' defenseman Larry Cahan and by the time they put me together again I came out of it with rib, chest and shoulder injuries and was out for a while. But it didn't seriously hurt the club. They did very well without me. The team was in first when I was injured and still there when I got back. Big Jean was leading the NHL in scoring but the figures that caught everybody's eyes were his penalty minutes. In 17 games he had 38 minutes, more even than Bert Olmstead and Rocket!

Blake was a big help to Big Jean. Just as he had the right touch with Rocket, Toe knew the buttons to push with Béliveau. And if the coach didn't prod him there were teammates around who would, especially Olmstead. Bert was one of a kind, an original, and completely fearless. One night Lou Fontinato cross-checked him in the head from behind after charging about 20 yards across the ice. Olmstead got up as if nothing happened. The guy was in the best shape of any player I have ever seen in my life. He never put on a pound. He would come to training camp at the right weight and finish the season at that exact weight.

Bert could be as tough on his teammates as he was on the opposition. One time I skated across from my side — the right — to his and all of a sudden I felt a whack. Bert had hit me on the behind with his stick. He barked at me, "Stay on your side of the ice. Half of the ice is yours and half of the ice is mine. Let Béliveau chase the puckhandler." When Olmstead talked Geoffrion listened.

Blake paid special attention to the power play and as good as it had been it got even better. In the first five weeks of 1955-56 we scored 17 times while the opposition was shorthanded compared with ten the previous year under Dick. Once against Boston we got three goals on one two-minute penalty and the league kept talking about changing the penalty rule to keep us from going wild on power play goals. "When they're playing that power play right," said Blake, "it is a beautiful picture to watch."

That was especially true at The Forum where we seemed to know every inch of the ice. When teams came to play us it had become almost a given that they would lose. They would throw up their hands in disgust. I remember Harry Howell of the Rangers saying to their trainer Frank Paice after a pregame workout, "Why don't we just give Montreal the two points and go on to Toronto!" Nobody wanted to come to The Forum.

Still there was no way I could repeat as scoring champion. I missed ten games with my first collection of injuries and then went down again on a Fontinato hit that reinjured my right shoulder. It really cost me. When the NHL announced the All-Star Team Rocket was first right wing and Gordie Howe was second. Big Jean was at center, Jacques Plante in goal and Doug Harvey on defense. I wasn't mentioned.

For a time it seemed as if the Red Wings might overtake us but a home-and-home series with them early in February 1956 said all there was to say about the changing of the guard. The first of the two games was on a Thursday night at Olympia Stadium, February 2.

Over two periods neither Jacques Plante nor Glenn Hall gave up a goal. The game remained scoreless for more than 15 minutes in the third. You just knew that whoever scored — assuming somebody could — would win the game. And you also knew that if a big goal was needed who would score it but Rocket.

Sure enough at 16:01 Rocket took passes from The Pocket and Dickie Moore and beat Hall. Big Jean got another a couple of minutes later and Plante kept the door shut the rest of the way. We left for home with a 2-0 win and resumed the rivalry two nights later. This time they opened the scoring, Ted Lindsay from Gordie Howe, but Béliveau got one back and we remained tied going into the third.

Overall we had better lines than Detroit. Lindsay, Howe and Alex Delvecchio was a great one and they could do anything. Howe was right behind Big Jean in the scoring race and after Plante Hall had one of the best goaltending records in the league. But line for line they couldn't match us, especially the way Henri had come on so fast.

On defense we had the experience of Butch Bouchard and Doug Harvey. Doug would play 35 to 40 minutes a game and make it seem as if he were on the ice for two minutes. He loved playing hockey as much as anyone I ever met and never seemed to get angry. Except once. I've already told you about the incident when Red Sullivan of the Rangers kicked Doug's skates out from under him. Doug was so mad he speared Red in the spleen and nearly killed him.

Tommy Johnson was a very good defenseman. He could hit, carry the puck and played the defensive zone almost as well as Harvey. Beyond them we had three up-and-coming players in Dollard St. Laurent, Jean-Guy Talbot and Bob Turner. The best Detroit had was Red Kelly, who was very good, followed by Bob Goldham, one of the top shot blockers in the NHL and Marcel Pronovost. After that there was Warren Godfrey, Bucky Hollingworth and Larry Hillman, who couldn't compare to our second-line defensemen.

The place where we really topped them was at center. After Béliveau and Pocket there was Kenny Mosdell and Donnie Marshall. Kenny was a terrific old pro and Donnie had become one of the league's best defensive forwards.

In the third period Bert Olmstead set up Big Jean and he fired the puck past Hall at 1:23 and that was all we needed. The final score was 2-1. Big Jean was racking up penalty minutes as fast as he was points. At the rate he was going he'd be the highest-penalized center in any season.

It was really strange. As Big Jean got tougher Rocket began mellowing. Mind you Rocket didn't get soft; it was just that he took longer to reach his boiling point so that he didn't blow up the way he did with Dick Irvin.

Without a doubt Blake was the reason but he was the kind of guy who didn't enjoy taking credit. Toe would say:

> *Your style of coaching has to depend on the players you have. If you try to change the styles of your players you're in trouble. I let the forwards do their thing and let the defense look after itself. Fortunately I have a defense that can look after itself. But I tell my players four or five stars don't make a team. Everyone in uniform is important.*

How good were we?

Detroit had finished first every single season since 1948-49. Seven championships in a row was nothing to sneeze at but we put an end to that streak in March 1956 and it wasn't even close. Our 100 points gave us our first NHL title since 1946-47 and put us 24 ahead of the second-place Red Wings. New York was third with 74 points. Big Jean not only led the league in scoring but finished with 143 penalty minutes. Rocket only had 89 minutes. To top it all Olmstead finished with 56 assists breaking Lindsay's old record from 1949-50.

I didn't even come close to retaining the Art Ross Trophy. Having missed 11 games with injury I played only 59 games and still managed to average more than a point a game. But 29 goals and 33 assists was not my idea of a good season.

Everyone agreed that as good as the regular season had been the year would not be a success unless we won The Stanley Cup. The first club standing in our way was the Rangers. We knocked them off 7-1 in the first semifinal at The Forum. Rocket got a hat trick and we had dreams of a sweep especially when we found out that Gump Worsley was out with a knee injury and New York had stuck an unknown named Gordie Bell in the nets.

Bell had been playing for Three Rivers in the Quebec League when the Rangers told him to get his derriere over to Montreal. But this was a goalie who had been playing pro hockey since 1942 and who had visited more towns than a traveling salesman. He had played eight NHL games for Toronto in 1945-46 and then went down to the minors — to Providence, Pittsburgh, Washington, Springfield, Omaha, Fort Worth, Louisville, back to Buffalo, Springfield, Syracuse, back to Springfield and finally Three Rivers.

We figured to vulcanize this poor guy. Instead Gordie Bell vulcanized the great Canadiens. We took 32 shots at him although admittedly most of them were either soft, short ones or easy, long ones. Rocket was checked into the ice by little Guy Gendron and Dave Creighton tied up Big Jean. Rangers broke a 2-2 tie with a pair of third-period goals and took us to the cleaners 4-2. What an embarrassment!

On the other hand it may have been the best thing that ever happened to us. We headed for New York where we beat the Rangers with Worsley back in goal 3-1 and 5-3 and then buried them 7-0 in Game Five. Rocket got five assists and after the game announced, "Now I've become a playmaker."

If there was a sad part to the victory it was the way our captain Butch Bouchard had faded. Butch couldn't keep up anymore and sat on the bench throughout the last game against New York. Toward the end fans began chanting, "We want Butch" and Blake turned to him and said, "Do you want to go on?" With a 6-0 lead at the time Toe had nothing to worry about. Butch just shook his head and grinned. "The boys are doing all right without me. Don't break up a winning combination."

Meanwhile Detroit had taken care of Toronto so we found ourselves head-to-head with the defending champs. It was exactly what we wanted. If anyone should take the Cup away from Detroit we wanted to be the ones to do it. We knew we could and so did the odds makers. They established us as two and a half to one favorites to go the route and we didn't want to disappoint them. Not only were we good but entering the finals we were healthy. Our physiotherapist Bill Head told Toe he had never seen the team in better shape.

The Rangers president General John Reed Kilpatrick said we were the best team he had seen in the 30 years he ran Madison Square Garden. He rated Doug Harvey as our most valuable player. "He's as good as any two men," said Kilpatrick. He wouldn't get any argument from me on that.

This would prove to be probably the most difficult play-off series I would ever play. Detroit had a great team with Howe, Delvecchio and Marty Pavelich. But with the team and talent we had combined with the spirit of Toe Blake behind the bench we felt we couldn't lose.

In the first game we had a shaky start but got on track. They had us 4-2 going into the third period. Jackie Leclair scored early for us and I tied it a minute later. Then I set up Big Jean for the winner less than two minutes after that. It wound up a 6-4 win which didn't make Jacques Plante happy but what the heck, a win is a win.

I got one in Game Two. So did Rocket, Big Jean, Marshall and Pocket. They got one to make it 5-1 and we were off to Detroit ahead in the series two-zip. Any thought of a sweep went down the drain in Game Three. Detroit rallied in the third and topped us 3-1. But that was their last hurrah. Plante shut them out 3-0 in the second game at Olympia and we went home and put the series to bed. Big Jean and Rocket got the first tallies of the game in the second and I beat Hall early in the third. The Wings got one later but it didn't matter. Nobody could take it away from us now and as the clock ticked off the final seconds Blake flicked a towel from Bouchard's neck and sent him over the boards with a pat on the back so he could finish his career as an active player on the ice with a Stanley Cup-winning team.

The game ended 3-1 and then came the ceremonies. Cooper Smeaton, league trustee for The Stanley Cup, presented it to Butch at center ice. I grabbed Toe by the left leg and Dickie Moore grabbed his right and we hoisted him over our shoulders.

Some of us shook hands with the losers but not Doug Harvey. "I didn't shake hands after the last two series we lost," Doug explained, "so I don't see why I should when we win." What can I tell you; he was his own man. Meanwhile the champagne bottles were opened and our dressing room turned into a crazy, happy place.

It was only the start of a four-day celebration that never seemed to end. The City of Montreal honored us with a 30-mile parade with each player riding in a car bearing his sweater and name. The parade started at City Hall where the team was greeted by Mayor Jean Drapeau. After we signed the city's Golden Book we headed for St. Helen's Island in the St. Lawrence River off Montreal for a reception and luncheon. Each of us received a ceramic lemonade set with our names baked into the clay.

While the celebrations continued the rest of the league worried about how much better we could become. My line — with Big Jean and Bert — finished up with 47 points, third best in play-off history. Big Jean and I would only get better. Bert was Bert and there was Rocket, Doug, Moore, Pocket and the rest of the gang.

Muzz Patrick, the Rangers' general manager, remembered watching the great Canadiens team led by Howie Morenz and Aurel Joliat. "There's no comparing that team with this one," said Muzz. "This Montreal team is many, many times better."

If that were the case we would have to win more than one Stanley Cup. Toronto Maple Leafs were the only team ever to win three Cups in a row. In spring 1956 we were taking aim at their record.

CHAPTER 8

The Greatest Team Ever

Rangers defenseman Bill Gadsby and Detroit left wing Ted Lindsay were the only non-Canadiens on the 1955-56 All-Star Team. We were represented by Jacques Plante, Doug Harvey, Jean Béliveau and Maurice Richard. Imagine. Even though he was in his late thirties Rocket still beat out Gordie Howe on right wing! Big Jean won the Hart (MVP) Trophy and Doug took the Norris.

Tom Johnson and Bert Olmstead made the Second All-Star Team. Frankly I thought Tom was a better defenseman than Gadsby and I'd take Bert as a corner man over Lindsay any day. But that only shows how powerful we were from top to bottom. And with youngsters like Phil Goyette and Donnie Marshall developing fast, we were only going to get even better.

How much better was the question and that would be decided by Toe Blake. He was masterful in his rookie coaching year but whether he could keep it going was another story. Let's face it; we were not necessarily an easy team to coach even though we had all that talent. There were a lot of strong personalities to contend with.

Pocket was coming along and Toe had to find a way to fit him in while not discouraging other young centers like Marshall and Goyette. Then there was the matter of keeping us from getting complacent. After all when you finished as strong as we did in 1955-56 there always is the possibility that we might get big heads.

As it turned out Toe was the perfect coach for the perfect team. When Butch Bouchard retired he named Rocket captain and nobody could argue with that, not with the way Maurice was steaming along. Rocket's mellowing had no effect on his scoring and when he reached the 500-goal mark, he said he would dedicate the goal to Dick Irvin. "He taught me everything I know about hockey," Maurice said.

Unfortunately Irvin's move to Chicago was not a success because Dick was in the throes of his fatal sickness. Chicago missed the 1956 playoffs and during that summer Dick's condition worsened. When training camp opened in September he wasn't behind the bench. He died in May 1957 and left a long line of friends and admirers, me among them.

Up until this time NHL players on opposing teams kept their distances from one another. Our dislike for the Red Wings for example was as intense as any rivalry in any sport, anytime, anywhere. In the six-team NHL jobs were scarce. Any player who challenged management faced the possibility of being sent to the minors. Remember how Johnny McCormack lost his job with the Maple Leafs because he got married in midseason? Well that's the way it was.

The players had absolutely no say in the way the league was run except in one small area, the players' pension fund. That had been started by Clarence Campbell years earlier and now there was a five-man NHL Pension Society. Campbell and two other league officials represented the owners and two players represented us: Ted Lindsay and Doug Harvey.

Even though we had Doug representing us we learned very little about how the pension was operated. We lived in fear of ownership. Campbell had showed us how tough he could be when he suspended Rocket in March 1955. Every year the president would come around and talk to us about league subjects and the pension plan. Most of us didn't know what he was talking about half the time because Campbell spoke a language all his own. Maybe that's what happens when you're a Rhodes Scholar.

The people who ran hockey then were very powerful. By contrast we were very weak but not altogether stupid. Lindsay was very intelligent and Doug, as easygoing as he was, was no dope either. Deadly enemies on the ice, they became colleagues off it. Harvey began to appreciate Ted's doggedness in trying to get answers from Campbell. Pretty soon these two totally different personalities were working together trying to get a better deal for the players.

Lindsay did most of the early spade work until he was convinced that the time had come for players from all six teams to get together in some sort of association the way they were doing in big-league baseball. Nobody in the league knew what Ted was thinking — not the owners and not the players — until we had the All-Star Game at The Forum in October 1956.

This was the one time of the year when players let their guard down. After all, the guys on the All-Star Team were from the other five clubs and they mingled as teammates while our guys, even though we were playing them, gabbed with some of them before and after the game.

Lindsay proposed to Doug and later to some of the others that we form a group to get better conditions for all the players. We didn't know it at the time but Ted had taken it upon himself to make a crusade of this players' association idea and we would hear more about it in the months to come.

The game ended in a 1-1 tie. Rocket scored for us and Lindsay scored for the All-Stars. The game produced $28,261 for the pension fund and some interesting changes.

Players began experimenting with the slap shot. I had perfected it to such an extent that there was a feeling that it really worked and could terrorize goalies. Frankly I was flattered that they felt that way.

The fellow who wasn't flattered was Jacques Plante. Now that he had established himself as our regular goaltender, it meant that he had to face my slap shot every day in practice. That was no fun but Jacques as I mentioned was very inventive. He was always looking for ways to make his job better and was now fielding pucks behind the net on a regular basis and sending passes to the forwards as if he were a defenseman.

He was also working on a revolutionary device. He had decided that since shots were coming at his head faster and harder by the year, it was time to find some protection. If a baseball catcher can wear a mask, Jacques asked, why not goalies?

Plante got together with an equipment expert and designed a plastic face mask which covered his brow, cheeks and chin. There were openings for his eyes and for his mouth. A leather strap held it in place. It was ugly but Jacques didn't care. He just wanted his head in one piece. Toe Blake wasn't impressed with Jacques' mask experiments but Toe eventually relented allowing him to wear it to practice.

At the time nobody thought of a goalie wearing a mask or of players wearing helmets. There was a macho feeling among hockey players. When asked by a reporter how he bounced back after nearly getting killed in a game in 1950, Gordie Howe replied simply, "Hockey is a man's game." That summed it up for all of us.

We had a championship team that promised to get even better in 1956-57. The season opened at home on Saturday night, October 13, 1956 and we beat Boston 3-0. We won the game but lost Henri Richard who left with torn knee ligaments. "It's wishful thinking if anyone figures we'll finish first again by 12 games," said Blake. "Injuries will be a big factor."

This would be a good test of our depth. With Pocket out Selke dipped into the farm system and called up an 18-year-old center named Ralph Backstrom. "He skates like Milt Schmidt," said Kenny Reardon. "He makes plays like Bill Cowley and has a heart like Elmer Lach."

You couldn't get higher praise than that. Backstrom made his debut between Rocket and Dickie Moore against Chicago but didn't score although Maurice got the goal on a pass from Dickie. It was a 1-1 tie. He didn't score in our next game either. But it was just a matter of time.

Our old nemesis Detroit was at it again. They started the season unbeaten in seven and took first place. We slipped to fifth. Besides Henri, Rocket and I were both sidelined with elbow injuries and Floyd Curry bruised his ribs. I needed surgery on my elbow as did Maurice. The good news was that Big Jean continued playing tough — 61 penalty minutes in 27 games — and led the league in scoring by 11 points again over Howe, Lindsay and Norm Ullman.

Now that Detroit had Ullman and Earl Reibel to back up Alex Delvecchio their center ice depth was almost as good as ours, so it promised to be quite a race. Blake figured that if we finished with 90 points we could take first place again.

As the race reached Christmas 1956 Lindsay quietly worked on the idea for the players' association. By now players around the league were well aware of what was happening because on each team fellows had to kick in money (dues were $100 a year) and some were understandably nervous about it and others didn't cough up any dough at all. Trying to keep this a secret from the hockey bosses was another story. In terms of the Red Wings Lindsay had to be concerned about his manager Jack Adams who was as tough and crusty as they come.

Adams must have gotten wind that something was up. Lindsay had been his fair-haired boy but all of a sudden in December 1956 there was an explosion in Detroit and it *had* to have something to do with Lindsay and his brainchild, the association.

What happened was that Marshall Dann, a hockey columnist from the *Detroit Free Press*, interviewed Adams and Jack ripped into Teddy. What made this so strange was that Lindsay was leading the Red Wings in scoring at the time and it was after a big Detroit win that put the club into first place. So you knew that Adams had other things on his mind.

"Lindsay has quit hustling," said Adams. "I don't know what has gotten into Ted. He had to be benched in Toronto because he wasn't hustling."

Then coach Jimmy Skinner chipped in, "Ted's not doing the job he's capable of and the worst part is that he acts like he doesn't care."

Anyone who had ever played against Lindsay knew that he always cared and I have the scars to prove it. Marshall Dann knew that something was afoot. "The climax of this intriguing plot is still ahead," he predicted.

It was!

On February 10, 1957 the Canadiens played Rangers at Madison Square Garden. I was still out with my injury and wasn't at the game. We got beat 5-4 on a goal by Dean Prentice with less than two minutes left. But that was nothing compared to the melodrama that would take place off the ice the next couple of days.

Harvey, Lindsay and the others got in touch with lawyer Milton Mound, who had worked with baseball players and on the day after our game at the Garden, they met in Manhattan to officially formulate our first players' association. The next day they called a press conference and announced that we were in business. Lindsay was president of the NHL Players' Association and Doug was first vice president. Two solid defensemen Gus Mortson and Fern Flaman were second and third vice presidents. Defensemen were all over the place; Jimmy Thomson was secretary and Bill Gadsby the treasurer.

Having played against them I can assure you that each one of these guys had paid his dues in blood and guts. Mortson and Thomson had won four Stanley Cups in five years — 1947, 1948, 1949 and 1951 — for the Maple Leafs. Flaman played for Boston and Toronto and ranks among the toughest, smartest players I ever faced. Gadsby broke in with Chicago and now was one of the NHL's top defensemen with the Rangers. You just couldn't argue with the quality of this group.

We knew that the owners would flip and preparations were made for that. One of the first things Lindsay pointed out was that this association was not a union and that we were not out to make trouble for Selke, Adams, Campbell and the rest of the power brokers.

Harvey returned to Montreal after the news conference. Selke was upset over the announcement but the reaction in Montreal was relatively calm compared to elsewhere. One reason for that was the changing of the guard at The Forum. Senator Donat Raymond, a wealthy and distinguished French Canadian and owner of the Canadiens, decided to sell the team to Senator Hartland de Montigny Molson. Head of Molson Brewery, one of Canada's oldest and most distinguished companies, Molson had the respect of both the French- and English-speaking communities of Montreal; he was an avid sportsman and had served as a fighter pilot during the Battle of Britain.

Neither Raymond nor Molson had much to say about our association. Selke, who still was the hands-on boss, wasn't at all happy about it but his reaction was mild compared to Jack Adams in Detroit and Conn Smythe in Toronto. The two of them exploded and set out to torpedo the association. Meanwhile we had a season to complete.

Toe Blake's comment about injuries being "a big factor," now seemed like prophecy. Big Jean went down with a hip injury and no matter what I did that year I couldn't keep myself out of the hospital. The bad elbow got infected again and I was in for more treatment. Vince Lunny calculated that when I was in the lineup our goal average was .825 and without me it was .325. "Boom should be considered for the Hart Trophy on that alone," he said.

March 14 was Floyd Curry Night at The Forum. The Busher was presented with a new car and a ton of other gifts including an 8-4 win over Toronto. My present to him was a pair of goals, one of which was a Harvey blast that rebounded off my left thigh into the net. Maybe my luck was changing!

That goal was number sixteen. I had missed half the year and I figured that if I finished with 20 goals I would be satisfied. I almost made it. I wound up with 19 and we finished second, eight points behind Detroit. Gordie Howe won the scoring title with 89 points and Ted Lindsay was second, only four behind. Big Jean was third with 84.

The play-offs have been an important part of hockey since long before I was born. They were invented by hockey pioneers Frank and Lester Patrick who devised the play-offs as a second chance for teams crippled by injuries or bad luck during the regular season. Since then hockey people have looked at any year as two distinct and separate schedules — the regular season and the play-offs.

No matter how badly a team or a player did during the year, the play-offs gave them a whole, new life. That's exactly how I looked at the 1957 postseason.

Since we finished second in the standings, we were pitted against the Rangers in the first play-off round. New York would not be easy. Their coach Phil Watson, a French Canadian despite his name, was a wild man and loved to antagonize us. They had future Hall of Famers like Andy Bathgate on right wing, Harry Howell and Bill Gadsby on defense and my old buddy Gump Worsley in goal. Then there was Leapin' Louie Fontinato on defense.

Louie was the most popular hockey player in New York where they loved fighters. Fontinato could fight, although he was not nearly as good as the Rangers' press agents claimed and he also could hit, as Big Jean, Rocket, Dickie, Bert and I well knew.

It seemed as if Louie nursed a special hatred for us. In those days the penalty box was — if you can believe this — shared by players from both teams. If double penalties were given out the opponents sat side by side on a single bench. One night Fontinato and Olmstead went off at the Garden. Bert sat down first and when Louie arrived a split second later he didn't like the room he was getting so he bodied Bertie right off the bench onto the floor. The cops had to be called to separate them.

Our series began at The Forum. Big Jean took a pass from Jean-Guy Talbot and gave me the puck. *Bang*! At 15:07 I had started a new life with a play-off goal. After that I assisted Rocket early in the third then scored my second and assisted Big Jean giving us a 4-1 decision.

Because of scheduling difficulties Game Two was at the Garden and it was a game for the ages. We were down 3-2 late in the third when I tied it up. In overtime we had chances galore but couldn't beat Worsley. Then New York counterattacked. Red Sullivan sent a pass to Andy Hebenton, a very quiet, hard-shooting wing, who put it past Plante, tying the series 1-1. It also sent us the message that we had better not take Watson's Rangers lightly.

We didn't.

We made up our minds that enough was enough. In the third game we were hot and I was back in the groove with a hat trick and an assist. Olmstead tied an NHL play-off record with five assists, Big Jean got two goals and Rocket got his third in three play-off games. We won 8-3. It made me feel as if those long days on the sidelines during the regular season were ancient history. Bert made me feel like a king. "Don't give me credit for the five assists," he told the reporters. "It's easy when Boom and Jean are popping them in."

I have to give the Rangers credit. Even though we bopped them out of the semifinals in five games, they never quit. In the last game they were down 0-3 but tied it up in the third. We didn't settle matters until overtime. Pocket set up Rocket at 2:11 of sudden death. What a way to end a series!

I couldn't have been happier. My scoring touch not only had returned but I had a league-leading seven goals.

Meanwhile in the other series everyone was predicting Detroit over Boston. The Red Wings had finished first and had an incredible team. Also the Bruins were using a second-stringer goalie by the name of Don Simmons from Eddie Shore's Springfield club. He was fantastic.

It was 1953 all over again only this time it took the Bruins only five games (instead of six) to knock out the Wings.

To us Boston was a lot like the Rangers. Instead of Fontinato they had Leo Labine. They also had several good forwards like Fleming Mackell, Don McKenney, Johnny Peirson and Real Chevrefils. Their defense was solid but didn't come close to ours. And we had it all over them in goaltending and outright firepower especially when Rocket was firing bullets which he was.

By the time we had beaten Boston 5-1 in Game One of the finals Rocket had eight goals in six games; so did his protégé — me. The play-off record was 12 held by Rocket and Big Jean. Although Rocket was almost 36 years old he was never better. Twice he missed great scoring chances because he was going too fast. Bill Durnan the Canadiens' goalie in the forties dropped into the dressing room and had a good crack about Rocket: "I don't think he'll be much good after sixty."

In that first game of the finals Rocket pumped four goals past Simmons, one short of his own 1944 record for a Cup game. Simmons had an interesting observation about Rocket. "What I remember most about the way he looked coming in at me is his eyes. Every time they were bulging. They looked like automobile headlights." Then showing he hadn't lost his sense of humor added, "That Rocket should go a long way. He shows a lot of promise."

So did Big Jean and yours truly. In Game Two I fed Le Gros Bill early in the second and the lone goal stood up through the end. We were two games away from our second straight Cup but Toe still wasn't happy and I didn't blame him. During the regular reason the Bruins had won seven and tied three with us and the next two games were in Beantown.

It was then that Blake showed just what a creative coach he could be. Even though we were clearly a better team than Boston Toe didn't want to give them any edge whatsoever. During the Rangers' series he had put together a new line with two of our promising kids, Phil Goyette and Donnie Marshall alongside veteran Busher Curry. Toe moved Donnie to the left wing with Curry on the right and Goyette at center. At first he used them mainly for defensive purposes but in the third game of the finals, Blake turned them loose as a regular attacking unit.

They were fantastic. They outplayed my line as well as Rocket's. Goyette and Curry both got goals and an assist while Marshall had an assist and would have scored except for a terrific save by Simmons in the third period. Their points gave us the margin we needed for a 4-2 win and a stranglehold on the series. "They were the best line on the ice," said Blake. "All of them played their best games of the season, both offensively and defensively."

Imagine the power we had now, not just three well-balanced lines but excellent defense and goalkeeping as well. Even though we were known for our scoring Blake always stressed defense and Harvey, Johnson, St. Laurent and the others made it awfully tough to get through for shots on Plante.

Doug was in his prime and there wasn't a better defenseman anywhere. He controlled the game like an orchestra conductor. When he wanted to speed up the tempo he'd dash from his end to the other one and set up a play. Likewise he could slow down the pace just as easily taking the puck and lazily moving it around until the speed was to his liking.

Both on and off the ice Doug was the sort of person you want on your side. There's an old army expression, "Here's a guy I'd like next to me in the trenches." Well that's how I felt about Harvey. When he was sitting next to me on the bench or playing next to me on the ice I always felt better.

Part of Doug's calm came from his confidence and that, I'm sure, had a lot to do with his natural athletic ability. He was a terrific baseball player and had played pro football with the Ottawa

Roughriders as well. When others were running around like chickens with their heads cut off Harvey was nonchalantly looking for someone open for a pass or easily relieving the opposition of the puck.

What fooled people about Doug was his easygoing quality. He was so laid-back that some people thought he really didn't care which wasn't the case. Red Sullivan could vouch for that. Remember my mentioning that Harvey once speared Sully so badly that they gave the Ranger last rites in the hospital. After the game some of the newspaper guys approached Doug and expected that he'd feel sorry for Red. He refused to apologize.

Harvey stood his ground for two reasons: He was unbelievably honest and candid. When you asked him a question he'd tell you exactly what he thought. Also Doug was angry with Sullivan for more than just kicking skates. Sully was the only guy in the league who would always try to nail Plante when he came roaming out of his net.

In those days the NHL didn't have the rules it does today to protect goalies and there was nothing to stop a forward like Sullivan from running down a goaltender if he came wandering far out of his crease as Jacques liked to do. Somehow most players chose to sidestep Jacques or if there was contact it wasn't vindictive.

But Sullivan was different. If he was on the ice and Jacques took one of his excursions to the sideboards or the blue line Sully would run him down like a lawnmower over a blade of grass. He did it again and again and Harvey resented it. Doug treated his goaltender like a son and if anyone was going to mess with Jacques he had to deal with Harvey. And that's why Doug was so mad at Sully and not particularly distressed that he had ended up in hospital.

Our aim in April 1957 was to prove that our previous Stanley Cup win was no fluke. We had hoped to knock off Boston in four straight games but to their credit the Bruins bounced off the canvas after three losses and beat us in Game Four at Boston Garden. Fleming Mackell, one of the fastest men in the league, got an early power-play goal for them and Don Simmons held the fort as well as any goalie in the league; we just couldn't beat him.

The Bruins dominated the whole game. They were inspired and smart, making almost no defensive mistakes which was a good trick against a team like ours. In the last minute still behind 0-1 Toe pulled Plante and threw out a sixth skater in the hopes of tieing the score but Mackell got the puck. Rocket fell back to play goalie but Mackell deked him and slipped it into the open net.

In a sense the loss taught us a lesson: no matter how good you are you can be beaten by a club that's willing to work harder. And they'll beat you with great goaltending. Even though we had a big edge on Boston on paper we all knew that there was something intangible about the Bruins that was scary. Toe sensed it and freely admitted that he too was worried.

"I'm afraid of the Bruins in this series," he said. "They're the kind of club that won't quit. Even when they're down they battle like demons."

The only consolation after being shutout like that was that we were going home for Game Five and had a very good chance of winning the Cup at The Forum. Another plus was the possibility that I could get my hot streak going again. I had ten goals heading into Game Five just two short of Rocket's record which he set in 1944 and which Big Jean tied in 1956. Also I was only four points away from Gordie Howe's all-time mark of 20 points which he had set in 1955.

Boston outplayed us in the first period and that's where Plante showed his stuff. So often a team will carry the play but get frustrated by a hot goalie and then the other club will get one chance and put it away. Jacques stoned the Bruins left and right and with less than two minutes left in the first period Toe tossed out a makeshift line with Donnie Marshall centering for a couple of newcomers André Pronovost and Claude Provost.

They were supposed to be our defensive unit. But moments later Simmons misplayed the puck and the rebound went to Pronovost who tapped it in at 18:11. We walked out of the first period with a lucky one-goal lead. I was worried because those Bruins were still showing me a lot of good hockey.

Early in the second I set up Dickie Moore for the second goal putting me only three points behind Howe's record. Then Bert set me up at 15:12. We were up 3-0 and I was two behind Gordie and one behind Rocket in the record department.

We held our three-goal lead until just past the middle of the third period. The Bruins made one last gasp. Down by three they kept coming at us and finally Leo Labine beat Jacques with a little more than six minutes to go.

Even with a two-goal lead Toe wasn't going to take any chances. He put out our best defensive forwards Donnie Marshall and Busher Curry and all they did was split the last two goals between them. When Busher scored at 18:31 the 15,286 fans in the building went out of their minds. It was 5-1 and there was no way Boston was going to rally from a four-goal deficit.

They didn't.

We ran out the clock in a rink that was so noisy we couldn't even hear the final siren. The green lights flashed at each end of the rink and Jacques Plante threw his hands up in triumph. We rushed to grab him. I put my arm around Jean-Guy Talbot and he put his around Big Jean and then Rocket came along.

All of a sudden Rocket and I broke away from the pack and went looking for Toe. As soon as he stepped on the ice I got hold of him around the right thigh and Rocket his left shin. One-two-three we put him on our shoulders and Toe lifted his right arm to salute the crowd.

As much as Montreal fans revered Dick Irvin there was no doubt that they loved Toe Blake even more. He had been a Montreal star his whole playing career and Blake's personality was one which fans found easier to embrace than Irvin's.

After we went through the hand-shaking ritual with the Bruins, Cooper Smeaton representing Clarence Campbell presented The Stanley Cup to Rocket at center ice.

As I watched Rocket accept the trophy I couldn't help but marvel at our team. There was Rocket the leader of our team; and there was Toe Blake the best coach in hockey; there was Big Jean one of the greatest players of all time and then there were Dickie Moore, Doug Harvey, Bert Olmstead, Jacques Plante. . . . Had there ever been such a team?

I was very pleased when Toe singled me out for special praise. It had been a tough year coming off the injuries but leading everyone in play-off scoring was just the tonic I needed in terms of my future. Little could I have imagined that in just nine months I would come this close to dying on the ice!

CHAPTER 9

I Almost Died; The Players' Association Did

After the dust had cleared from our second straight Stanley Cup championship my teammates and I had another run of celebrations, took a vacation and relaxed. At least we tried to.

Still unnerving events were taking place during the off-season like nothing I had ever experienced before. One of them had to do with the Ted Lindsay-Doug Harvey NHL Players' Association which had been made public during the winter.

Although it was never our intention to go to war with the NHL owners some of them reacted to our player's association the way the United States had to the attack on Pearl Harbor. League power brokers like Conn Smythe in Toronto and Jack Adams in Detroit had fits when they learned that we wanted more control of our players' pension fund and also to have the proceeds from broadcasting our All-Star Game funneled into the pension package.

Even though Canadiens' ownership still was in a state of flux with the Molsons taking over from Senator Raymond, Selke seriously considered trading Harvey to punish him but then came to his senses and realized that he could never replace him. Not only would he lose the best defenseman in the league but afterward we would have to play *against* him! Selke wasn't about to cut off his nose to spite his face. No deal was made and Selke contented himself with hoping that his buddies in the NHL high command would kill the association in their own way while he left his Canadiens alone.

Every so often the players' association made news. Milton Mound, who was the counsel for the players, made a revelation that was surprising for the time. He announced that Canadiens were the highest-paid team in hockey with a payroll in 1956-57 totalling $192,000, an average of $10,670. But he also revealed that "high-priced" players like myself, Rocket, Harvey, Moore and Béliveau put several Canadiens in the category below $10,000 a year. This marked one of the first times team salaries were made public and it bothered a lot of people, especially the owners.

In Detroit it was another story. By now every player connected with the players' association knew that Ted Lindsay was in deep trouble with Jack Adams. Right after his Red Wings were knocked out by the Bruins Adams went on record saying there were only five "untouchables" on his club — Gordie Howe, Alex Delvecchio, Red Kelly, Marcel Pronovost and Al Arbour. You knew that Lindsay was at the top of Adams' Hate List because Teddy was First All-Star left winger and still was not an untouchable.

Before summer was over Adams had dealt Lindsay and Glenn Hall to Chicago in a monster deal that shocked everyone, especially Teddy. He got hold of the media in Detroit and ripped into his old boss although never once mentioning him by name. Adams shot back that Lindsay was "disloyal" and then Jack went a step further and sent Teddy's business partner — and one of Detroit's best-ever defensive forwards — Marty Pavelich to the minors. Not long after that Marty hung up his skates for good.

If Adams hated the idea of the players' association Smythe hated it ten times more. Jimmy Thomson had been his most consistent defenseman when Toronto won four Stanley Cups in five years (1947-1951). In 1956-57 he had been named team captain and was a solid player. But when Thomson got involved with the players' association Smythe targeted him just as Adams had Lindsay. "The way I looked at it," said Smythe, "the association was causing a good deal of trouble and I was annoyed that our captain was one of the vice presidents."

Smythe sold Thomson to Chicago for only $15,000 and was then convinced that by eliminating Lindsay and Thomson, who were two of the most active participants in the plan, he had "isolated the association." Looking back I have to admit that he was right. The association lasted through the summer of 1957 and sputtered on before actually dying in February 1958.

When I checked in to training camp in September Toe was telling reporters that "a healthy, injury-free Geoffrion" was his biggest wish. I had news for him, that was my biggest wish too!.

I was also hoping that our club could regain first place. Even though winning The Stanley Cup was important it would have been nice to have finished ahead of Detroit in the regular season. When I looked around camp I knew we were loaded with talent. In addition to the nucleus of our Cup team there were several promising newcomers.

One of them was a goaltender named Eddie Johnston, who would eventually make a name for himself in the NHL, but not with us. Our Rochester farm team had sent us a big forward, Ab McDonald, and a little one, Murray Balfour. Both had NHL written all over them. Toe's favorite was Marcel Bonin, quite a character who liked to brag that he wrestled bears and ate glass for the fun of it. He could do those things but he could also play hockey and eventually would become a key part of our club.

On the eve of The All-Star Game in Montreal the annual *Hockey News'* writers' poll had us finishing first. I found out about it from a hospital bed. Just before training camp ended I got a terrible case of the flu and doctors ordered me to the hospital as a precaution. I dreaded the idea of another tough-luck year like the last one.

The All-Stars beat us 5-3 and I missed the game. I had heard there was more talk about the future of the players' association. The word was that Jack Adams was putting a lot of pressure on his players to quit the organization. Adams had already gotten rid of Ted Lindsay and Marty Pavelich. Now he was going after his prize Gordie Howe.

"Howe won't miss Lindsay a bit," Adams said when he was in Montreal. "He helped Lindsay more than Lindsay helped him. Hockey made Ted Lindsay and now he turns on hockey. It gave me a laugh when Lindsay called a press conference to state his case, whatever it was." But the big laugh was Adams saying, "I traded Lindsay for no personal matter."

Who was he kidding? Adams traded Lindsay to help kill our association and in November 1957 Jack's pressure paid off. Gordie Howe, Red Kelly and Marcel Pronovost quit the players' association at a press conference. Adams was there with a big grin on his face. Without the Red Wings the association was kaput! By the end of the season the great idea of Lindsay and Harvey was history.

My flu kept me out of our first five games of the season. When I got back into the lineup against Toronto on October 17, 1957 we were in first place and Rocket was leading the NHL in scoring. For what else was going on, Marlene will tell you.

Things were slowly changing off the ice, too. We hockey players' wives were starting to be a little less sheltered, to do a few things on our own.

Lucille Richard and I often drove together to pick up Rocket and Boom after a road trip but I always picked her up because Rocket hadn't encouraged Lucille to learn to drive. So I suggested she go to driving school and she did just that.

A few months later Lucille Richard actually picked me up for the first time on a miserable midwinter night. We were going to pick up Boom and Rocket at the train station. To Maurice's surprise Lucille announced that she had learned how to drive. By the look on his face you could tell he was skeptical.

Rocket took the wheel and was driving up Guy Street, a very steep hill, in rush hour when guess what we ran out of gas!

Maurice turned to his wife and said, "The first thing you have to learn about driving is to fill up the gas tank."

Something which simply wasn't done back in those days was wives traveling to watch their husbands play away games. It was kind of an unspoken but understood rule of management that wives just didn't show up on the road.

But finally Lise Richard, Pierrette Talbot and I decided to be really brave and travel by train to New York to watch the Canadiens play the Rangers. We had friends make all the arrangements for us so our husbands didn't know we were going and my Aunt Charlotte would take care of our children Linda and Bobby while I was gone. I was so excited; I was about to go on my first trip to New York.

Wouldn't you know it! Boom got sick the day before I was to leave for New York. That meant I had to tell him about the plans because all of a sudden it looked as though he might not make the trip. He was amazed when I told him what we were planning but he said immediately, "Oh no, you must go. This is only a cold. I'll be fine. I'll fly down tomorrow."

So off we went, spent the night in New York City and the next day — game day — ran our feet off sightseeing. I was having such a great time. We got back to our hotel room around four in the afternoon to get ready to go over to the Garden when the phone rang. It was my sister-in-law Margo calling from Montreal: "Marlene, you better get back here. Boom's in the hospital with pneumonia!"

Now I had to get back home all by myself because there is no way Lise and Pierrette are coming back with me. Someone at the hotel told me how to take a bus out to the airport. By some miracle I caught the right one, because I really didn't listen to what he was saying, I was so scared and worried about Boom. But I got to the airport, managed to get on a flight to Montreal and was home late that evening. Boom was sick as a dog for a whole week.

So that was my adventurous trip to New York City! That trip made me grow up in one afternoon. When two or three girls are together it's much easier to be brave and daring. But when you're alone it's not quite as simple.

By game time that horrible night Toe Blake had heard the rumors that wives were in New York City and he supposedly told the team before the game, "I found out that some of the wives are here. If you don't win this game you have a $500 fine to pay." They won the game.

In the meantime it was a good thing I decided to get my wanderlust out of my blood that early in the season because I was pregnant again, the baby due in late January.

On Saturday night October 19, 1957 at The Forum in my second game of the season I got my first two points — a pair of assists. But that wasn't the story. On the previous Thursday when we were home against the Maple Leafs Rocket beat goalie Ed Chadwick midway through the third period for his 499th NHL goal.

The entire City of Montreal, not to mention much of the rest of the hockey world, became obsessed with Rocket's five hundredth-goal. In *The Hockey News* Ron Laplante wrote, "It would not be inaccurate to say that almost everyone in the Province of Quebec sometime during the day either discussed or thought about Richard and his imminent accomplishment."

When Rocket stepped on the ice with us for the warmup skate he was given a rousing ovation. I could almost hear goalie Glenn Hall saying to himself ". . . Not on me. Please don't score number 500 on me!" Chicago had a formidable team with Lindsay, Hall, Jim Thomson and Gus Mortson in the lineup and for more than 15 minutes they played us even.

Rocket was in top form. He tested Hall early and often but the goalie was sharp. The break happened shortly after we had killed a penalty. Jean Béliveau, who normally would have been on a line with Bert Olmstead and me, was out with Maurice. Big Jean sent out a pass, Rocket flicked his powerful wrists and the twine bulged behind Hall at 15:32. The crowd noise seemed to lift The Forum right off its foundations.

When the ovation subsided the public address announcer said, "Goal by Mister Hockey — Maurice Richard." Once again the place erupted as I've never heard it before. Now you know why my assists on goals by Harvey and Béliveau were overlooked that night.

While Toe Blake had cooled down Rocket's temper he didn't dilute any of Maurice's endless drive for goals. Even out of town crowds, which normally would give Rocket all kinds of abuse, had come to appreciate him. When he scored a hat trick at Olympia the Detroit fans gave him a standing ovation. "It took 16 years," said Detroit writer Marshall Dann, "but the time finally came when Rocket Richard drew more cheers than jeers in Detroit."

Another visiting player who brought down the house at Olympia was Ted Lindsay. He came back as a Blackhawk and drew a thunderous ovation. The Detroit fans were turning against Adams. His trades had backfired and his Red Wings had sunk to near the bottom of the league.

By contrast we were better than ever. The NHL scoring leaders were: Rocket, Pocket, Dickie Moore and Big Jean. At the rate he was going Rocket looked good enough to win the scoring championship he had lost to me in 1955.

But it wasn't in the cards. On November 13, 1957 tragedy struck at Maple Leaf Gardens. Rocket had taken a shot on goal when he collided with Toronto defenseman Marc Réaume. The two fell to the ice but as Réaume scrambled to his feet his skate blade caught in Maurice's tendon guard and sliced into his Achilles tendon snapping it almost in half.

"He was lucky," said Dr. Jim Murray, the Leafs' physician. "Just a shade more and the tendon would have snapped. Had this happened it could very well have meant the end of his career."

As it was we figured on losing Rocket for most if not all of the season. Watching the medics take Maurice off the ice I realized again how vulnerable we were and how quickly our careers could end. I knew from firsthand experience. Paul Meger my former linemate had been one of the most talented prospects in the NHL when he came up to Canadiens with me. But one night he had been involved in a collision and the back tip of a Boston player's skate cut right through Meger's scalp almost to his brain. The damage was permanent and Meger never played in the NHL again. Then there was Gil Mayer, a promising Maple Leafs goalie who was blinded when hit in the eye with a puck. In 1950 Gordie Howe missed a check on Ted Kennedy and pitched headfirst into the boards suffering a fractured skull. He nearly died.

I prayed that my friend, my mentor, my hero would be all right. But even without Rocket we climbed to first place. Then lightening struck again and Big Jean got hurt. They brought up a kid named Gene Achtymichuk from Montreal Royals to center my line. It felt strange playing without Big Jean but something clicked between Gene and me. Len Bramson wrote, "Boom Boom is playing some of the greatest hockey of his career."

Despite the injuries the whole team was playing super hockey and by January 1958 we were so far ahead of the pack the other teams were becoming frustrated. If teams couldn't beat us with goals they tried to do it with their fists and sticks.

One of the most memorable brawls took place on New Year's Day, January 1, 1958 at Boston Garden. We beat the Bruins 4-3 and I got our second goal but that was incidental in terms of what else was going on that night.

I must emphasize that during our run through two straight Stanley Cups we played hockey the way the game was meant to be played. Some writers liked to call it "Firewagon Hockey" and others had different names for it, but the bottom line was that we stressed the best parts of the game. Rocket and I were the explosive shooters; Big Jean was the best playmaker who could also score from any angle; Bert was the best digger I've ever seen and Dickie had the grit to go with his intelligence. On defense Doug and Tom were the two best behind the blue line and Jacques had become the best goalie.

With all this skill we had no use for so-called "policemen" in our lineup. We fought our own battles. When Lou Fontinato picked on Rocket, Maurice slugged it out with him. When Ron Murphy high-sticked me in New York, I didn't look around for somebody else to do my dirty work, I did it myself. That's the way it was up and down the line which is why that New Year's free-for-all at Boston Garden was so important for our hockey club.

Every one of the other five NHL clubs knew our lineup inside and out and they were jealous of us. Because some of them didn't know better a couple of coaches got the idea that they could slow us down by running The Pocket. After all Henri was one of the smaller guys in the league and they were hoping that Maurice would get distracted trying to defend his kid brother. If that happened not one but two Canadiens would be neutralized.

It is important to remember that the Bruins had plenty of skilled players to go with their fighters. Bronco Horvath was right up there with me near the top of the scoring race and so were his line teammates Vic Stasiuk and Johnny Bucyk. They had future Hall of Fame defensemen like Fernie Flaman and Leo Boivin. But they also had the fighters like Jack Bionda and Leo Labine and Flaman could handle his dukes with the league's best. They made Boston one of the least fun places to play.

On this night Labine put them on the score sheet early in the first. Claude Provost and myself briefly lifted us ahead and then Horvath tied it at two before the period ended. There were five penalties, two for us, but no indication of what was going to break loose.

What was clear however was that the Bruins had taken dead aim at Pocket, who just happened to be one of the NHL's leading scorers right behind Dickie Moore. Boston players pounded Henri at every turn, but true to form he bounced off them like a rubber ball.

Flaman was giving Henri the business again and was about to get a two-minute penalty when Pocket decided he had had enough and laced into the big defenseman. Next Bionda and Harvey went at it and just like that every single player on the ice except the goalies was swinging.

It was like a tag-team wrestling match with everyone changing opponents. The real star of fight night at Boston Garden was Pocket. He fought Flaman, Bionda and Labine in order and never backed away. It was an amazing sight because each of them was much bigger than Henri.

More important, it delivered a message to the Bruins and the rest of the league that Pocket Rocket wouldn't be intimidated by the biggest guys on the opposition. Even Lynn Patrick, general manager of the Bruins, was impressed:

> *I saw little Richard take on Fernie, Jack and Leo one right after another. Let me tell you he didn't lose a decision to any one of them. He must have fought by himself for five minutes but he didn't back up once. How he did it, I don't know but he's a heckuva fighter. You don't need any policemen to take care of him!*

And speaking of policemen the fight got so out of hand that some of Boston's finest went onto the ice to restore order. But they didn't have skates and the ice was slippery. When one policeman fell to the ice, losing his cap he was helped to his feet by Flaman. Captain Leo Hoban, officer in charge of the Garden police division, consulted with referee Frank Udvari at rinkside: "Your men don't have any footing out there," Udvari pleaded. "If you call them off we can get things straightened out."

The police retreated to the sidelines and the fights finally petered out. The scars remained for some time. I was cut and bruised around the face. So were Labine and Bob Armstrong of the Bruins as well as Pocket, Moore and André Pronovost. Labine, Flaman and I came out of it with damaged hands. Labine also had a five-stitch cut on his forehead and tore a tendon in his finger that required surgery.

Some fun.

"The Bruins learned something," said Toe Blake. "They learned that Henri is in this league to stay."

They also learned that we could play the game anyway the other team wanted to play. And if they wanted to brawl we could swing with the best fighters they had.

Pocket came right back in the third period and scored at 6:38 and Claude Provost and Phil Goyette combined for our fourth goal. We won the game 4-3 and won more respect around the league.

I had 23 goals in 36 games and felt fantastic. Big Jean returned to the lineup on Sunday January 19, 1958 when we were in Boston for a return engagement against the Bruins. This was an important game for me because I was only one shy of my two-hundredth NHL goal and Marlene was expecting our third child Danny.

After the New Year's fight, feeling between our teams was running high. I wasn't worried about that. I was hot. Going into Boston I had 24 goals even though I had missed the start of the season. Now I not only was in shape but the puck was bouncing for me. If I reached the 200 plateau I'd be only the twenty-eighth guy in NHL history to do that. (Rocket, Toe Blake, my late father-in-law Howie Morenz and Elmer Lach had done it for Canadiens.)

The score was zip-zip in the first when their defenseman Allan Stanley went off for two minutes. The power play went into motion with Dickie Moore, Big Jean, Marcel Bonin (filling in for Rocket), Doug and me. We moved it into their zone. Dickie gave the puck to Big Jean and he got it to me in front of the Boston net.

Flaman was there right in front of me with his arms apart when I noticed Bonin standing by their goalie Harry Lumley. I shot the puck trying to miss Flaman and hit Bonin for the deflection. Lucky for me it didn't hit anything except the inside of the net. The red light went on and number 200 was mine!

I got another one later in the game as well as an assist en route to a 6-2 win. We were hot and everything was falling into place after a shaky start.

One other thing about that game in Boston that bears retelling because it says so much about the way every one of us on Canadiens was thinking in those days. The score was tied 1-1 in the second period when the linesmen blew the whistle for an offside as the Bruins were coming into our zone. Jacques Plante had relaxed as he usually did after the whistle blew but for some reason Flaman fired the puck into our empty net.

Doug Harvey was closest to Flaman and he took the puck and fired it right down the ice at the Boston goal. All of a sudden referee Eddie Powers points his finger at Doug. "Hey, wait a minute," Harvey shouted, "Flaman shot the puck into our net. Nobody scores on our net at any time during the game if we can help it and that's the way it's always been for us."

Powers gave Doug a misconduct penalty and a game misconduct but I still say Doug did the right thing. We constantly fought to score and to not let anybody score on us at anytime during the game, misconduct or no misconduct.

Big Jean was back in the lineup and Rocket was practicing again which meant that he too would be with us and we'd be stronger than ever. I didn't think things could get any better but they did! On January 24, 1958 Danny Geoffrion came into this world. Mom and the new babe were just fine but because big brother Bob was home with scarlet fever the doctor decided to keep them in the hospital a full week. I visited Marlene and Danny every night that I didn't have a game. I was one happy hockey player.

What I didn't know was that the thing Dick Irvin used to call "The Unseen Hand" would play a very dirty trick on me, one that almost cost me my life.

The date was January 28, 1958 and it was an ordinary practice at The Forum. During the workout the guys were checking pretty closely. At one point André Pronovost took the puck from me and I wheeled and came back. The two of us collided and I felt a burning sensation but I kept on skating. Everything seemed all right.

But it wasn't. About a hundred feet further on the pain overcame me and I fell to the ice.

My teammates were used to my clowning around and thought I was at it again. Later Tom Johnson told reporters, "We thought Boom was joking. We all started to laugh." But this was no joke. I wanted to scream but I couldn't make a sound. Doug Harvey was the first one over to me.

I wanted to talk to Doug but I couldn't say a word. If I could have spoken I would have shouted, "*J'etouffe, j'etouffe.*" (I can't breathe.) I thought I would die right then and there. Doug grabbed my two legs and started pumping me but I passed out. That's when everyone realized that it was no joke and called our physiotherapist Bill Head who may well have saved my life. Bill instantly knew that something terrible was wrong and that pumping on me was the wrong thing to do. He looked at me and said, "Don't touch him! Boom has to go to the hospital right away!"

Nobody knew what was the matter until I got to the hospital which fortunately was just across the street from The Forum. No sooner had they moved me into the Emergency Room than the doctors discovered that I had a ruptured bowel. They took me into the operating room for two hours of emergency surgery. Later Bill Head said it was the first time he had encountered an injury like that during his long career dealing with athletes.

After I regained consciousness I realized how close I had come to losing my life. I picked up the *Montreal Gazette*. Queen Elizabeth's visit to Montreal was on page two. On page one the headline read: "Hockey Star Bernie Geoffrion Fights for his Life in Hospital."

Marlene can tell you the rest:

> It was about two in the afternoon and I was standing at the hospital window with a plant in my hand trying to find a better place to sit it. I had the radio on. Suddenly I heard the announcer say something awful, something about how they had no definite word yet on the injury to Bernie Geoffrion but one report said he was near death.
>
> The plant fell from my hand and shattered on the floor. I turned to run out of the room and as I did a doctor and a nurse walked in. He tried to reassure me but I'm starting to yell and they quickly got me into the bed. The next thing I knew somebody was sticking a needle in me and then I was out like the proverbial light.

I regained consciousness hours later at about seven at night and here was Boom's family all standing around the bed looking at me. At first I thought I had dreamed the whole awful thing and I started to tell them about this terrible nightmare I had had when they began to tell me what had happened and why no one had told me.

Boom was hurt four days after Danny was born and the doctor wanted to keep me in the hospital a whole week but the next morning there I was trying to get off the maternity floor and out to see my husband. I just had to see with my own eyes that he was going to be okay. The elevator door opened and there stood my doctor coming to see me. He just turned me around, escorted me back to my room and that was that.

Fortunately the Canadiens were very supportive. Senator Molson sent a messenger to tell Marlene that I was in good hands, that the surgery was successful and not to worry, which was nice of him.

But the fact was I had come pretty close to death and I knew it, the doctors knew it, and Marlene knew it. If I had not been moved so quickly to the hospital, I would have been history. No question!

My recuperation was slow. I had lost more than 15 pounds and felt very weak. I couldn't even think about playing hockey. As soon as I saw Marlene I said, "You don't have to worry. I'm not going to play hockey any more."

She knew what I was talking about. Her father Howie Morenz broke his leg in a game against Chicago. He was taken to hospital, complications set in and he died there. My injury had taken place exactly 21 years later to the day! My father-in-law's accident had taken place on January 28, 1937.

Naturally Marlene didn't want me to play any more and I certainly understood her feelings. I was very nearly killed and it shook me up. All I wanted to do now was follow my doctor's orders. They told me to rest completely for a month and a half which meant that I could forget about hockey for the rest of the season.

That was easy to say but not so easy to do. Hockey had been my entire life since I first laced on a pair of skates; it had been my career and my means of earning a living. I didn't have a day job. I had a wife and three kids, one just an infant, to support. I was worried.

And there was plenty to worry about but I decided that I would make the best of it, which meant having the best time possible at the moment. The team helped with that. They were kind enough to send me down to Florida for a vacation. It was the best thing that could have happened at the time. There I slowly began to regain my strength and to put on weight again. I could relax on the beach and try not to think about the future. By the time I returned to Montreal I was feeling better than ever. Some of my teammates were recovering from injuries too. One of them was Rocket. Another was Dickie Moore.

When Richard's Achilles tendon was injured in November 1957 it was widely predicted that his career might be over. After all he was 36 years old and as his sportswriting pal Andy O'Brien put it, "It was just too much to expect that the Rocket's leg could ever recover enough to obey the orders from his mind to swerve, spurt and come to jolting stops."

Rocket would hear none of that. He suffered though the months of rehabilitation and on February 20, 1958 Maurice The Rocket Richard was back wearing number nine. The Forum was jammed — 14,528 fans came to see his return. Rocket had six terrific scoring chances, put two of them past Harry Lumley and led Canadiens to a 4-0 win over Boston.

Dickie Moore's story was just as amazing. It would be hard to find a hockey star reaching such heights in 1957-58 under more difficult circumstances. How many players could have skated through the tough, final five weeks of the NHL schedule with a hand in a cast and still go on to win the scoring championship? Yet that's what Moore did. He finished the 70-game schedule with 36 goals and 48 assists for 84 points beating out Pocket by four.

After a while I got back on skates and began working out to get into shape. I hadn't changed my mind about quitting hockey I told myself. The club finished first by miles but what happened on the last weekend of the season was disturbing.

What made us think twice about the team was the manner in which they finished. On the final Saturday home game we got trashed 8-5 by Boston and Sunday at Detroit the Red Wings took us 4-2. Even though the games were meaningless Les Canadiens do not like to enter the play-offs dropping two straight, especially since the last game was against the same team we'd meet in the opening play-off round. Detroit was scheduled to face off against us on March 25 to launch our Stanley Cup defense.

By now I was antsy from not playing and the Tuesday morning of the opener I told Marlene that I was going to visit The Forum.

"What for?" she asked. "You told me you were finished, that you couldn't play anymore."

"I know," I said, "but I just want to go down there and see the guys."

I meant it too.

But when I got to the corner of St. Catherine and Atwater Streets I began to feel differently. And when I sat in on the team meeting I felt part of the team for the first time since my accident. After the meeting I went over to my locker and pulled out my skates. Slowly I laced them on while continually asking myself, "Boom, what are you doing?"

For about half an hour, I skated around The Forum ice. My legs weren't in mint condition but they were holding me up. That did it!

I drove home, walked into the house and told Marlene I wanted my steak and potatoes, my honey and ice cream. She asked me what was up. I was very defensive.

"Hey, Marlene," I said trying to put up a good front, "I used to eat at this time before, so why change things now?"

An hour or so later we left for The Forum. As far as Marlene was concerned the two of us were merely driving down to watch a play-off game between Detroit and Montreal. When we got to the rink I said good-bye and went to the dressing room. "Don't worry," I said, "I will never play again!"

Famous last words.

What did I know? I meant it at the time. I knew that it would be stupid for me to try a comeback especially at this time after the doctors had warned me about making any premature attempts at rejoining the team. I didn't want to be a dead hero. I kept telling myself that as I walked to the dressing room.

But as I entered the room I suddenly got the urge to play. I put on the *bleu, blanc et rouge* uniform with the number five on the back and decided to take the ice during warmup just to see how I felt. Toe had no objections. I think that deep down he was hoping that I would come back in time for the play-offs although he never mentioned it to me.

Frankly I wasn't thinking about anything when I stepped on the ice. When people starting clapping and yelling I wondered what the commotion was all about. Soon everybody was on their feet and I realized that they were cheering *me*! This was too much.

Marlene stood up in her seat to see what all the cheering was for. I had told her I was retiring so she never dreamed the applause was for me. Just then a fan rushed by her and shouting "Boomer is back!

Boomer is back!" She was stunned — and not too happy because she had been assured by me and the medical staff that I needed the entire summer to recuperate and that I was finished playing hockey. No, Marlene was not tickled to see me on the ice at all!

I was nervous, I'll tell you that. I sweated through "O Canada" and wondered what would happen if I did play. I say "if" because I had no idea what plans Blake had now that I was on the bench. Rocket made it easier for all of us by scoring before the game was two and a half minutes old. Then at 3:57 Detroit got penalized which meant it was time for our power play. Toe looked down the bench and signaled me to go on with Rocket, Harvey and the others.

I felt weak but I could keep up. We were on for less than half a minute when I fed the puck to Rocket and he beat Terry Sawchuk and we were up by two. After that Béliveau scored at 6:02 and when the Red Wings got still another penalty Toe gave me the signal, along with Rocket and Pocket. The Richard brothers moved the puck around as if it was on a string. *Bang! Bang!* Over to Boom and I bombed it past Sawchuk. A goal and an assist in the first period of my comeback!

The cheers were wonderful and the 8-1 win was easy. But do you know what? I made a big mistake coming back like that. I was still weak and I really needed more time to recuperate. People were telling my wife that I was stupid and they were right. I should never have done it.

We slaughtered the Red Wings 5-1 in Game Two, then went off to Detroit for two straight in the Motor City. In the final game we trailed 3-1 going into the third period. Rocket made it 3-2 and then they got a penalty. Toe sent me out again on the power play. Big Jean and I teamed up getting the puck to Dickie Moore. He rifled it past Sawchuk and then 49 seconds later Rocket followed with the winner. Detroit was gone in four games.

Toe was still cautious. "We haven't won The Stanley Cup yet," he insisted in the dressing room after we had disposed of the Red Wings. "When we do then it will be time enough to celebrate."

I admired Blake's attitude. Nothing is ever in the bag. The trouble was nobody else in the hockey world believed him.

How could they? Rocket was superhuman. "I never saw anybody so goal hungry," said Toe. "You'd think Rocket was still going for the first goal of his career."

Dickie Moore was never better. Ditto for Doug Harvey. My pal Big Jean was the best center in the NHL with Pocket right behind him. At this point in time it would not be unfair to say that we had the best team man-for-man and position-for-position in history.

"Canadiens have a good clutch goalkeeper and the best defenseman in the game," said Billy Reay who was coaching Toronto at the time. "They've got the two leading scorers (Moore and Pocket), three good centers and on top of that they've got the Rocket. Who's going to beat them?"

The Bruins had knocked off the Rangers in the other play-off semifinal and on a Tuesday night April 8, 1958 they would get their first chance to dethrone us as champions.

Right off the bat their strategy was obvious; hit us at every turn and wear us down. Leo Labine and Fern Flaman got penalties in the first minutes but we couldn't make our power play work. Later when Boston got socked with a bench minor for too many men on the ice Toe gave me the eye and I was back out on the power play.

It didn't take very long. In less than a minute Harvey and Don Marshall combined to get me the puck. Big Jean screened Don Simmons. Donnie gave me the puck and I put it in at 12:24; the lead held up until Allan Stanley beat Jacques Plante early in the second. A little bit later I was taking off on a rush when Labine tripped me. With Labine in the penalty box Moore put us ahead again. Nobody scored after that and we skated off with a neat 2-1 win and a one-game lead in the series.

Game Two was a disaster for us although I managed a goal early in the first period to tie the count at one. Simmons was hotter than molten lava while Plante was not. The 5-2 loss was a wake-up call for us. And we needed it because the series now moved on to Boston Garden where the rink was smaller and the bodychecks harder.

"If we get the first goal tonight," said Blake, "we'll win."

That was simple enough strategy. The game was scoreless until late in the first period when Bronco Horvath went off at 16:17. Just as the penalty expired I set up Rocket and he put it away. That turned out to be the winner although the Richard brothers each got one in the third. Plante was perfect in the net.

I have to give that Boston team credit, they wouldn't go away. They outskated us, got a pair of goals from Don McKenney and skated off with a 3-1 win in Game Four. All of a sudden the series was tied at two games apiece and we were having second thoughts about this Bruin club. Simmons really was coming up big and their top-liners like McKenney, Fleming, Mackell and Doug Mohns were giving us fits.

The series returned to Montreal for Game Five and the Bruins stuck to form. McKenney put them ahead in the first but Big Jean and I traded second-period goals and we looked pretty good going into the third. Just past the ten-minute mark Horvath beat Plante and a game we thought was all sewed up went into overtime. A loss would send us back to Boston down three games to two. It was almost unthinkable.

For the first five and a half minutes nothing happened. In retrospect it was the perfect script for You Know Who. Later I was told that a Boston reporter turned to another and said, "When the game goes into sudden death the number I fear most is nine."

Here's how the last act unfolded: Pocket won the face-off and got the puck to Moore. Maurice was tearing down the right side and Dickie fed him the rubber. While Rocket maneuvered for his shot, Pocket skated interference in front of Simmons and Moore acted as a decoy, creating the impression that Rocket intended to give him a drop pass.

Rocket fired and Simmons never saw the puck.

On the train ride back to Boston I wondered whether I would have anything left for Game Six. If I did I figured maybe we could finally put these guys away and win another Cup. But I wasn't kidding myself about my condition. I still felt weak and didn't have the urge to play regularly; yet I still wanted to play.

Team spirit is something that is hard to explain to someone who has never experienced it. For me it was something special right from the beginning but especially after I got my confidence and was able to imprint my personality on the dressing room. While Rocket tended to be terribly intense and Big Jean was quiet I had become the locker room performer. Sometimes I was a balladeer and other times I was the team clown.

Most of all I liked to sing. Every so often a bunch of us would wind up at a nightclub. Once when Marlene and I were on vacation with Rocket and Lucille we went to a club. Somebody who knew I liked to sing urged me to go up on stage. Rocket was worried. "Boom," he said, "are you sure you know the words?"

I said, "Rocket, don't worry. If I don't remember the words, I'll make them up."

So I went up, belted out the tune and got a standing ovation. They asked me to come back again the next night which was fine except that I only knew that one song. I went back and for three straight nights I did the same tune and had a ball.

Actually my favorite type of music is opera. I developed my love of it when I was a kid and we had an old windup Victrola record player in the house. We had 12-inch records of the great Italian tenor Enrico Caruso singing "Pagliacci." I'd crank up the Victrola and worship every note the Great Caruso thundered over the machine.

I never lost that love of opera. When the Canadiens visited New York for a game with the Rangers, instead of taking my afternoon rest, I would sneak out of my hotel room and go to the Metropolitan Opera House. For five bucks I could get a seat way up in the back. Being at The Met was as much a thrill as playing in The Stanley Cup finals. Well, almost.

Speaking of the finals, my nerves were wound awfully tight on the night of April 20, 1958 when we took the ice at Boston Garden. The Bruins really impressed me with their overall toughness and defense, especially their captain Fernie Flaman. They had a rookie center Norm Johnson who looked good up front along with Jerry Toppazzini, Don McKenney and Fleming Mackell. They were all game-breakers.

We were thankful that Tommy Johnson had returned to our lineup after missing the first four games of the finals with an injury. Tommy wasn't in good condition and hadn't played in several weeks but he showed a lot of courage in getting out there. Along with Doug Harvey, Tommy was a steadying influence on our team when we needed it most. I was tickled that he'd be in the lineup again for Game Six because we had lost Dollard St. Laurent with a broken cheekbone in Game Four.

As we took the ice I remembered what Toe had said the last time we came to Boston; get the first goal and we'll win the game. Now I figured if we got the first goal we'd not only win the game but The Stanley Cup as well.

I was pleased that Blake sent our line — Big Jean, Bert and me — out for the opening face-off. The Garden was jammed and screaming as the national anthems were completed. There was only one way to quiet them down — that was with a Montreal goal.

Right off the opening face-off we went to work and within 46 seconds we had the result we wanted. Olmstead had worked the puck deep into the Bruins' zone and shoveled it off to Big Jean in the corner. Le Gros Bill sent me a waist-high pass and I deflected it behind Simmons. It was a bang-bang play, nice and early, just what we needed.

A minute and eight seconds later Rocket took a pass from Moore and beat Simmons with a 20-footer just inside the post. Simmons saw it all the way but — Rocket is Rocket!

We needed that two-goal cushion because Boston counterattacked in waves. In succession Plante had to make big saves on Vic Stasiuk, Mackell and McKenney. Finally McKenney took a pass from Mohns and beat Jacques with a drive that he partially stopped but the puck dropped between his feet and rolled over the line into the net. The first period ended 2-1 for us.

This was a hockey game.

When the Bruins came out for the second period the crowd greeted their heroes as if they had already won The Stanley Cup. We expected that and went about the business of building our lead. The key was forechecking. Our forwards went deep and penned Mackell, McKenney and Stasiuk in their own end for long periods of time.

Having scored one I was feeling a lot better about myself. Early in the second period Harvey put me in orbit with a pass on the right. I noticed Big Jean moving into good position at center so I flipped it to him. Up until this point Béliveau — like Rocket and Pocket — specialized in the forehand wrist shot and the backhander. I was the only one who regularly slapped the puck.

But Big Jean had been practicing the slap shot during scrimmages waiting for a perfect opportunity to try it out. On this particular play Simmons must have been expecting a wrist shot because he seemed awfully surprised when Le Gros Bill wound up and cranked a slapper. It beat him at 6:42 and the score was 3-1 for us.

It's funny what a goal can do for you both physically and mentally. All of a sudden all my aches, pains and fatigue were gone. I felt like flying and I did. With less than a minute left in the second period Bruins' defenseman Leo Boivin began moving toward our blue line from center ice.

I took a chance and lunged for the puck. The next thing I knew I was there alone with the puck in front of Simmons. Clean breakaways like that don't come often and I wasn't going to let this one go to waste. I raced in on Simmons, faked a slap shot and put it up and in with my backhand.

A 4-1 lead heading into the third period felt awfully good. Maybe too good. I suspect that more than a few of us already were seeing The Stanley Cup in our heads before we took the ice for the third period. Toe cautioned us about getting carried away but after all a three-goal lead is a three-goal lead. Right?

Wrong, when you forget to play defense. Sure enough the Bruins began chipping away at us as soon as the third period began. Norm Johnson finally scored at 5:20 to make it 4-2 and now they came at us with even more drive. We managed to keep them at bay until the 13-minute mark when Labine and Flaman brought the puck into our zone and dished it off to Larry Regan. The slick center circled our net and slid the puck past Plante.

With more than six minutes left the Bruins were alive and well. We were staggering and the 14,000 Boston fans knew it and turned the old rink into a noise factory. Now there was no room for fooling around. We tightened up like the champs we were and denied their every rush until the final minute when Bruins coach Milt Schmidt lifted Simmons for a sixth skater.

Harvey intercepted their pass and moved straight up the ice with only Regan back acting as their "goaltender." Doug shot and Regan made the save but couldn't hold on. Harvey just slapped the rebound into the yawning net. That did it. We had won our third straight Stanley Cup, the first team to turn the trick since Toronto won a trio in 1947, 1948 and 1949.

The victory celebration was not what you would call glamorous. At Boston Garden the visitors' dressing room was tiny, dirty and with all the media trying to push in quite a mess. Since this was our third consecutive Cup we tended to take it a little more matter-of-factly than the first two but really the only thing holding us back was the closet that passed for a dressing room.

Believe me we had plenty to shout about. Sure we finished first and won the Cup with relative ease but when you think about *how* we did it, the feat is all the more amazing. Over the season Rocket, Big Jean, Plante, Harvey, Olmstead, Johnson, St. Laurent, Busher Curry and I had each been out with injuries.

The credit for keeping us together and rolling forward has to go to Toe Blake. As a coach he was never better. "About the only existing thing Toe can do with The Stanley Cup," said his old friend Milt Dunnell of *The Toronto Star*, "would be to lose it."

We weren't about to do that. Our club was bursting with talent. Rocket was still a fixture on the right side. Pocket, who hadn't even reached his prime, almost won the scoring title and Moore won it with a cast on his arm for more than a month. Plante was the best goalie and his backup, little Charlie Hodge, did the job almost as well as Jacques. And Doug Harvey won his fourth Norris Trophy in a row!

Considering my physical condition I consider my play-off pro-duction one of the most amazing things I ever accomplished. In ten games I delivered six goals and five assists for 11 points. This from a guy who said he would never play hockey again.

CHAPTER 10

Full Recovery and Another Cup

I needed a vacation very badly in the summer of 1958. My play-off heroics on our run to the third straight Stanley Cup took a terrible toll on me both physically and mentally. No question I did good by the team but it was at great expense to my body and my family. Now I was glad to relax with Marlene and the kids and think about my future.

Marlene will tell you the details:

This was the time of year we would entertain — the only time I could rely on Boom being there. We had several close friends who were completely outside of hockey by this time and while these friends had entertained Boom, myself and the kids whenever possible in the wintertime, we would reciprocate in the summer after we had come back from the annual trip to Florida (which we took thanks to other close friends like Jimmy and Betty LaPorte and Ernie and Dee Carradori, who loaned us their condos in Boca Raton, Florida for years).

These nonhockey friends — Dr. Marcel and Eileen Remy, Dr. René and Pauline Poirier, Dr. Robert and Thérèse Gareau, Dr. Roger and Claire Pontbriand and Jean-Paul and Lucette Hamelin — were gracious people who taught both of us so much about elegance, gracious entertaining and friendship. They invited the whole family out to Mount Roland (near ski country) for the winter holidays for several seasons. The kids and I would go out and be entertained royally then Boom would join us for a night or two right on the holiday. He couldn't ski of course because he had to play hockey but the kids and I could. While I spent some lovely times with these wonderful friends, it was 11 years before I spent a New Year's Eve with my husband! Still despite the hardships and injuries these years and the summers we had together with our friends were some of the best years of our lives. . . .

The ruptured bowel had given me the scare of a lifetime and I realized that I was lucky to be alive. It was only natural that I should think about retirement. But if I quit the game now at age 27 what was I going to do? I loved to sing and believed that I could have a career in show business. My sister Margo took me to a music teacher and I spent an hour with her. When I got out I turned to my sister and said, "My music career is over! If I have to go through all this forget it. I quit."

As the summer unfolded I felt stronger and better in every way. I thought about Rocket who was now 37, had recovered from a serious Achilles tendon injury and was preparing for training camp as if he were a rookie. I was reminded of a goal he had scored in the play-offs the previous spring against Detroit.

"Rocket looks like he'll go on forever," was the word around The Forum. That's what I wanted them to say about me too. If Rocket was coming back, Boom Boom was coming back as well and there I was at training camp raring to get going for the 1958-59 season.

The first thing on the agenda was the annual All-Star Game. Frankly, Canadiens' record against the All-Stars was somewhat embarrassing. In 1953 they beat us 3-1. In 1956 we tied 1-1 but in 1957 we lost again 5-3. The sum total was a tie, two losses and only five goals in three games.

The game on October 4, 1958 was played at The Forum before a crowd of 13,793, third largest since the All-Star Game was inaugurated a dozen years earlier. From the very start I knew that this would be a different kind of game for the *bleu, blanc et rouge*. How did I know? All I had to do was read Rocket's face. He scored the first goal at 9:19 of the first period and I whacked in the second behind Glenn Hall less than six minutes later.

Donnie Marshall and Pocket put us up 4-0 in the second before Bob Pulford finally beat Jacques Plante. After that we cruised to a 6-3 triumph. It's worth remembering that Rocket not only got the game's first goal but the last one as well. The other thing I remember about the game but not too fondly was that I suffered still another injury scare.

Midway through the game I was coming out of my own end and reached for a pass. Red Wings' defenseman Red Kelly caught me with a solid bodycheck harder than the collision that had ruptured my bowel. It was a good, legal check; Kelly always hit clean, but I was caught off guard. I went down in a heap and lay there with shooting pains in my neck and chest. I kept saying to myself, "I've done it again!" In The Forum clinic they thought I had a broken shoulder blade. I couldn't help but remember my brush with death the previous season. Canadiens' physiotherapist Bill Head told me later that they had lost my pulse for fifteen seconds. A ruptured bowel can be fatal — I had been given last rites — and I had a foot-long scar down the middle of my stomach to remind me that I was in a very, very dangerous business. I figured that if the shoulder blade was broken it was a sign that it was time to hang up my skates.

On a closer examination the doctor said that this time I had only pulled muscles in my neck and chest and I could play in our first game if I wanted to. I did some heavy thinking and realized that hockey was what I knew best. I knew then and there that I loved the game too much to think about quitting.

I was back in the lineup in nothing flat. Not that Toe Blake desperately needed me because we were so loaded with greatness. Frank Selke had so many talented young players knocking at the door that he actually let go of Bert Olmstead, Dollard St. Laurent and Busher Curry in the off-season and hardly thought twice about it. Busher retired, St. Laurent was traded to Chicago and Bert went to Toronto.

I would miss Bert. I loved him for a lot of reasons but mostly because he was one of the most intense players I had ever known. It wouldn't be easy to replace him on the line with Big Jean and me. You don't find digging left wingers like Bert very often.

Bert Olmstead had helped me enormously during my first two NHL seasons. On nights when I was ready to toss my skates in the corner Bert would give me an encouraging pat on the back but he'd also lift the skin right off my hide when I made a foolish mistake or got too cocky.

How do you replace really good people like that? We added a rugged defenseman named Ian Cushenan and had Ralph Backstrom to fill in for Curry up front. Ab McDonald was to replace Bert.

When somebody told Toe Blake that King Clancy of the Maple Leafs had said "The Canadiens have a lock on everything," he snarled, "It doesn't matter how good you are — you can't let down. If we do they'll beat us."

We didn't. Boston, who many pundits picked as our biggest challenge, came to The Forum and we topped them 3-2. I assisted on the first goal. We raced to the head of the pack and after nine games I was tied for the scoring lead with Rocket and Pocket, with Big Jean only one point behind us. The bowel injury was by now ancient history and I was loving the game again.

Bouncing back the way I did filled me with new energy and an appreciation of life. My sense of humor was at its best and my teammates were liking me for what I was. "Before a game we can tell how Boomer is going to go," Tom Johnson told a reporter. "If he's doing handstands in the dressing room then you know he'll get one or two goals."

I had a comeback for every question. When a newspaperman asked me what I liked about playing hockey I shot back, "The money!"

Another night after we had been defeated at The Forum a fan gave me a hard time as Marlene and I were walking along Atwater Street.

"Mister," I said, "if you're so smart, for the next game, I'll let you wear my skates and I'll sit up in your seat. And we'll see how good you are."

I was as good as I ever was. My shot still was the hardest in the league even though more and more players were copying the slap shot and I was stickhandling as well as I ever had. My imitations of opera star Mario Lanza were never better. I had seen him in the movie, "The Great Caruso" nine times!

Nobody could bother me not even the league's great needlers. One night King Clancy, coach of the Maple Leafs, really got on my case."You're a bum Geoffrion," Clancy shouted from the Toronto bench. "Just a bush leaguer."

I skated over to him and barked, "I may be a bush leaguer but at least I'm playing for a big-league coach!"

Toe Blake was very happy with me because I was doing the job for him even without Olmstead. Playing alongside Big Jean was fantastic. His passes were crisper than ever and his view of the ice was about the best there was. I figured that if I could stay healthy I might even have a chance to tie Rocket's 50-goal season record. The trick for me was to be able to last the entire schedule without missing any games.

As pleased as he was with the team Toe was wise enough to know that he could have problems ahead. Rocket wasn't getting any younger and perfectionist that he was the time was coming when he would have to settle for less simply because he wouldn't be able to get around the rink as quickly as he would like. For the moment at least there was no concern because Maurice was still keeping up with Pocket and Dickie Moore. Together they formed one of the best lines in the NHL during 1958-59.

Jacques Plante was the NHL'S best goalie but ever creative he was taking more chances leaving his crease and clearing the puck. Jacques had expanded his repertoire. Instead of merely skating behind the net to stop the puck for his defensemen Jacques had decided to play defense himself and was passing the puck ahead to our forwards to launch plays.

Critics marveled at the way Plante was revolutionizing goal-tending. They continued to praise him until one night in a game with the Blackhawks at The Forum early in the 1958-59 season. It was the first period and Earl Balfour, one of the Chicago players, had snapped the puck into the corner of our zone and typically Jacques went after it. He wanted to clear the puck into the oppo-site corner out of danger but underestimated how fast Balfour was coming at him. When he finally realized that the Blackhawk was almost on top of him he rushed his clearing attempt.

Instead of skimming along the boards behind the net and around the other side to one of our players, the puck hit the side of the net exactly where Balfour happened to be! He said "Thank you very much, Mister Plante," circled in front of the gaping net, and slipped it in for the easiest goal of his career.

The Forum crowd booed unmercifully.

Jacques was shaken. After the game which Chicago won 4-2 he was pale and drawn in the dressing room. As he pulled on his coat to leave he muttered, "Why did it have to happen here? Why here of all places?"

By mid-November 1958 Plante's goals-against average had climbed to nearly 3.00 per game, almost one full goal over the mark he had maintained in winning the Vezina Trophy for three straight seasons. Blake complained:

Worse than that is Plante's nervousness. Our home fans have been riding him and he's let it get his goat. It's affecting his work. He's got to get over it. After all he is a professional. The only way

*to shut up a guy who boos you is to play better. This ought to make
Plante fight back. Instead he's getting worse. We can't win a championship with bad goalkeeping.*

Toe himself was feeling the pressure. The more Stanley Cups we
won the more demands he felt to win another one and now we were
aiming at a record fourth in a row, so you can imagine how intense
he had become. Where in the past he might have joked about an
incident now Blake was reacting in a more negative way. One game
more than any revealed this turnabout in his personality.

We were in New York on November 26, 1958 for a game against
the Rangers. The real focus of attention on this night was Rocket
who had 599 goals going into the game. Late in the first period he
grabbed the puck at the right side of the Rangers' net. He tore
behind the goal in a semicircle and wound up at the left corner
where he jabbed the puck into the little air between Gump
Worsley's pad and the goal posts. When the puck slid across the
goal line Maurice broke into a smile and leaped to his feet.
Ironically referee Frank Udvari who once had been Rocket's tor-
mentor fetched the puck for him. Number 600 was his.

At first the Garden crowd was silent, then they realized that
hockey history had been made before them. There was early, scat-
tered applause and then as if by chain reaction fan after fan began
applauding. It was a heartwarming scene.

Unfortunately it was not enough to win the game. Rangers rallied for three straight goals and beat us 5-3. In the dressing room
afterward steam was coming out of Blake's ears. There was a knock
on the big, steel door. Blake opened it and saw two New York
reporters standing there waiting to come in and interview Rocket.
Toe slammed the door so hard you could hear the reverberations
in Montreal. That kind of behavior told me that Blake had become
a lot edgier. It was clear that the pressure had gotten to him.

As for Rocket the six-hundredth goal got him thinking. "I've
got 600," he said, "but I don't think I'll ever get 700. I'll play
another year but if I get another bad injury this year it could be
my last."

Soon after that comment Rocket collided with Red Kelly leaving
his mouth painfully swollen. However it wasn't enough to cause
him to retire.

Both Rocket and Toe recovered quickly with the best tonic of all,
a couple of huge wins over the hated Red Wings. The first was a

Can you believe the Boomer once was an altar boy? I got my start here at my First Holy Communion.

My mom, Florina Geoffrion, was a rare beauty in every imaginable way. The picture speaks for itself.

My dad, Jean Baptist Geoffrion was the kind of dad every son would want to have.

I never could have been a professional hockey player if I hadn't played on this team for the Immaculate Conception Parish in 1942, and my first coach, Father Robitaille. I am the one mugging for the camera, second from the left, bottom row.

In 1948, at the age of 17, I played junior for the Montreal Nationales. Notice our very classy uniforms. How about the patch over the knee?

You're looking at a guy who has fulfilled his childhood dream. I'm wearing the bleu, blanc, et rouge of Les Canadiens, in the 1951-52 season.
(Photo courtesy of Imperial Oil-Turofsky/Hockey Hall of Fame)

Some would call this a match made in ice heaven—the daughter of Hall-of-Famer Howie Morenz marries the Canadiens' sharpshooter. Marlene was an accomplished figure skater when we met. The above photo was taken the day before our wedding, May 3, 1952. After 44 years of marriage I can say without a doubt that marrying Marlene was one of the best moves I ever made—on and off the ice!

Beating Red Wings ace Terry Sawchuk always was a big event. But when I did it for my 100th career goal during the 1954-55 season, it was even more special. (Photo courtesy of Photos and Archives CHC)

By the 1960-61 season, my slapshot was terrorizing the league. That was the season I scored 50 goals, only the second player in the league to do so after The Rocket Maurice Richard. (Photo courtesy of Hockey Hall of Fame)

Here I am against goalie Johnny Bower and the Toronto Maple Leafs. Ron Stewart (12) moves in on my right while Bob Pulford defends from my left.
(Photo courtesy of Imperial Oil-Turofsky/Hockey Hall of Fame)

No team besides Toe Blake's Canadiens ever won five straight Stanley Cups. Here's Jean Beliveau (left), Pocket Rocket Henri Richard (right), and yours truly around our friend "Stanley" in 1960.
(Photo courtesy of Hockey Hall of Fame)

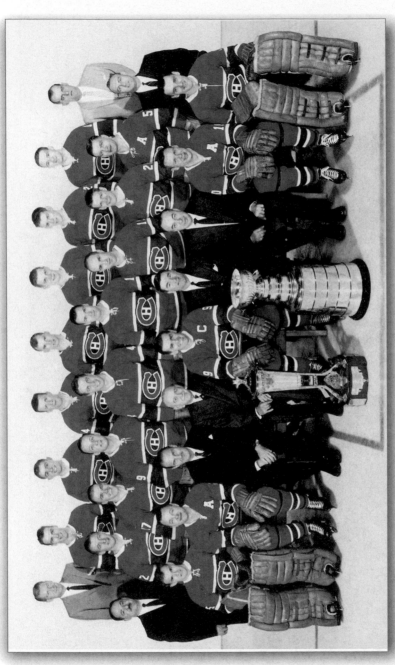

Our fifth straight Stanley Cup in 1960 (Photo courtesy of Hockey Hall of Fame)
Front row (left to right): Charlie Hodge, Doug Harvey, T.H.P. Molson (Vice-president, Canadian Arena Company), Frank J. Selke (Managing Director), Maurice Richard (Captain), Ken Reardon (Vice-president), Toe Blake (Coach), Tom Johnson, Jacques Plante.
Second row (left to right): Camil Des Roches (Associate Publicity Director), Dickie Moore, Jean Guy Talbot, Albert Langlois, Jean Beliveau, Ab McDonald, Bob Turner, Phil Goyette, Bernie Geoffrion, Frank D. Selke (Associate Publicity Director).
Third row (left to right): Larry Aubut (Assistant Trainer), Henri Richard, Bill Hicke, Claude Provost, Don Marshall, Ralph Backstrom, Andre Pronovost, Marcel Bonin, Hector Dubois (Trainer).

A first place team in my first year of coaching is about as good as it gets when you're behind the bench. This is a team shot of my Quebec Aces in 1964-65. Gump Worsley is at the far right and Doug Harvey is third from the left in the front row.

That's me, Broadway Bernie, scoring one for the New York Rangers. Madison Square Gardens was my home for only two years (1966-68), but what a ball I had in the Big Apple. (Photo courtesy of Frank Prazak/Hockey Hall of Fame)

It's said that coaching in the NHL will give a guy ulcers. I'll vouch for that although my Rangers in 1968-69 were a great bunch of guys.

NHL hockey in the Deep South? Some said impossible! I said, "Y'all come and see my Atlanta Flames" and they did and big league hockey became a hit in Dixie. (Photo courtesy of Hockey Hall of Fame)

What seemed like my ultimate accomplishment—coaching Les Canadiens to a winning record in 1979–80—turned out to be a disaster. (Photo courtesy of Bruce Bennet Studios)

Our personal ice palace, the Montreal Forum, closed late in the 1995-96 season. I'm pictured here at one of the closing ceremonies with some of my old buddies: (left to right) Henri Richard, Dickie Moore, Jean Beliveau, me, Maurice Richard, and Tom Johnson. (Photo courtesy of Photos and Archives CHC)

Here's an early family photo in a typical setting. Marlene and I with our children (left to right) Bob, Linda, and Danny.

Marlene visits the Hockey Hall of Fame in Toronto, Canada, where her father, Howie Morenz, is immortalized.

Best friends are like gold. Some of my 14-karat friends are (left to right) Ernie and Dee Carradori, and Jimmy and Betty LaPorte with us in Palm Springs, California.

Being married for 40 years is a terrific family milestone. Marlene and I celebrate with our kids, (left to right) Bob, Danny, and Linda at the bash our family threw for us in Georgia.

You would never believe that Marlene had just recuperated from major heart surgery. Yet, here we are celebrating our health and happiness in 1993.

We couldn't be happier and every parent knows the reason why. Marlene and I with our family: (front row, left to right) Linda, Blake, Sebastian, Brice, Brittney, and Nicholas; (back row, left to right) Joey, Shane, Mechelle, Hartland (Linda's husband), Marlene, me, Nancy (Bob's wife), Bob, Kelly (Danny's wife), and Danny.

6-2 shellacking we administered to them at The Forum but that was small potatoes compared to what we did at Olympia. It was 7-0 for us and I had a hat trick. Better yet I had moved into a tie for the scoring lead with New York's Andy Bathgate and we had taken a four-point lead over Detroit in the battle for first place. Once Doug Harvey recovered from his leg injury we opened the gap even more.

When Big Jean was sidelined Toe put Ralph Backstrom between me and Ab McDonald and we clicked immediately. When Béliveau recovered someone asked Blake where he was going to play Le Gros Bill. "I think I can find a place for him," Toe said facetiously, "but I'm not going to break up Boomer's line while it's going well."

We were hot. I was hot!

We had won a dozen games in a row and I had stretched my lead over Bathgate to seven points. Knock wood I wasn't getting hurt but I was getting attention. Bruins' general manager Lynn Patrick picked me as the greatest scorer he had ever seen, "Boom Boom has the best chance of beating Rocket's record," said Patrick.

I saw no point in arguing with him.

Naturally life was too good to be true. Something awful just had to happen and sure enough it did. In mid-January we were on a power play when the puck came to me at the point. Rocket was moving to his right as I shot and the rubber hit him square on the ankle. He was gone for six weeks.

Ordinarily that might have been considered a catastrophe but we kept on winning. Our lead over second-place New York had climbed to 16 points and counting. But my lead in the scoring race disappeared. I began to feel a terrible pain in my groin and the doctors diagnosed it as pulled muscles. Treatment was very slow and very frustrating. At one point Selke sent me to Florida for recuperation. "When I come back," I told The Boss, "I'll pay you back with goals."

That injury cost me my chance to win the scoring race but I wasn't depressed because Dickie Moore had moved into first place. I was his biggest fan. From the days when we played against each other in juniors my respect for Dickie as a player and as a person could not have been greater.

Moore was a player's player. He was never interested in self-promotion. All he cared about was winning. I have already mentioned how he played regularly wearing a cast on his hand during the homestretch of 1957-58. That told you everything you needed to know about his character and perseverance. You just knew that he'd be out there even if he wasn't getting paid.

Another thing about Dickie was his versatility. When Rocket was injured Blake shifted Moore from left to right wing and he still led the league in scoring. Now he was doing it again playing with two new linemates Big Jean and Marcel Bonin. It was no accident that both got hot as soon as they started skating alongside Dickie. Moore became the first Canadien ever to win two straight scoring titles.

We finished first, a fat 18 points ahead of second-place Boston but actually we were involved in a dramatic battle for a play-off berth right down to the final game of the season.

This unusual twist came about because the Rangers pulled the biggest choke in NHL history. With two weeks left in the season New York looked good enough to finish second. Rangers had a seven-point lead on fifth-place Toronto. But there was a revolt in the New York dressing room; players were furious over the way Phil Watson was handling them and in the last two weeks Toronto came on strong while the Rangers faded.

Here's how we came into the melodrama. On the final Thursday of the season, March 19, we were host to the very hot Leafs. Jacques Plante was injured and had been replaced by Charlie Hodge who was doing a good job. But on this night Blake dressed a kid named Claude Pronovost as our starting goalie. It was an unusual decision to make in a heated play-off race because Pronovost had bounced around the minors for a long time.

That is, unless Blake and Selke had an ulterior motive which could have been Blake's keen dislike for Phil Watson and some of the Ranger players and Selke's unhappiness with the Rangers organization that went back a long, long way.

On the other hand it could have been an ordinary decision to see what Pronovost could do in a tough situation. Whatever the reasons — and Toe and Selke took them to the grave — Toronto killed Pronovost 6-3 and you could hear the screams all the way down in New York.

Muzz Patrick, the Rangers' general manager, claimed that Toe had no business starting Pronovost in such an important game, blah blah blah. But what was done was done and now Toronto was right on the Rangers' tail. As it happened our last game of the season was on a Sunday night, March 22, in New York. That same night the Leafs were in Detroit.

Here's how it would shake out: if the Rangers beat us they would clinch a play-off berth. But if we won the game and Toronto beat

Detroit then the Leafs would take fourth place, the final spot for the play-offs.

Toe started Hodge against New York but before the game was six minutes old Harry Howell beat Charlie giving the Rangers a one-goal lead. Less than a minute later Moore tied it and exactly one minute after that Big Jean beat Gump Worsley. After that we never trailed. Charlie was superb in goal and Pocket scored early in the third to give us a two-goal lead. It ended 5-3 for us. In Detroit the Leafs rallied for a 6-4 win. The Rangers — and Watson — were dead.

Nobody in our dressing room was in mourning.

Besides we had more important things to think about, starting with the defense of The Stanley Cup.

For a change we weren't facing either Boston, Detroit or Rangers. Chicago which had been gradually rebuilding into a formidable outfit finished third and went up against us in the opening play-off round.

This was not going to be a cakewalk. Chicago's goalie Glenn Hall had become one of the NHL'S best. They had a solid defense and some terrific young forwards led by Bobby Hull and Eddie Litzenberger who we had given them in the "Help the Poor" movement.

The series was tied two games apiece with Game Five at The Forum. I remember it well because I got the fourth goal — our insurance so to speak — in a 4-2 win. Then we returned to Chicago for what turned out to be one of the wildest games I ever had the pleasure, or maybe displeasure would be the more appropriate word, to play in and witness.

They call Chicago "the Windy City." Well on Saturday night April 4, 1959 an ill wind blew over the town and seeped right through the cracks of Chicago Stadium.

First let me point out that Blackhawks fans had been suffering through more years of mediocrity than followers of any other NHL team since the franchise began in 1926. Chicago had only two Stanley Cups to its credit, the last being in 1938. Stadium fans were dying for a winner and finally they had a team that at the very least was competitive, if a bit of a long-shot to take the silverware away from us.

Second you should know that the referee on this night was Red Storey, a Hall-of-Famer, an official of consummate integrity who took absolutely no guff from anyone. Red had been a professional hockey player, a great pro football player and one who was respected and loved by just about everyone who skated in the NHL. When he took to the ice we knew we'd get a fair shake and so did the opposition whether we liked his calls or not. If nothing else Red Storey was a straight shooter.

With this in mind you should have a better understanding of the craziness that unfolded; a craziness multiplied by the 20,000-odd fans who jammed the rink well beyond its legal capacity. From the noise alone I would have guessed there were 100,000 maniacs in the joint.

We quieted them but good within minutes. Only 13 seconds after the opening face-off Glen Skov got two minutes from Storey but we couldn't beat Glenn Hall on the power play. Nevertheless Dickie Moore and I controlled the puck in their zone after Skov got out of the penalty box. The two of us set up Doug Harvey for the first goal at 2:20. We were off and running or so we thought.

Ted Lindsay beat Plante at 13:05 and the first period ended tied at one. From there the game seesawed back and forth. Litzenberger put them ahead in the second but Moore and Claude Provost put us back in the driver's seat 3-2.

The third period was total madness. First Litzenberger, then Moore, then Lindsay scored and now it was tied at 4-4 with less than six minutes remaining in regulation time. Up until this point Storey had refereed a fair game although he had given us more penalties than Chicago. (I got one at 9:05 of the third but luckily we killed it with no damage.)

But at 15:38 Storey got the fans crazy when he hit Blackhawks defenseman Al Arbour with a two-minute minor. Chicago managed to defuse our power play and now it was still tied with only two minutes and change left in the third. It was anybody's game.

Except for my first period assist I hadn't been a major factor in the game. Our best line had been Don Marshall, Phil Goyette and Claude Provost. They buzzed around the ice like waterbugs on a pond and were on the ice when the Hawks attacked our blue line.

Bobby Hull, one of the most powerful skaters in the game, went one-on-one with Al Langlois our young defenseman. As Hull reached the edge of our zone Junior put on his radar and perfectly lined up Hull for a hit. Although classic, old hip checks were going out of style, Langlois delivered one that would have made Butch Bouchard proud. Hull went up in the air and then landed with a thud.

From the home team bench I could hear the screams directed at Storey. "Tripping, Red. Call it!"

But there was no whistle. Storey correctly figured it for a clean check and never did the tweet-job on Junior. For a second or two the Hawks seemed to let up. They were so upset that Red had let Langlois off that it threw them off their game just enough to give us an opening.

Marshall, Provost and Goyette took over and made a beeline for Glenn Hall. Before the Hawks could recover Provost put it in at 18:32. The goal didn't officially kill them but the Blackhawks were mortally wounded and as far as their fans were concerned the murderer was Red Storey.

From the upper reaches of the side balcony, as well as the mezzanine and end arena torrents of garbage came hurtling on to the ice. Our bench area wasn't covered in any way so we had to duck the bottles and other pieces of protest that came our way but most of it was aimed at Storey.

As the blitz got more intense Red moved to center ice which was about the safest place in the building but not completely fool-proof. One fool came running out on the ice, sneaked up behind the ref and doused him with beer. Before Storey could deal with the guy Doug Harvey did the job for him. A couple of seconds later another crazed fan dashed out and tried to jump Red. Doug whacked him with his hockey stick.

What Doug did was send a message to the rest of the incensed fans — come after Red and you've got to come through me. They got the message. Nobody else came out after that. But the storm of debris lasted almost half an hour. It was nearly as crazy in its own way as St. Patrick's Day 1955 at The Forum when the tear gas bomb exploded.

On that night Clarence Campbell had been the center of attention and he would be again this time only in a different way. We later learned that Storey had tried to contact the president in order to determine whether or not to halt the game but Campbell refused to walk over to the penalty timekeeper's area and help poor Red.

Eventually the ice was cleared and we played out the final minute and a half. The game ended 5-4 for us. In terms of the real drama that was only act one. After the game Campbell spoke with an Ottawa journalist named Bill Westwick. Campbell claimed that he was talking off the record but Westwick thought otherwise. He quoted Campbell as saying that Storey "choked" in the final minutes and that he had "frozen" on two calls which should have been penalties against Canadiens. The article had the president using other derogatory expressions about the referee including "chicken" which should have been the last thing anyone would have said about Red.

When Storey learned about the remarks it hit the fan. Campbell admitted that he made a mistake talking to a reporter about one of his best referees. But Campbell added, "I'm not taking anything back. I'm not crying for help. I feel I was the victim of bad faith that has precipitated a most unfortunate mess."

Meanwhile Storey had told referee in chief Carl Voss that he was through and refused to even see Campbell. "If I had gone back to Campbell's hotel room," said Red, "there would have been one less president in professional sport."

Many of Red's friends tried to talk him out of retiring. Some like former referee Bill Chadwick said that Storey was too hasty and should have cooled down before making his decision. But Red stuck to his guns and that was that. My teammates and I were very upset with Campbell and very sorry for Storey because you never want to see a class act like he was leave the game. What a way to end a career!

We couldn't dwell on the Storey saga very long because we still had a Stanley Cup to defend. The Maple Leafs, who made the final play-off spot on the final night of the season, continued to amaze. They beat Boston in a seven-game semifinal and went up against us in the finals. Only four more wins and we would have a record-breaking four consecutive Stanley Cups. Ironically the record we would break was set by Toronto which won its third consecutive Cup in 1949, exactly ten years earlier!

For us it looked like a breeze but the truth was that we were hurting. Rocket was still out with his broken foot and my stomach had been bothering me through the last half of the season. That's where our depth paid off. Little Marcel Bonin had been slipped into Rocket's spot, to the point of borrowing Maurice's gloves. In the six-game Chicago series Bonin had seven goals and three assists playing on a line with Le Gros Bill and Moore.

Toronto had a promising team with a blend of good youngsters like Frank Mahovlich and Carl Brewer as well as solid veterans including a first-rate goalie John Bower. Their coach Punch Imlach oozed confidence. "We'll beat Montreal in six games," he said in a press conference.

When Toe heard that he nearly had a fit. Then he simmered down and smiled. "Don't you think Imlach should be a little nicer to us? After all we had something to do with getting Leafs into the play-offs."

There was nothing easy about the finals. We kicked it off on April 9 at The Forum and it was tied 3-3 after two. Bonin finally got us ahead at 11:59 and then he fed Moore a pass at 15:02 to give us the insurance. Game Two was the same tied at the end of two (1-1) and then a pair of third period goals put it away for us.

Imlach kept harping on the fact that his team wouldn't quit and he was right. Dickie Duff, a fine little left winger, won Game Three for them in overtime. Plante complained that the shot hit Tom Johnson in the ankle and caromed in but Blake wouldn't buy the alibi. "I've seen Jacques stop tougher shots than that one," he snapped.

Duff's goal not only put Toronto on the win sheet, it also gave the Leafs new life. Some of them actually were chirping that they could still win The Stanley Cup and end our streak. To tell you the truth the way they played for two periods of Game Four they came close. Some experts said it was a game that the Leafs could have won had they gotten a break early in the third period.

I've always said that hockey is a funny game that reflects life. Sometimes you think you're doing everything right and still the breaks go against you, and that's exactly what happened to Toronto in Game Four. Neither team scored in the first two periods but early in the third Toronto's right winger George Armstrong fired a shot that beat Plante.

There was only one problem; Armstrong's shot was so hard it went right *through* the net and neither the goal judge nor referee Frank Udvari saw it. Imlach cried but after conferring with the goal judge Udvari ruled that it had never gone in. "If it had counted," Imlach later said, "we might have won and gone back to Montreal tied in games." (Films later showed that the puck actually went through the webbing and should have counted.)

Toronto did get the game's first goal but it wasn't enough. Blake had put me on a line with Backstrom and McDonald and we clicked like perfectly meshed gears. I set up Ab for our first goal, set up Ralph for the second and I scored the third, which happened to be the winner. It put us ahead three games to one and broke Toronto's back.

That sent the series back to Montreal for Game Five and gave us the opportunity to set the new record for consecutive Cup wins at home. It was *my* game. I set up the first goal, scored the second and our fourth which turned out to be our insurance goal. It was 5-1 for us until just past the 12-minute mark of the third period. Toronto got two late tallies but it didn't matter. We were champions for the fourth year in a row. No other hockey club could make that statement!

In the dressing room Selke came over and patted me on the back. He remembered what I had promised him when he gave me the tickets to Florida. "You said you'd pay me back," said Selke, "and you have."

CHAPTER 11

The Drive for Five (Straight Cups)

There *is* such a thing as the law of averages. You can look it up. If you flip a penny often enough it'll start to come out heads after you've been getting tails for a while; and if you've been getting tails eventually you'll get heads. It's the law.

The law of averages applies to hockey teams as well. We Canadiens knew it. Nobody had to tell Rocket, Big Jean, Frank Selke or me that we would go on winning Stanley Cup after Stanley Cup forever.

When you think about it winning four in a row was spectacular. Since the invention of hockey nobody had won four in a row — except us. So for us to think about making it *five* straight was really pushing the law to its limits. But that's exactly what we went about doing when we reported to training camp in September 1959.

Let me point out here and now that five other teams were trying very hard to make sure the law of averages worked against us. They did it on the ice and in the boardrooms behind our backs. Just before the 1956-57 season, they pushed through the stupid rule that ended a penalty, sending a player back on the ice, after a goal is scored. That was aimed directly at us because our power play was so good.

Now that Jacques Plante had redefined the role of goaltender — leaving the crease to stop the puck, making passes and otherwise participating in the play — our enemies were at it again. This time they tried to push through a rule aimed directly at Plante to keep him anchored in his goal crease. Fortunately we fought so hard against it that the rule was never passed.

Toe Blake said:

It was aimed at Plante and it was thought up by the Red Wings. They used to score a lot of goals by shooting the puck behind the net and having a guy come in fast to grab the rebound. Plante stopped all that by leaving the crease and intercepting the puck behind the net. And the reason Jacques can do it and the other goalies can't is that he's faster than the other guys.

Still the other NHL teams kept after us. When the first rule failed they adopted another one aimed at Plante. This one, which was pushed through over our objections, made a goalie subject to a minor penalty if he fell on the puck behind the net. None of us was happy about it but we figured that Jacques was good enough to get around that obstacle and we still could make good on our drive for five.

One of Plante's problems that year came outside the NHL in the tiny town of Sturgeon Falls, Ontario. Our favorite goalie was appearing at a local celebration onstage singing a few selections from his repertoire of French Canadian hits. Suddenly someone in the audience ran up on the stage, grabbed the microphone from Jacques and yelled into it, "Don't sing that song!" Then the mike swung back and hit him right in the mouth breaking one of Jacques' front teeth. When he recovered he joked that he never thought he would be injured singing!

Toe Blake was singing the same old song when he opened camp; nobody was going to give us the fifth Cup in a row; we were going to have to take it. There was no room for slackers. If anyone got lazy he knew that Selke had at least two possible replacements in the minors.

I knew that even though I had become a fixture there were younger guys ready to jump into my slot. One of them was Billy Hicke, a Regina kid who had been rookie of the year in 1958-59 in the American League. Hicke was a chunky winger with good speed and a hard shot. Somebody made the mistake of saying that Hicke was heir apparent to Rocket's right wing position. It was a mistake for two reasons: nobody could follow Rocket and it put too much pressure on a young guy who hadn't even come close to proving himself.

Maurice showed up at camp and dispelled any rumors that he was about to retire. Selke signed him to his eighteenth NHL season in a meeting that took less than 15 minutes. "I never have any contract problems with Maurice," said Selke. "I tell him what I'm going to give him and he signs!"

Imagine that happening today.

At age 38 Rocket had a good camp and predicted that he would score "25 or 30 goals." Actually Rocket came to camp with more incentive than usual. In addition to Pocket a third Richard brother made an appearance. His name was Claude and he played left wing. Claude lasted only four days in camp before Selke shipped him down to our Ottawa farm team in the Eastern Professional League. There would be no favoritism and no publicity gimmicks on Canadiens.

If Selke wanted some free ink he could easily have gotten it from Plante. Jacques continued to push to use the face mask during regular games and he finally went to the NHL with his idea. To everyone's surprise NHL President Clarence Campbell took Plante's side.

Jacques brought a model of his mask to Campbell's office and after study the president authorized its use. "We're anxious for goalies to wear anything that will cut down injuries," said Campbell. "After all the goalie is the most important man in our game."

Jacques showed his mask to the media, posed for pictures wearing it and generally gave the impression that he was sick and tired of suffering facial lacerations and fractured cheekbones. The mask was his solution.

Toe Blake was against the mask — adamantly. His argument shared by all the other goalies was that the mask suggested that the goalie was afraid. Blake, who was a man's man, made it very clear that Plante was going to wear the mask over his dead body. But Campbell didn't agree: "It's completely ridiculous for anyone to think a goalie who wants to wear a mask is chicken because anyone who would stand up to a 100-mile an hour projectile is no coward. No goalie has to play without a mask to prove his courage as far as I'm concerned."

But Toe Blake was coach of Canadiens not Clarence Campbell and Jacques Plante started the 1959-60 season unmasked.

Jake The Snake, as some of the writers were calling him — others nicknamed him Jacques Be Nimble — was stopping pucks without the mask as well as ever. In the All-Star Game at The Forum Plante was the best man on the ice as we whipped the All-Stars 6-1.

"We've won four Stanley Cups in a row," said Blake when the game was over, "and we may as well make five especially since everybody expects us to do it."

When you have four consecutive Stanley Cups under your belt you tend to get a swelled head — and midsection. Which is exactly what happened to us. Some of the players had come to camp overweight and needed the first few weeks of the season before they were in mint condition. By the end of October we were back at the top and everyone was feeling good about himself except Plante who still couldn't get Blake to budge on the mask.

As for me I just prayed for a season without major injury. Just one. If I had that I knew I was capable of leading the league in scoring the way I had in 1954-55. I was playing the best hockey of my life. Late in October 1959 I had three goals and three assists in three games.

I hit my stride when we played the Red Wings on October 25, 1959 at Olympia. Detroit had jumped off to a terrific start; they were undefeated (5-0-1) and all of us knew that this would be a test to see just who was going to rule the league.

The game was typical of several classics we played with the Wings over the past six years. Donnie Marshall put us ahead in the first; Detroit tied it in the second and we remained locked at one apiece well into the third. Jacques was never better in goal and Terry Sawchuk looked like the Sawchuk of the early 1950s when he was the league's best puckstopper.

For a time it appeared that the game would end in a tie so evenly matched were the two teams. But Canadiens never played for one point. We were always after a win and with less than a minute and a half left on the clock I found myself on the ice with Pocket at center instead of Big Jean.

Pocket was a great center and I could play with him anytime. He made me skate and he had great moves. This time he worked his way through the Detroit defense and fed me the pass. I was 20 feet out and beat Sawchuk clean. It was my two hundred and thirtieth career goal and it won the game for us. Plante's goals-against average was just a shake over 2.00 and he gave every indication that he would remain the NHL'S best even without the face mask.

Leading the league we had come to New York for a Sunday night game with the Rangers at Madison Square Garden. The date was November 1, 1959 and as far as I'm concerned it was as important to hockey history as any other landmark event including my introduction of the slap shot.

Early in what otherwise was a typically hard-fought New York-Montreal game Andy Bathgate of the Rangers went down the right side over our blue line. He moved diagonally toward the goal, going from right to left and let a hard backhand shot go. It was probably traveling upwards of 60 miles per hour at a screened goaltender.

Jacques never saw it. The puck smacked him right between the nose and mouth. He went down like a redwood that had just been chainsawed. Blood was gushing everywhere. Plante was badly cut.

The trainers stopped the bleeding, took him to our dressing room and a time-out was called. In those days most clubs had no reserve goaltender. If a goalie was hurt and couldn't continue the home team would "loan" a house goaltender for the night. Often these were guys who were out of shape and came to the rink just to get a free ticket. We wanted none of that.

Jacques was a mess when they stretched him out in the dressing room; his face was swollen and his white jersey was caked with blood. The Rangers' doctor got out his needle and put seven stitches through his nose and upper lip. Plante winced but his mind was on more than his wounds. Once he had regained his senses he knew that he would be expected to return to the ice. It was the goalie's creed; you go back in the nets unless you can't stand up on your skates.

The person responsible for getting Jacques back on his skates was one of the great characters of NHL medical history. Dr. Kazuo Yanigasawa was a slightly burly Japanese fellow who always seemed to have a cigar plugged into his mouth and always seemed to be playing gin rummy in the bowels of Madison Square Garden. They used to say that "Yana", as we called him, was the only person in captivity who could smoke a cigar, play gin and stitch up a hockey player at the same time! He was also reputed to carry a gun with him everywhere he went. That was the man who went to work on our favorite goaltender.

The wait seemed interminable while he patched up Jacques. Some of us stayed at the bench; others went into the dressing room to check out our goalie. After the stitches were in Jacques said he would return but only if he could wear the mask. Toe was opposed but what could he do; Plante made it clear that he wouldn't continue without the mask.

Much as it pained him Blake agreed. We were used to seeing Plante wearing the mask in practice but the Rangers and the 15,000 people filling the Garden were shocked. Jacques looked like something right out of a horror movie.

The grotesque-looking mask sent murmurs through the crowd as Jacques took his position in front of the net. History was being made before our very eyes. If Plante could play up to his pre-mask ability there was no question that he would continue wearing it. But if his game deteriorated as Blake and others firmly believed then the mask would be history.

Those who insisted that the mask wouldn't work pointed to the vision problem. These critics claimed that the fiberglass covering made it more difficult to see the puck especially from the side and when it was at his feet. This could cost us two or three goals a game they predicted. The only way we would know for sure was when the Rangers started throwing pucks at him.

If Jacques was nervous he didn't show it. Actually he was over-joyed because the very fact that he was wearing the mask was a tri-umph over Blake and the other critics. Plante's confidence was evident as the Rangers fired shot after shot at him.

Dickie Moore gave Jacques a one-goal cushion late in the first. André Pronovost got another early in the second. I was on a line with Big Jean and Marcel Bonin. We had worked well together the previous season and made some beautiful music on this night as well. Jean and Marcel got the puck to me in front of my old pal Gump Worsley and it was in faster than you could say Montreal three Rangers nothing!

Jacques was near-perfect. He took the three-goal lead into the third period and gave nothing to the Rangers until Camille Henry finally beat him with just over nine minutes remaining. That was it! The equation went like this: 27 saves versus one goal equalled one very good mask.

Plante had won his battle; Blake had lost his — although he did-n't know it at the time. As much as he relished winning the game Toe was hoping that the mask would just fade away. That of course was not to be. A horde of reporters invaded our dressing room after the game and surrounded Jacques. Our victory was virtually ignored, as the mask became *the* story. Plante had center stage and was deter-mined to make the most of it. He was still wearing his bloodstained white jersey when the first volley of questions came at him:

"You played well Jake."

"It's always a good game when you win."

"For a while it looked like you were hurt bad."

"That's why I made this mask. Here, feel it, hit the thing with a ham-mer and you couldn't break it. It's molded to fit my face perfectly, see."

"Jake, doesn't it bother you at all?"

"It doesn't bother me . . . well naturally sometimes it gets a little uncomfortable, I was a little nauseous tonight. I think it can be improved but I don't know how."

"Do you think other goalies should wear masks?"

"I do. You have to realize that the game has improved so much it's become much tougher on goalies. They're starting to realize it. Take (Terry) Sawchuk. He never used to wear a mask, now he uses it in practice. He says he could practice all day in a mask, that's how much he likes it."

"Why didn't you wear one sooner?"

"I asked the coach and he said the people wouldn't go for it. I guess he figured if I wore the mask and played a bad game the fans would say `that's what did it.' I think it's just in the people's mind."

The questions were machine-gunned so fast Plante barely had time to remove his bulky leg pads. Now, he took a breather and pulled off his jersey, the thick, black chest pad with the letters CH in red and white in the center and his other equipment. Then he continued the interview in his tan, sweat-stained long johns.

"Would you have returned to the game if you didn't have a mask?"

"I would have to but I think I would have been nervous."

"You're lucky Bathgate didn't hit you with his forehand."

"If he had I'd be six feet under. The face of the goalie gets the worst beating of all in hockey."

"Did you play better after you put on the mask?"

"My stops were about average, some hard, some easy. I didn't have a chance on the goal they scored. I split to stop Bathgate and Henry hit the open net."

The mask was the talk of the town if not the hockey world. Rocket said he thought it caused "blind spots." Gump Worsley, who faced Plante at the other end of the rink that night, couldn't understand why Plante wanted the mask:

> *How can a mask protect you when it's flush against the face? They say you don't get cut, just bruised when a puck hits the mask. Well sometimes it's better to get cut than bruised.*
>
> *My objection to the mask is that it's not necessary. Why all of a sudden after hockey has been played for 70 years do they decide we should wear masks?*
>
> *Don't tell me that and don't tell me the game has changed. Besides you don't see college goalies wearing masks and they're a careful bunch. Do boxers wear masks?*

Plante may make a pot full 'o money on that mask idea. He can have it, I don't want the thing.

Neither did a lot of other NHL people. Even though Clarence Campbell supported Jacques other members of the hockey establishment did not. They came up with all kinds of crazy arguments to put down Plante and his mask. One of them was Muzz Patrick, general manager of the Rangers, who had once been Canadian heavyweight boxing champion. Muzz hated the whole idea of the mask and you can tell by what he said:

Our game has a greater percentage of women fans than any team sport I know. I'm talking about real fans — ones who give you the scoring averages and the All-Star lineups. Those women fans want to see men not masks. They want to see the blonds, the redheads — and the bald spots. That's why I'm against helmets and masks. They rob the players of their individuality.

We start out with goalies wearing masks. Every club has a defencemen or two who goes down to smother shots. Soon they'll want masks. All the forwards will wear helmets. The teams will become faceless, headless robots all of whom look alike to the spectators. We can't afford to take that fan appeal away from hockey.

Today every goalie wears a mask and most players wear helmets. So who was right, Muzz or Jacques? Actually I shouldn't say that because after that game even we didn't know who was right. Jacques had only played part of one game with the mask. It would have to prove itself over time. And Toe made it clear that if Jacques started losing with the mask it would end up in The Forum dumpster.

In our next game we beat the Rangers 8-2. I helped out Jacques with a hat trick and two assists — five points in one night! Next we tied Chicago 2-2. I only got one goal! Then it was a 3-0 shutout of the Maple Leafs in Toronto and 8-1 over Boston.

The mask now had four full games — three wins and a tie. Plante was on a roll. At Boston Garden on November 15, 1959 we won 4-1 and it was the same at Maple Leaf Gardens. For Jacques and the mask the score was 5-0-1.

Chicago Stadium had become one of the most challenging rinks for us yet on November 22, 1959 Plante made it look easy: 3-1. The Red Wings went down 4-2 and then 1-0. Jacques was laughing. After nine masked games his record was 8-0-1!

Plante's injury started the front office thinking about what might happen if he got hurt again and couldn't come back. Selke signed an alternate goalie for the road. He was my pal, French-language sports columnist Jacques Beauchamp, 31, overweight and out of shape.

When asked about how he rated himself as a goalie Beauchamp replied, "I am not good — but I am ready!"

We returned to Beantown for a 4-2 decision and then shutout Toronto. Jacques and his mask were undefeated in ten games. We had 19 out of a possible 20 points. Those were Stanley Cup-winning numbers. Then Don Simmons of the Bruins declared publicly that he would be the next goalie to put on a face protector.

All good things must come to an end and so it was with our undefeated run. On December 2, 1959 Toronto beat us 1-0 on a Frank Mahovlich goal and that was that. Still we were in first place six points ahead of Detroit and feeling pretty good.

Toe was still not happy about the mask but he did admit that we were a better club than the 1944 Canadiens with him, Rocket and Elmer Lach on the famed Punch Line. "It was an outstanding team," Toe allowed, "but we didn't have the players to compare with Béliveau, Moore, Pocket, Harvey and Boom Boom. The 1944 team," he explained, "only had one line that could score. This team has three."

Three that is, when we were healthy but as usual injuries dogged us through the season. I missed 11 games because of a severe skate wound after a collision with Doug Mohns of Boston. Then the flu put me down for another four games.

Rocket missed 19 games with injuries and there was more talk about his retirement. "I've felt awful for the last three years," he said. "It's not that I'm sick but that I've been hurt so often. I just can't keep up the pace anymore. Some of the younger fellows can skate all night. I can't."

By a normal player's standards Rocket wasn't having a bad year. Even with the injuries he looked like he could make it to the 20-goal plateau and Selke gave his vote of confidence. "Two-thirds of the younger players in the game can't match Rocket's skills," he said.

But Detroit's Jack Adams had the best insight: "When the time comes that he doesn't get 20 goals he will hang up his skates. It's pride that makes The Rocket go."

It was true. Rocket was proud and he had a lot to be proud of especially the way the team was going. After the new year we put another lock on first place leaving Toronto, Detroit and Boston in the dust. Our club was so strong Selke sold future stars like Bill Hay and Murray Balfour to the Blackhawks for $20,000 each. By midseason Hay had become one of Chicago's best forwards and Balfour would come back to haunt us in a few seasons.

Once I shook off the injuries in February 1960 I got right back into the groove. I got a hat trick against Boston's Harry Lumley and came back with one the next night against Gump Worsley. My 22 goals lifted me back into the top ten point getters which was not bad considering that I had been out for 15 games.

Just about everyone in hockey was predicting that we were good enough to win a fifth straight Stanley Cup. One of the main reasons was Big Jean who was leading us as never before. When Béliveau got hurt in midwinter we stumbled momentarily and then got on track again.

I remember once when we were in Boston for a game and someone told the Bruins' general manager Lynn Patrick that we were missing Big Jean. "We are too," Patrick quipped. "We're also missing Geoffrion, the Little Rocket, Moore and Harvey."

If there was anything disturbing about our homestretch drive it was in goal. For reasons that nobody could really understand Plante's goaltending began an alarming decline and Glenn Hall of Chicago began challenging Jacques for the Vezina Trophy. Some Canadiens' officials claimed that Plante was growing weary of the NHL grind and needed a rest before the play-offs.

Others blamed it on the mask. After wearing it for 50 straight games Jacques was finally persuaded to play without it for at least one game. That happened on March 8, 1960 at Detroit. The Red Wings didn't do Plante any favors and neither did we. Normie Ullman beat him in the first period, Len Lunde followed up with another in the second and Len Haley rounded out the scoring in the third. Detroit 3, Us 0. The winner in the end was Jacques' mask. He never played without it again.

"The decision over whether he wears the mask or not belongs to Jacques," Blake said in his concession speech. "I won't force him to discard it anymore."

Plante was tickled pink and went on to beat Hall for the Vezina. I was just as happy. I wound up with 30 goals in only 59 games just two points behind Gordie Howe who played all 70 games and was ready for our drive for five.

As a team we were in excellent shape. We won more games, had more points, scored 255 goals — three less than in 1958-59 — and finished a fat 13 points ahead of second-place Toronto. The Blackhawks, who were third and 23 points behind us, would be our first-round opponents.

I was ready. In the opener I got the game winner and two assists; it was 4-3 for us. I got two assists in Game Two but the real hero was Doug Harvey who beat Hall at 8:38 of sudden-death overtime. Dickie Moore actually made the play happen when he got the puck after Bill Hay had missed a wide-open net. Dickie raced down the left side and put the puck on Pocket's stick. Henri swerved around the back of the Chicago cage and fed Doug on the point. Hall never saw the 50-foot shot.

Now the series moved west to Chicago where we figured the Blackhawks would give us some grief. Some of our guys were noticeably tired so Blake took a gamble and put together a makeshift line of Ralph Backstrom, Don Marshall and Bill Hicke, who had been called up from the minors.

Talk about genius. After a scoreless first period Hicke beat Hall in the middle of the second and then Backstrom and Marshall fed Jean-Guy Talbot for number two. Marshall got his first of the game and then yours truly dropped the curtain to round out a 4-0 shutout for Jacques.

The most frustrated guy in Chicago was Blackhawks' coach Rudy Pilous. "I had Glen Skov tie up Béliveau and he did a pretty good job," said Pilous. "I had Ted Lindsay on Boom Boom and he did okay. So what happens? Somebody named Hicke came off the bench and scored. Everything we tried, even if it worked, was no good. People tell me Canadiens are a lucky hockey club. Maybe they are lucky. They're also good. A big difference is that they don't give the puck away as often as other teams do."

Two nights later Jacques Plante did it again — two-zip and the four-game sweep was over.

Toe had a theory: "I was wearing my lucky suit," he explained. When someone asked how many suits he had Blake jokingly replied: "Just one."

The Chicago media referred to us as the "Montreal Monsters." There were demands that Clarence Campbell break up the Canadiens. They said that our dominance was bad for the league. To his credit the president stuck up for us this time:

I disagree that this is harmful to the league. I believe that it is always a good idea to have a good standard to shoot for. If the Canadiens are that good and everyone is trying to equal them it is good for the league and the standard of its play.

And the Canadiens' play must be very good over the long haul because there hasn't been an unsold seat in The Montreal Forum in 15 consecutive years now.

As for breaking up the Canadiens I believe our internal draft takes care of the situation nicely and will be felt more and more as the years go by. Under this system a club can protect only 18 players and two goalkeepers. All other players owned by it become subject to draft by the other five clubs.

Of course the draft serves another purpose; it frightens clubs into making deals ahead of it. The Hawks acquired Murray Balfour and Billy Hay in this manner.

We were four wins away from our fifth straight Stanley Cup. As luck would have it our opponents would be Imlach's Maple Leafs. Already Punch had changed his strategy. Now he was trying to soften us up. Whenever he'd see a reporter Imlach would refer to us as "The Mighty Montreals."

Any time Punch complimented the Habs I was suspicious. So was Toe. "The biggest battle I have with our club," he said, "is keeping them from becoming complacent."

The bookies helped our complacency. They listed us at 5-1 to win it all again. The best reason was that we had three 30-goal men — Pocket, Big Jean and myself — while Toronto's highest scorer Bob Pulford finished with only 24 goals.

Two of our three 30-goal men delivered in Game One of the 1960 finals which pretty much explains how we beat Toronto 4-2. I wound up with three assists setting up Dickie Moore with the opening goal early in the first period and then doing the same for Big Jean in the middle of the first putting us up 3-0. Toronto made it close scoring twice in the second but I fed Pocket at the start of the third and he beat Johnny Bower.

I don't want to make it sound as if winning the game was as easy as snapping my fingers but I must say that as a team we were never more on top of our game. Even when the contests were close as in Game Two we always seemed confident that we would eventually put them away.

We got the jump on Toronto early in the game. Rocket gave the puck to Pocket who gave Dickie a goalmouth pass, and with a little half-slap the puck was in. Less than five minutes later Big Jean converted passes from Marcel Bonin and Jean-Guy Talbot. We were up 2-0 before the six-minute mark.

"You can't spot those guys two goals and then expect to beat 'em," said Stafford Smythe who replaced his father, Conn Smythe, as Maple Leafs' boss. And he was right. We gave up one goal and held on for the 2-1 win.

So far Rocket had one assist. Everyone was watching Maurice because we all knew that this Final could be his last and it was interesting to see how he handled it. Rocket's age was showing. He wasn't skating quite as fast or shooting the puck quite as hard but the drive was still there in his eyes. What we all wanted most of all apart from another Cup was for Rocket to at least score one more play-off goal.

That would happen in Game Three at Toronto. If you can believe that Toe had a "problem" going into that one, he did. But it was a problem most coaches would die for: how to cram all of the good players into the lineup. Johnny Gottselig, who had been a Blackhawks' star and now was their press agent, couldn't believe that we were so top-heavy with stars.

"They've got so much talent they can keep guys like Ralph Backstrom and Billy Hicke on the bench for a year," said Gottselig. "And when they do get into the game they beat you."

Sure enough they did. Toe played them in Game Three and Hicke set up Donnie Marshall for the first goal. It was 3-0 for us before Toronto finally scored late in the second period. But the goal that was most important came at 11:07 of the third.

Up to this point Rocket had had a number of good scoring chances but Johnny Bower had managed to make the saves. Not this time. Dickie took the shot; Bower made the save but gave up the rebound. It was like old times. Maurice swooped in to bang it into the net for our fifth and last goal of the game. As soon as the red light flashed for his eighty-second play-off goal Rocket did an unusual thing. He reached into the net, picked up the puck and pocketed it. We won 5-2 but when it was over everyone was talking about Rocket.

The big question on everyone's minds was why he wanted the puck. Did it mean that he was retiring?

"I don't know why I picked it up," he said. "I haven't got the puck that was used when I scored my first play-off goal but I'd like to have the one that was used when I scored my last one. If I get another play-off goal I'll keep it and some kid can have this one.

But that doesn't mean I'm going to retire because I don't know what I intend to do."

We finally shut Punch Imlach's mouth for the season on April 14, 1960. Big Jean had a pair, Pocket one and Harvey the other. I finished with three assists and we walked out of Maple Leaf Gardens with a 4-0 win and The Stanley Cup. Pocket, Red Kelly of Toronto and I finished in a three-way tie for first in play-off scoring with a dozen points each.

Five consecutive championships! What more was there to say except quote Conn Smythe: "We lost to the greatest team of all time."

It was thrilling but I had the haunting feeling that this team would never be the same. All I had to do was look across the room at Rocket to know that I had better watch old number nine take off his uniform because I might never see it again.

CHAPTER 12

Fifty Goals or Bust

Before leaving for the summer Rocket remained vague about his plans for 1960-61 although just about everyone was speculating about his future. I'm no detective but I had a pretty good clue that Maurice was going to hang up his skates. He had just opened a tavern and hung a big sign outside with the number 544 — his regular season goal total. Why would he do that if he didn't expect to quit? I wondered.

I was interested in his decision for two very personal reasons. First I loved Rocket as a friend, a teammate and a fellow athlete. I wanted his decision to be the best for him. Second I knew that if he did pack it in Canadiens would have to select a captain to replace him. There were several possibilities. Doug Harvey, Tom Johnson, Dickie Moore, Jean Béliveau and I seemed like the favorites.

I remember Dick Irvin telling Butch Bouchard, "When Rocket retires there's only one man who's going to take his place as captain and that's going to be Boom Boom Geoffrion." But Harvey had the seniority and everybody loved Doug.

All this of course depended on The Rocket's decision. We waited through the summer without any word. The longer we waited the more likely it appeared that Maurice would try just one more season in the *bleu, blanc et rouge.*

While he waited Selke went about the business of fortifying the club for a sixth straight Stanley Cup. He knew as we all did that sooner or later the law of averages would catch up to us. Friends would tell me that we couldn't go on winning the Cup forever and even that it would be good for hockey if some other club took the silver.

I didn't agree. I felt that as long as we kept winning it was a great thing for the Habs and for Boom Boom Geoffrion.

As usual trade rumors abounded. Bob Turner, who had become a solid defenseman, was mentioned. Another report said that Ralph Backstrom and Bill Hicke would head for Toronto and that we would get left winger Dick Duff in return. That amused Toe Blake to no end.

"When and if Backstrom goes to Toronto," said Blake, "it will be over my dead body so it won't hurt much."

The opposition already had us pegged to repeat. Milt Schmidt who coached the Bruins was another who called us one of the greatest teams of all time. "Playing those Canadiens is like sitting on a horse with a noose around your neck," said Schmidt. "The minute the horse gets hungry and moves for a bite of grass you've had it. Make one mistake against them and you're dead."

The pressure to keep winning had begun to tell on Toe as early as our third straight championship. It got more intense the next season and worse the year after that. "I get another ulcer every year," said Blake.

But winning relaxed him as did the tavern he opened near The Forum. During the off-season Toe would hang out there and be the funny, easy-going and wonderful fellow he had been as a player.

Toe Blake's Tavern soon became a landmark in Montreal and a hangout for hockey people in and out of season. At the time it was one of the few places where United States' currency was accepted at par with Canadian money. (At that time the Canadian dollar was worth more than its American counterpart.) One day a waiter walked into Toe's office to tell him that a customer had given him an American bill to pay for a beer.

"You know our policy," said Toe, "no discount."

"But Mister Blake," the waiter insisted, "it's a hundred-dollar bill."

"Give him back the bill," said Toe, "the beer is on the house!"

Summer 1960 came and went with still no word from Rocket. Finally on September 15 the Canadiens suddenly called a press conference at the Queen Elizabeth Hotel in downtown Montreal. We all knew that Rocket was going to announce his decision. Three major injuries in the past three years were just too much for Rocket.

His bones were older and so were his legs. When he stepped to the podium to underline his decision nobody could disagree.

"For two years," said Rocket, "I have thought more about retirement than anything else and it is difficult to come to this decision. I owe the public a debt that I can never repay."

As much as I would miss this best of friends, best of linemates and best of players I was sure that Rocket had made the right decision. Maurice The Rocket Richard was great for the game of hockey and the best role model an aspiring player like me ever could have had. And maybe one of the best examples he set was to show when to hang up his skates.

It was the end of an era.

Toe Blake said "It leaves us with a big hole to fill. Tell me where I can find another leader like him."

He was right of course. We needed a new captain and in our closed vote Doug Harvey won it almost unanimously. There was one other vote. Doug cast his for me!

If it was up to management Harvey never would have won the captain's C. Frank Selke had had it in for Doug ever since he combined with Ted Lindsay to organize the NHL players' association. The only reason The Boss hadn't traded him was that he just happened to be the best defenseman in the world and proved it by winning The Norris Trophy every year. Selke was just waiting for Doug to make one false move or have one lousy season and he would be gone. Selke's lieutenant Ken Reardon felt the same way.

Still the players loved Doug Harvey and for the moment that was all that mattered. The great thing about Doug was his disposition. If I went a couple of games without scoring I'd be miserable and snap at everybody. I couldn't shake a bad game the way Doug could. He had the right idea. If he played a bad game he knew it and he knew what he had done wrong. And he could go back the next game and forget all about it.

We opened the season amid keen speculation about how Rocket's absence would hurt us. The critics said we would miss his leadership and ability to come up with the big goal when it counted. But when we opened the season on October 6, 1960 against Toronto at The Forum we showed the naysayers.

I banged the puck past Johnny Bower only 66 seconds into the game. Pocket got a pair while Billy Hicke and Marcel Bonin rounded out the scoring. Jacques Plante, who now had Toe's blessing to wear the mask forever, blanked the Maple Leafs. We were off and running.

After seven games I had seven goals, Dickie Moore had nine and Pocket was right behind. The big surprise was Hicke, who was our fourth-leading scorer.

When you win five straight Cups you automatically become a target for the opposition. Every club we played wanted to be able to say that they beat the Canadiens. Which meant that every game was played to the hilt although none were tougher than our games against New York.

For some reason the Rangers gave us a lot of grief and the best reason was that their fiery center Red Sullivan seemed to get great pleasure going after us. In a game on October 23, 1960 at Madison Square Garden Sully belted Phil Goyette right out of the game with a three-stitch cut over the eye, a cut neck and a bruised shoulder.

Dickie Moore, Pocket, Bobby Rousseau and myself all went after Sullivan and we each wound up with two-minute penalties. When Lou Fontinato went after me it was the main event of the night. The bout ended in a draw and we both wound up in the penalty box snarling at each other. When it came time to leave we fought over who would get out of the box first. Two burly Madison Square Garden cops intervened and while I argued with them Fontinato got the jump on me and leaped back onto the rink.

Not many other players got the jump on me that season. I was healthy and I was putting the puck in the net. My confidence was better than it had been in years. Toe said he had never seen me so chipper and full of spirit. By November 13, 1960 I was leading the NHL in scoring. I had 11 goals and 17 assists in 18 games. I honestly believed that I was good for 40 or even 45 goals if I could play every game.

Rocket went a step further. "If anybody in the league today scores 50 goals it will be Boomer," he said.

Because I had made a name for myself with the slap shot I got stereotyped as only a big shooter. That wasn't fair because even though I wasn't stylish like Pocket I was a strong skater and I could stickhandle with the best. I could also check. Some people made fun of my skating because my strides were choppy. I had been a terrible skater when I was young and I still wasn't a free skater. Some nights when my legs were tight I really had to force myself to skate. When the legs were loose, it was a little easier.

The big thing at this stage of my career was my shot. I was the kind of player who could score in any number of ways. I got my shot off very fast and it was usually very accurate. I also could deke the goalie but for some reason I didn't score as much from in close.

To this day I give Frank Selke credit for helping my scoring. When I was younger I was reluctant to shoot until I was sure of my shot. I used to pass back to a teammate near the blue line. After one game Selke asked me why I chose to pass to a player who was in poorer position.

"I don't want to be a puck hog," I told him.

That bothered Selke because he figured I was hurting the team with such an attitude. What he did was rewrite my contract the following year and one which he kept in force ever after. It was designed to ensure that I did what I did best — shoot. Under a clause in the contract I got an extra $100 for every goal I scored over 20. I also got a flat $1000 for scoring the first 20.

Dickie Moore should have swung the same deal because he had 19 goals in his first 20 games. At the same time I had a dozen but we were tied for first place in scoring with 29 points. Big Jean was right behind with 26.

With all that we weren't running away from the rest of the pack as all the experts had predicted in training camp. By early December the Red Wings had pulled ahead of us but that wasn't the half of it. There was major concern that our number one goalie had at last lost it. In his first full season wearing the face mask Jacques Plante had become such a target of The Forum boobirds that we were becoming concerned that they would run him right out of town.

Remember these were the same fans who once chanted "We Want (Paul) Bibeault" when the great Bill Durnan had a bad night. And when Gerry McNeil went sour, they screamed *for* Plante. Now they were screaming *at* him. Jacques' average was very high for him, 3.28 goals against.

It got so bad that something unprecedented happened; Selke and Reardon tried to go over Blake's head and demanded he bench Jacques in favor of Charlie Hodge for a game against Detroit. Toe wouldn't hear of it. "I told Jacques, `I don't care how many goals you let in as long as you win the Vezina Trophy again,'" said Blake.

Plante was between the posts for us against Detroit. He beat them 4-2 to show his appreciation to the coach. From there we began our climb back to the summit. When Plante got hurt Hodge stepped in without missing a beat.

For me the crazy and happy part of the first three months of 1960-61 was that I wasn't injured and played every one of our 26 games and I had moved to the top of the point parade with eight more assists than I had goals (15-23-38). "Geoffrion is leading the league," commented *The Hockey News*, "because he has suddenly become a fine playmaker."

I wasn't a Jean Béliveau that's for sure but the points were coming and a three-way race developed between Big Jean, Dickie Moore and myself for the scoring leadership. By Christmas 1960 we had a six-point lead over second-place Toronto.

A few moves by Selke didn't hurt either. He dealt André Pronovost to Boston for Jean-Guy Gendron, a solid left winger. Blake put Gendron on the line with Big Jean and me and we clicked immediately although I don't think anyone could have guessed how well our gears would mesh in the new year.

Nevertheless Toronto always seemed to be a threat to us. Punch Imlach had put together an amazing team and now had one legitimate superstar up front — Frank Mahovlich otherwise known as The Big M. Frank was a powerful skater with long, strong strides who packed a heck of a shot. Between Mahovlich's shooting and Johnny Bower's goaltending the Leafs had a nice one-two punch. As Jack Adams liked to say, "The big guy puts 'em in and the old guy (Bower) kicks 'em out."

By February the Big M was leading the league in scoring and it looked like he might even top Rocket's 50-goal season. The difference of course was that Rocket got his 50 in 50 games and now we were playing a 70-game schedule. Mahovlich had 43 goals on February 12, 1961. I had 32. Everyone was talking about Big M having Rocket's record in his sights. Nobody, justifiably I might add, mentioned my chances.

Mahovlich needed less than a goal a game to crack Rocket's record but once he entered the homestretch the pressure mounted and he found himself under intense checking. Slowly but surely Frank began to slow down and where he decelerated I accelerated.

I bounced back from an injury that had sidelined me for six games and now was averaging 1.4 points a game. The gap between Big M and me was narrowing. On March 5, 1961 he had 47 goals but I was only four behind.

Then I made my move. In one week we won three games and scored 19 goals — I had six of them. On March 12, 1961 we visited the Windy City. The night before at home I had two goals in a 7-5 win over Boston. Gilles Tremblay, a sweet, speedy young left winger, had moved onto the line with Big Jean and me. Let me tell you we were cooking with gas.

I was tied with Mahovlich at 48 goals but he was tiring and I was getting hotter. Against Chicago I got number 49. This set the stage for our March 16 game against Toronto at The Forum. I didn't sleep the night before.

Even though the Maple Leafs were in second place right behind us Punch Imlach was more subdued than usual. On this night he had tall, lanky Cesare Maniago in goal and a really solid defense with Bob Baun, Carl Brewer, Tim Horton and Allan Stanley. They rarely gave you any room to maneuver. They were strong and they had spirit and usually played well on the road. "Aggression doesn't mean you have to be fighting all the time," said Imlach and he was right.

But when Montreal and Toronto collided a fight was almost inevitable. This time it was Eddie Shack and Marcel Bonin early in a scoreless first period. In the second we traded goals for a 1-1 tie. Billy Hicke and Pocket got a couple of quick ones in the third before Shack put in Toronto's second goal.

This had turned into another nip and tuck Habs-Leafs game until Ralphie Backstrom teamed up with Bonin and Hicke for our fourth goal. A two-goal deficit meant that Toronto had to do what they normally didn't like to, open up the game. But Imlach had no choice and that gave me my chance.

Béliveau carried the puck into the Toronto zone and popped it into the left corner. Gilles Tremblay beat both Bob Pulford and my former linemate Bert Olmstead into the corner and passed the puck back out right onto my stick. I didn't hesitate even for a fraction of a second but slapped it right past Maniago. He never saw a thing.

The Forum crowd rose as one and gave me the ovation of my life. I thought to myself that this made up for 1955 when I beat out Rocket on the last night of the season and my fans booed me. The glorious moment made all the hardship of the past years seem worthwhile and I soaked it up until the cheering stopped. I finished the final few minutes of the game in a daze.

That was my last goal and point of the season. We had two more games left on the schedule: Saturday night at home to Chicago and Sunday in Detroit. We lost 4-1 to the Blackhawks and then went to Detroit. Toronto was still on our tail after beating Boston 6-2 the previous night. We needed a win at Olympia to clinch first place.

This time Big Jean and Jacques delivered. Béliveau broke a zip-zip tie in the second and Plante blanked the Red Wings the rest of the way. Actually it was a 1-0 game down to the wire when rugged, underrated Claude Provost got an open-netter with one second left.

I won the scoring title with a total of 95 points; Big Jean was second with 90 and Mahovlich was third with 48 goals and 36 assists.

It would have been the happiest season of my entire life if we had won our sixth straight Stanley Cup. But as Dick Irvin would have said the unseen hand would intervene — again.

CHAPTER 13

Our Reign Is Over

As good as we were having finished first and with five straight Stanley Cups under our belt we were not the same Canadiens team as before.

Some would say we were better, especially with the addition of Gilles Tremblay on left wing, while others would say we weren't. After all we didn't have Rocket to lead us anymore.

We were different; that's for sure. And we could be had.

No matter how good you are when a club wins five championships in a row some kind of complacency sets in no matter how well it's concealed. And even if we weren't complacent we had some awfully good opposition on both sides ready to take us, especially Chicago.

The Blackhawks had played us hard all year and we wound up splitting the season series with them right down the middle. What's more *The Hockey News* gave an enthusiastic boost to Chicago in its Stanley Cup Preview. The Hawks had a terrific goalie in Glenn Hall and well-balanced lines. But most of all Rudy Pilous who coached them had instilled a toughness in his lineup.

Their defense was big and scary. Jack Evans was one of those quiet guys who could pound you through the boards if you didn't watch out. Moose Vasko was as huge as his name implied and Pierre Pilote, even though he was small for a defenseman, would flatten you if you didn't watch yourself. Plus they had a lanky, bespectacled defenseman who never seemed to make a mistake. His name was Al Arbour.

Up front they had two young superstars-in-the-making. Bobby Hull, The Golden Jet, had copied my slap shot and was shooting the puck almost as hard as yours truly. Stan Mikita was a little center who could make plays as well as anybody in the league. He could hit as hard as anyone in the NHL as well.

The Chicago Blackhawks were a hard driving, hard shooting, hard hitting team, one that would be called a "physical" team, in later years. One of their more boisterous members was a chunky guy who could play either forward or defense. Reggie Fleming not only could fight and throw hard bodychecks but he also had enough talent to play in the NHL. I knew about Fleming because he had grown up in east end Montreal and had come up through the Canadiens' system. He had played on the Junior Canadiens with Phil Goyette, Claude Provost and Pocket.

Fleming stayed in our system for a while until we traded him to Chicago. Right off the bat he made a name for himself by slugging Rangers' goalie Jack McCartan, the hero of the U.S. gold medal team in the 1960 Olympics, during a hockey riot at Madison Square Garden. Fleming got a total of 37 penalty minutes in that one game!

I wouldn't say that Reggie was a policeman but he was setting the stage for the Dave Schultzes of the NHL who would come along a decade later. Fleming's minor league coach in Shawinigan Falls was Fred Shero who turned Schultz and the Philadelphia Flyers into the Broad Street Bullies.

Chicago wasn't a bully team but they were tougher than any team we had faced in the past few years including Punch Imlach's Maple Leafs. They also were motivated because several of them had been dropped by the Canadiens' organization for one reason or another. These included Fleming, Dollard St. Laurent, who had become one of Chicago's best defensemen, Red Hay, Murray Balfour and Eddie Litzenberger. Also it had been so long since they had won The Stanley Cup they could taste it.

The semifinal opened on March 21, 1961 at The Forum. Toe was confident and so was I. "This team can do anything," Blake said and the way we handled Game One showed that we were still Stanley Cup champions.

Big Jean and Tremblay set me up for a goal before the game was three minutes old. Chicago stayed close, it was 2-2 after two, but we blew them out with four unanswered goals in the third and skated off the ice with a 6-2 win. There was only one hitch; the Blackhawks had given us an awful pounding and a few of our guys were really hurting.

We didn't know it at the time but the most telling blow of all was dealt by Jack Evans against Le Gros Bill. Big Jean was checked into the boards behind the net by the Chicago defenseman and struck his head on the glass as he was falling to the ice. The next day Béliveau still was complaining of a headache and would not be the same for the remaining games. If one check could turn a series, that was it.

We were home again two nights later and for a while it looked like the same script had been written. We were tied at the end of two but that's where the similarity ended. Hull shot them ahead at 8:23 of the third but Goyette got us back in at 10:26. Litzenberger, the same guy we had "donated" to Chicago years earlier, beat Plante with less than three minutes left and they beat us 4-3.

With the series tied at one game apiece we moved back to Chicago for what would be one of the wildest nights I've ever experienced. Before telling you about it let me first point out that Red Storey's walkout as a referee two years earlier after that hectic game in Chicago was still having repercussions in the NHL officiating staff.

Red had been well-respected by his colleagues and several of the zebras like Eddie Powers and George Hayes were angry that he had left, especially the way it had happened. They also were unhappy with the way Clarence Campbell and his referee in chief Carl Voss were handling the officiating. This had a trickle-down effect to the players, coaches and managers who weren't crazy about the way some games were handled. Nor were they crazy about certain referees.

We'd had trouble with one of them all season. Dalton McArthur was one of the younger referees and he and Blake had had their share of shouting matches — Toe did most of the yelling — during the season. Now as luck would have it McArthur was handling Game Three.

This was not a game for the faint-hearted. Chicago Stadium was like a volcano waiting to erupt even before the opening face-off and it stayed that way throughout as bodies crunched bodies. McArthur called three double-minor penalties in the first period but there were no goals.

It stayed nothing-nothing until late in the second when Balfour, playing on a line with Bobby Hull and Red Hay, beat Plante. Meanwhile Glenn Hall was terrific in goal for Chicago. He nursed the 1-0 shutout through the third period until McArthur hit Hay with a minor penalty at 18:40 of the third.

What a break. In 44 seconds Pocket had tied the score and into overtime we went. Usually referees are reluctant to call penalties in sudden-death and McArthur swallowed his whistle in the first period. But in the second he hit us for two minors and Chicago with one. Incredibly neither team scored.

In the third overtime he penalized Ron Murphy of the Hawks just eight seconds into the period. We had a great chance to put it away but Hall was unbeatable. At 11:44 McArthur sent Dickie Moore off and Chicago went to their power play once more. Right away they moved the puck into our end. Stan Mikita and Pierre Pilote were passing it around until it reached the front of our net where a wild scramble took place.

Murray Balfour had his back to the net when the puck came to him. He took a blind whack and the puck slipped along the ice right past Plante. It wasn't a hard shot but it sure had good eyes. The rubber went in at 12:12 of the third overtime but then the fur really began to fly.

Toe went berserk. Instead of heading to the dressing room with the rest of us he went over the boards and made a beeline for McArthur who was directly across the ice exactly 85 feet from our bench.

The referee already had gone to the stat man to give him the final details. At the timekeeper's bench in Chicago Stadium they had glass that came right around and only one opening where the door was to the penalty bench.

As a result McArthur had to lean over and talk in to the scorekeeper. Because of all the cheering for the winning goal the scorekeeper couldn't hear the referee so he had to holler, repeating his report three times. That delay was pivotal because it gave Blake enough time to reach McArthur. Just as the official pushed himself backwards to turn and go down to his dressing room, he turned right into Toe. Blake threw a right cross at McArthur's head. The ref didn't know what hit him.

Meanwhile Clarence Campbell was watching the whole thing and in his presidential manner had to do something about it. After reviewing the reports Campbell fined Toe $2,000, the largest single fine ever leveled in NHL history up to then.

When he heard about it Blake had a wonderful comment for the media, "Well there goes my new car for next year!" In a more serious vein he admitted that he had blown it, "I know I broke the rules. I have no appeal. A suspension would have hurt me more."

What hurt me was my knee. I got badly whacked in the triple-overtime game and had torn ligaments in the left knee. That left me out of Game Four in Chicago which we won 5-2 and Game Five at home which we lost 3-0.

"That was the worst we ever played in a play-off since I've been here," moaned Blake. "But I still have confidence we'll pull it out of the fire. Our team always plays its best under pressure."

Our predicament was clear. We were a game away from having our Cup streak ended.

My predicament was complicated. Dr. Larry Hampson had put my leg in a cast until April 7. But our do-or-die game in Chicago was April 4. What to do?

I hobbled on to the train with the rest of the guys for our trip to Chicago. No question we were in bad shape physically, mentally and on the scoresheet. The Blackhawks were kicking the stuffing out of us. Their tough defense had practically nullified our offense. To give you an idea how much our attack was affected our leading scorer for the series wasn't Big Jean or Dickie or Pocket or me, it was little Phil Goyette. Béliveau didn't have a single goal. I had only two.

Worse than that was the fact that we didn't have an antidote for their roughhousing. Where they could throw out Fleming, Evans or Pilote we simply lacked an aggressive fighter to neutralize them. Something had to be done and Doug Harvey had an idea. While we were sitting in the parlor car Doug laid it right on the line. "Boom," he said, "we really need you tomorrow night."

"Doug," I shot back, "I want to help but I've got this cast on my leg. What am I gonna do about that?"

"Why don't we cut it off, see how you feel without it? If you think it's okay, try working the power play."

It sounded crazy but the more I thought about it the more I decided why not, what was there to lose — except maybe my leg!

Doug got a knife from the train kitchen and the two of us sneaked into the ladies' washroom. With my leg up on a chair I watched my captain saw away at the heavy plaster cast. He cut it lengthwise and the way the train was bouncing around it was a miracle I wasn't cut. It seemed to take hours to complete the job. I breathed a sigh of relief when he was done but soon had second thoughts. Pain shot up my leg when I stood up. I began to consider the repercussions of what we had done. I had plenty of time to think it all over because the leg hurt so much that I hardly slept a minute on the train that night.

The next morning my cast-less leg was the talk of the team and Doug was feeling like a surgeon who had just performed a delicate operation. With a big smile on his face he said, "I didn't do it in record time but you have to take into consideration the rolling train."

Toe and our trainer were furious. But I begged them to freeze the knee and they relented. For a few hours after the shot I really didn't feel too bad.

I wasn't trying to be a hero by biting the bullet and all that but I did have a sense of loyalty to the Habs and if ever they needed a boost this was it. After all how many times do you get to go for six straight Stanley Cups?

Blake saved me for the power play and sure enough we got on midway through the first period. All the Chicago guys knew about my predicament and they also knew that they had a better chance of winning the series with me out of the lineup. As the power play began the puck was passed to me and I managed to skate from blue line to blue line. But as I neared Chicago's line I looked up and there was Bobby Hull skating right at me. As I saw him coming I said to myself, "Here we go again!"

Sure enough Hull connected. In fact he connected so hard that I crashed backward onto the bad knee. I knew then that they were determined to get me out of the game. I hobbled back to the bench and begged for one more chance but when it came on another power play they just knocked me right off my gimpy leg once more and that was really it. I was finished.

And so were the Canadiens. We did nothing. Glenn Hall wound up shutting us out for a total of 137 minutes and 29 seconds in Games Five and Six. Unbelievable. Hay, Hull and Eric Nesterenko scored for them in the second period and that was that — 3-0.

I don't know what was more painful, the thought of losing a sixth Stanley Cup or the pain that was rushing through my knee now that the painkillers were losing their potency. Blowing the series *was* awful but in my entire hockey career I never experienced anything as terrible as the pain that shot through my leg that night.

On the miserable train ride from Chicago to Montreal I threatened to take that kitchen knife to Doug if he ever suggested I do anything as harebrained again. "At least you tried," he said.

By the time our train pulled in to Montreal's Windsor Station the pain was so intense that tears were streaming down my face and I had to leave on crutches. But then the whole team was so woebegone that even on crutches and crying I didn't look much worse than the others. Most of my teammates were sporting cuts, bruises and assorted shiners all testifying to the physical pounding we had taken.

Writing in *The Hockey News* Gil Smith observed, "Even the gloom of the station itself seemed to blend perfectly into this cheerless homecoming scene." It was over. The dynasty was history and to a man we knew that things would never be the same. Selke announced ominously: "There will be drastic changes made before next October."

I knew I was safe. Selke wasn't going to unload his best goal scorer and even though he may have frowned on my "cut the cast caper" The Boss understood that I had done it out of loyalty to the team. Big Jean, Dickie and Pocket also were obviously untouchable but that left some other big names on the fence.

One of those was Doug Harvey. Doug had an off year and both Selke and Ken Reardon were fed up with him. Losing The Stanley Cup would be the perfect excuse for them to get rid of him which they eventually did.

Another question mark was Jacques Plante. Toe Blake was becoming more and more disenchanted with the goalie's eccentricities and Selke complained, "He's got to take things more seriously."

Nobody said anything but Toe himself was a concern because the strain of five straight Cups and the attempt for a sixth was getting to him. He once said, "I'd like to coach Canadiens for a hundred years but the tension is too terrific. On the days of some games I was almost not human."

The loss was disappointing but it was also inevitable. All dynasties, from the Yankees to the Packers, eventually get old and creaky. Sooner or later either injuries or complacency or both knock a champion off the pedestal. We were the only team to win five Stanley Cups in succession and I honestly don't think another club will ever duplicate that.

The other reason we were defeated was because of the change in hockey strategy or philosophy, if you will. Chicago had shown that rough hockey can produce winning hockey. Jack Evans' brutal check on Big Jean against the plexiglas at The Forum symbolized the entire series and the new direction hockey was taking.

"Canadiens are going to be a lot tougher next season," Selke warned. "We have been playing nice, clean hockey a little too long.

The Blackhawks deliberately racked up five of our best players and not one of the Canadiens put a hand on them in retaliation. I'm tired of hearing fans calling our players `yellow-bellies.' This is going to change."

That change would have a profound effect on Montreal hockey — and on me.

CHAPTER 14

A New Captain Leads the Habs

Frank Selke wasn't kidding. When he said there'd be changes made he meant *changes*.

The Boss dropped the bomb right after Chicago's Stanley Cup win over Detroit and just before the June draft. Doug Harvey was no longer a Canadien. He and defenseman Al Langlois were traded to New York for Leapin' Louie Fontinato and John Hanna. Any time a club trades the best defenseman in the history of the game it's front page news.

But it was hard news for us to take. We all loved Doug and we knew he still had good hockey in him but politics figured into this deal as much as anything. Selke had never forgiven Harvey for helping launch the players' association but it was more complicated than that. Selke wanted to shake up the club which had been getting too complacent. He was annoyed at our getting pushed around by bigger, rougher clubs like the Blackhawks. And Hanna and Fontinato were known to like mixing it up.

But everything has a price and we would miss Doug, who was still the NHL's best defenseman and had won his sixth Norris Trophy in eight years (Tom Johnson and Red Kelly had each won it once).

The Rangers' manager Muzz Patrick wanted Doug to be both player and coach the way Sid Abel had been with Chicago in the early 1950s. Abel took the Blackhawks to a play-off after a long drought and Doug would do the same for the Rangers.

Doug's departure was the most unpleasant surprise of my year. My most pleasant was winning the Hart Trophy as the NHL's most valuable player. I shouldn't call it a surprise as much as a shock when you consider the competition.

In the first balloting at half season Toronto's goalie Johnny Bower was the leader with 48 points, Frank Mahovlich was second and Gordie Howe was third. With only 29 points I was buried in fourth place. But my homestretch drive for 50 goals changed all that. In the second half I picked up 55 points. Bower got only 23 and Howe took 30. The final tally was Boomer 84, Bower 71 and it was a decision that gave me one of the biggest thrills of my career.

I had dreamed of winning the Hart but when you're surrounded by greats like Rocket, Doug, Big Jean, Moore, Pocket and Plante you know your chances are slim. In fact I was so sure there was no way I'd ever get the Hart that when a reporter phoned me and said that I had won it I was sure he was putting me on. "Yeah, yeah," I said, "What else is new?" and hung up on him.

There was another vote in 1961 — to replace Doug Harvey as the captain of Canadiens. No doubt about it that would have been a real feather in my cap being the successor to such top leaders as Rocket and Doug.

Several players had the qualifications. Dickie Moore would have been a great captain and so would Tom Johnson who, along with Dickie and me, was one of the elders. Big Jean was a great playmaker and a great leader although he didn't have the seniority. Did I think I had a chance? Sure I did. I had the track record and had proven my dedication over and over again. I believed that I could lead the Habs to another Stanley Cup just the way Rocket had in the 1950s.

We had the vote just before the 1961-62 season opened at The Forum. On the first ballot there was a tie between Big Jean and me. This surprised me a bit because the C always went to the player with seniority.

On the second ballot Big Jean was declared the winner and for a moment I was crushed. Then a large misunderstanding developed. The rumor mill suggested that I was jealous of Jean but that wasn't it at all. I was never angry at Big Jean. I was happy for him but for a day or two my feelings were hurt because I finally had to face the fact that I wasn't the most loved guy on the team. So if I didn't get it I knew the best guy to be captain was Béliveau. I congratulated him on winning the C although I obviously didn't really hide my disappointment either.

Béliveau admitted in his book that he didn't vote for me because I "didn't convey enough seriousness to be captain." The guy who wears the C had to go into the dressing room and talk to the players. It was something I had done throughout my hockey career. And while I was at it I had a lot of fun with it but somehow the fact that I could have fun while I was trying to motivate the guys was seen as "not serious." I had played 11 years with Montreal Canadiens. You don't have that kind of longevity if you're "not serious."

Wonderful and sensitive individual that he is Big Jean was concerned about my reaction and finally decided that it might be a better idea if he gave up the captaincy. He told Blake that he would be just as happy wearing the A (for alternate) but Selke wouldn't hear of any change. The vote stood and the episode ended.

Within a day or two I got over what felt at first like a snub. Besides, there were so many good things going on around me that I couldn't let the captaincy issue get me down, especially with a show business career developing on the side.

I had made a successful television debut on a Canadian Broadcasting Corporation network show with Joan Fairfax. I sang "Dear Hearts and Gentle People" and "C'est Magnifique" and got great reviews from all over the country.

The producer wanted me to do two more shows. *The Dinah Shore* show in the States was talking about having me on and I got an offer to appear at the plush Bonaventure Room of Montreal's Queen Elizabeth Hotel. It was all very flattering but when the reporters asked me about my singing career I told them straight out, "Hockey comes first."

I wasn't kidding myself. I owed everything I had to hockey. If it wasn't for my name in hockey I wouldn't have even had one appearance on TV. Of course my name in hockey wasn't exactly making me a rich man, at least not by today's standards. Remember the NHL still was a six-team league, we didn't even have a players' association and hockey on television was in its infancy. Big money wasn't being tossed around as casually as it is today. I had that lesson hammered home to me when I visited Selke's office after my 50-goal season.

At age 30 I wanted some security. To me that meant a five-year contract and when a reporter asked me about it I told him exactly what I wanted. What a mistake!

Selke hated players who "negotiated through the newspaper" and this was no exception. That was never my intention but I should have talked to him first. When I went up to his office for our meeting Selke was sore, really sore. I left with nothing more than burning ears and heard not a word from The Boss or his people for the whole summer.

Finally August came to an end and it was time to get ready for training camp. It had been two months since I had seen Selke and I had heard from the grapevine that he had signed every one of my teammates except me! Uh-oh. I phoned him and headed down to The Forum. When he made me an offer I accepted it in a flash.

I was happy. I was still playing big-league hockey; I was a star and by the standards of 1961 I was getting paid good money. Selke gave me a bonus for winning the scoring title, another bonus for tying Rocket's record of 50 goals and he gave me the same bonuses that I had the previous season. All things considered I felt very good.

If there was a concern it was left wing. Dickie Moore had undergone surgery and Marcel Bonin had played the past three years with a chronic back ailment. Gilles Tremblay had looked great as a rookie but Selke hedged his bets. He sent defenseman Bob Turner to Chicago for a prospect named Fred Hilts who had scored 45 goals in Sault Ste. Marie. Hilts and Tremblay were vying for the same job so naturally I was rooting for my teammate Gilles. He kept his job and went on to have a great season with 32 goals. He was one of the best left wingers I ever had the pleasure to have on my line.

Even though we had been knocked out in the opening play-off round and had lost Harvey and Langlois several experts picked us to rebound and finish first again. Selke said he wasn't worried either. "Plante will make the difference," he said. "Jacques is starting out with a different attitude than last year and his morale is marvelous. Don't be surprised if he has the best season of his hockey career."

The Boss was right again. Despite his idiosyncrasies, phobias and allergies The Snake was at the top of his game and would become a First All-Star once again. And even though Big Jean and Dickie were out with injuries at the start of 1961-62 we were unbeaten in our first five (4-0-1).

Nobody was on the spot more than Fontinato, who had replaced Harvey. The Forum fans, who were quite capable of running a guy right out of the NHL, watched Leapin' Louie closely in the first few games. He didn't let them down. When we went to New York and beat the Rangers 5-2 Fontinato was the best player on the ice. As much as I missed Harvey I had to admit that Louie was doing the job for us.

The real surprise was up front. Claude Provost had been one of our best defensive forwards but one month into the season he also was leading the league in scoring.

He told me how he did it. Claude had watched Gordie Howe during the All-Star Game and noticed that Big Gordie had an unusually short stick. Claude picked up a saw and hacked the top off his shaft. "The thought occurred to me that my stick was too long," he explained. "All of a sudden with the shorter stick shots that used to hit the post were on the net. I didn't miss the goal so much."

Provost used to be dreadful on breakaways. One year he had 19 goals with three games to go and desperately wanted to reach 20. In Detroit he got two breakaways on Terry Sawchuk. He fired the puck right at him both times and never did get his 20 goals. This season he had already had three breakaways and scored each time. It just shows you how little things can change everything.

I knew I probably wasn't going to have another 50-goal year but I did expect to be up there. After a slow start I started coming around before Christmas. Toe said it was because I was backchecking. "You have to have the puck to score and you can't get it unless you check," he said. I checked, got enough points to be second in scoring and then hurt my knee again and was out of the race.

With all of our injuries and age catching up to some of the veterans we could have slipped badly. But I give Selke credit. He had built a terrific farm system and more importantly maintained it with top people in the field.

By far the best of all was Sam Pollock, who had come through the Montreal Junior ranks and was running Selke's farm club in Hull-Ottawa. He gave us a steady stream of good, young players, from J.C. Tremblay on defense to Bobby Rousseau, a rookie right winger who became the sensation of 1961-62.

The way the Canadiens got Rousseau in the first place showed how our club operated in those days. When Bobby was playing Junior B hockey with a team at St. Jean, Quebec Pollock spotted him and liked what he saw. The problem was that the team was sponsored by the Red Wings. Sam talked Selke into buying the rights to all the players on the team. Pollock didn't care about the rest of the kids but he did get Rousseau.

Bobby came up to us in 1960-61 and only scored once in 15 games. He was small but had talent and speed and when we brought him back he became a top candidate for rookie of the year. His slap shot was second only to mine in speed and accuracy and he managed to score 16 goals in 24 games.

The night I got hurt — December 23, 1961 — was the night he became a true big leaguer. Until then he was only killing penalties but when I got sidelined Toe put him alongside Big Jean and Gilles Tremblay and he got two goals. When I came back Blake left Rousseau where he was and put me with Ralph Backstrom and Donnie Marshall.

We hung onto first through midwinter because the second and third liners were coming through. Aside from Rousseau and Provost, Gilles Tremblay, Ralph Backstrom and J.C. Tremblay were playing outstanding hockey.

By early March 1962 we were solidly in first place but I was so far down in the scoring list you needed a guide to find me. That's when my moodiness showed. One day during my slump *Toronto Star* columnist Milt Dunnell, one of the nicest people in the business, asked me to sing a tune for him. I had to beg off.

"When goals don't come there is no song," I told him. "That's wrong I know but how can I sing when I am not happy?"

When I would pick up my seven-year-old son Bobby at school he would say, "Hey Dad, the kids at school want to know why you don't score goals like you did last year."

Marlene knew that I fretted too much. And she was right. I had been fighting myself. Sometimes even the muscles of my legs tightened up. I knew I had to relax and realized there was no point putting myself under more pressure. Toe told me the same thing.

The Montreal fans surprised me. They treated me as graciously as if I were headed for another 50-goal season. I had no complaints with them nor with the media although for the first time in my career there were reports that I might be traded.

Writing in *The Boston Globe* Tom Fitzgerald said, "How'd you like to see Boom Boom Geoffrion in a Bruin uniform?" He went on to say that it was not impossible what with all the young Canadien forwards doing so well. "Montreal needs some reinforcements on defense," he went on, "and would love to pry away the likes of Doug Mohns or Leo Boivin."

I didn't let it worry me. I didn't want to leave Montreal but if Selke felt he had to deal me so be it. In the end Mohns and Boivin weren't as appealing as the young defensemen like Terry Harper and Jacques Laperriere, who were being developed on our farm teams.

Besides my game started coming around just at the right time. I got my twentieth goal in a 5-2 win over Boston on March 10, 1962 and followed that with number 21, which gave me a career total of 325.

Even though I had made a relatively small contribution compared to the previous year I was satisfied with the team's final result. So was Toe. We had won our fifth straight league season championship, the sixth in seven seasons. "Of all the league titles we have won this one pleases me most," said Toe.

Selke was pleased as well. His acquisition of Fontinato turned out to be a very wise one. Leapin' Louie reminded me of myself in some ways. He was high-spirited and it was catching. It rubbed off early on the young fellows like Rousseau and Gilles Tremblay and some of us veterans couldn't help but be affected by it. We would need Fontinato's presence against defending champion Chicago in the opening play-off round.

For a while our prospects of bringing The Stanley Cup back to Montreal looked great. We shut down Chicago's offense in Game One and beat them 2-1 on goals by Moore and Béliveau in the third period. Game Two was even better. After being down 1-3 we rallied for three late third-period goals and a 4-3 edge. With a two-game edge we left for the Windy City.

Little did we know that that would be our last win. In Game Three I twisted my chronically bad left knee after my old buddy Dollard St. Laurent dumped me into the boards. I couldn't help the club after that and we lost four straight to exit the play-offs for the second straight year.

You can theorize forever about why Chicago beat us for the second straight year. Sure injuries hurt us and Plante tailed off in goal but Toe put it best when he simply said, "Not enough of my men played well while every last one of the Hawks managed to get up for the series."

I wondered who would face the chopping block after the loss. Would it be me?

CHAPTER 15

The Beginning of the End

There was no need to panic. True, for two years in a row we had failed to win The Stanley Cup and were knocked out of the play-offs in the first round.

But, we had won five straight Cups before that and look at the awards we received. Jacques Plante not only won the Vezina Trophy (2.37 goals-against average) but the Hart Trophy as well. Bobby Rousseau took the Calder and our Hull-Ottawa Canadiens won the Eastern Pro League championship. That team was loaded with prospects. Billy Carter, Keith McCreary, Brian Smith, Jacques Laperriere, Terry Harper, Jim Roberts and Claude Larose were among their best. Most of them would make a name in the NHL. (You might have heard of their chief scout Scotty Bowman.)

But Montreal was not like the other five NHL cities. Our fans were used to success and weren't satisfied with just a first-place finish if we didn't win the Cup. For the first time since he had been named coach in 1955 Toe Blake's effectiveness was being scrutinized for every sign of weakness.

Questions began being asked after the blowup with referee Dalton McArthur in the 1961 play-offs. When Chicago knocked us off again in 1962 Toe faced even more questioning. How could a team that finished 23 points ahead of third-place Chicago fail to take them out in the play-offs? We even heard talk that Toe might quit. He was as crushed by the defeat as anyone but wasn't about to walk out on the Canadiens.

"I'm not giving up," he said. "I'd hate to bow out a loser. If the club will have me I'll be back on a one-year contract."

One aspect of the play-off defeat that bothered Blake as much as it annoyed me was our lack of toughness. The additions of Lou Fontinato and John Hanna helped a little behind the blue line but Louie had been injured a lot leaving us as vulnerable as we had been the year before. Opponents found it easy to zero in on Big Jean, Pocket and me. Béliveau missed 27 games through injury in 1961-62 and still the front office expected him to be among the scoring leaders. That wasn't fair and he went public with his unhappiness.

Nevertheless Selke didn't add any noticeable beef. When Marcel Bonin retired after back surgery Selke brought in center Red Berenson who had gone to the University of Michigan which was unusual for NHL players in those days. He also wore a helmet which didn't win him a lot of points with Blake and most of the players. Everyone despised helmets. We figured that Canadiens looked soft enough as it was and now we add a university guy who wouldn't play without a helmet.

Actually Berenson was a pioneer of sorts. Helmets would eventually become part of the landscape and hockey was beginning to change in a lot of ways. For one thing salaries were starting to climb. Doug Harvey got a bundle from the Rangers and Frank Mahovlich was asking a ton from the Maple Leafs.

When Punch Imlach balked at Big M's demands Blackhawks' owner Jim Norris startled everyone in the business when he offered to buy Mahovlich from the Maple Leafs for one million dollars. At an owners' party on October 2, 1962 Norris made the offer and put it in writing in front of some of the governors, "I promise to pay one million dollars for Frank Mahovlich. Signed. Jim Norris."

Harold Ballard of the Leafs' signed the note. At the time this was startling news. In Canada it replaced the World Series as the top sports story.

In the end Imlach and Smythe killed the deal but it just pointed to the direction hockey was moving. Big money was coming to the NHL and eventually the players were going to benefit. Big M signed a Toronto contract for $25,000 which wasn't a million but wasn't bad for the time.

We had a good training camp in September 1962. I felt fine and the reporters were impressed by the way I looked. "He's like a champion thoroughbred when he's in the right mood," wrote Pat

Curran in *The Hockey News*. "He appeared that way in training and should score handily again."

I didn't score handily in our opening game on October 11 at Boston, in fact none of us did. The Bruins shellacked us 5-0 and even the score didn't tell the half of it. We didn't score and we did- n't even hit. "Nobody threw a good bodycheck all night," snapped Blake when it was over.

Jacques Plante was a different kind of concern. Before we took the train to Beantown Jacques complained that he was under the weather. As a precaution Blake brought young Ernie Wakely of Hull-Ottawa as a backup. Jacques insisted that he could play but didn't look sharp as five beat him.

"That's the last time I'll ever be talked into using a player when he's sick," said Blake. Jacques agreed when he said, "I'll never go into the nets again in this condition." His ailment was diagnosed as an infectious allergy related to his asthmatic condition. When we returned to Montreal to open the season at The Forum Jacques phoned to say he wasn't well enough to play. Wakely went out and beat New York 6-3. "Jacques has to show me his attitude is right," Selke insisted.

Plante's attitude never would be right again, not as far as The Boss was concerned. The season wasn't even a week old and I could sense that we were in trouble. It was the beginning of the end as far as our dynasty was concerned. If our Hart Trophy winner was being doubted by the general staff what did that say for the rest of us?

Mind you the collapse was neither sudden nor complete. Nobody was running us out of the league but little things were going wrong. And there was a big one, too — our power play. There was a time when taking a penalty against Canadiens was suicide for the opposition but now they were laughing at us and continuing to go after the smaller guys.

By far the worst incident of all took place in Chicago on October 23, 1962. Reggie Fleming, who by this time had become one of the most intimidating players in the league, collided with Gilles Tremblay, who always played the game hard but clean.

The incident began when Gilles passed the puck behind the Chicago net and Fleming hit him with a shoulder check. They met again coming back up ice near our blue line. That's when they started sniping at each other. Tremblay whacked Fleming across the glove and then both sticks started to go like a fencing match.

Each of them wound up taking eight to ten swipes at the other and pretty soon Tremblay was bleeding from the head. He needed 13 stitches in his scalp.

Clarence Campbell ordered a hearing with the result that each player was hit for $750 and suspended for three games. That had little effect on our club because we were going nowhere — in a hurry! Some critics whispered that we were over the hill. Others said the new kids didn't really care and Toe just wrung his hands in frustration.

"There are no reasonable grounds for thinking that fellows like Boomer and Béliveau are not capable of playing as well as they ever did," said Blake. "I'm sure they are. They just haven't hit their peak quite as quickly as I expected."

Dick Irvin had a theory that once you hit age 30 you have to drive harder just to break even and every season after that it became more work and less fun. I was still in the top ten on the scoring list but I was working harder than ever before. Early in December I had yet another scare.

We were at Maple Leaf Gardens en route to a 2-1 loss. Our goal was mine but it proved to be very painful one. We were on a power play when Donnie Marshall and Big Jean put me in the clear against Johnny Bower. As I went in on him Bower tried to deke me. He moved one way then back and I ran into him. My wrist hit his chin just as I lifted the puck over him and into the net.

The X-rays showed a possible fracture which could have killed my season but when we returned home another set of X-rays indicated no break at all. What luck!

Tom Johnson wasn't as lucky. He also had a wrist injury but that was only the half of it. Tommy was one of the best defenseman I had played alongside on Canadiens over the past ten years. But as good as he was he was not appreciated by the Montreal fans. When his playing slumped the fans booed. Finally The Boss dropped the bomb: "Tommy shouldn't have to take that sort of thing," said Selke. "In appreciation for what he's done for us in the long time he's been with Canadiens I would be glad to make a trade."

There were even reports that Dickie Moore was on the block. How had we fallen so far? In the first half All-Star balloting not one Canadien made it to the first team. Even though he was a bit on the crude side Lou Fontinato would have gotten a vote from me.

It was interesting to see how Louie had been welcomed into our dressing room after being so hated when he played for the Rangers.

The thing was whoever came into the room became a Montreal Canadien and we didn't hold a grudge. We welcomed Louie and we liked him because he was funny. Louie was so close with his money he wouldn't buy you a pop. I used to tease him about it and he'd laugh. But nobody on the opposition laughed at him. Louie was tough. He wasn't afraid of anybody.

My wrist injury put me on the shelf for a dozen games and when I did return it was with a bang. It was January 31, 1963 with the Maple Leafs visiting us at The Forum. Toe had planned to bring me back into the lineup slowly and didn't put me on the ice until the third period. The score was 2-2 at the start of the third when Toronto pulled ahead.

On my first full shift in the middle of the third — we were now losing 4-2 — I drove for a rebound at the Leafs' net and banged into goalie Don Simmons. Carl Brewer, an annoying Toronto defenseman, went after me and we started to scrap. For some reason Brewer was bugging me more than usual and I kept chasing him both at the net and the penalty box. I wound up getting a minor, a misconduct, a game misconduct and a $75 fine.

We lost the game 6-3 and then Toe lost it. He blew up at the referee Eddie Powers claiming that he had handled the game as if he had bet on the result. Those are fighting words for any referee and Powers expected Clarence Campbell, who had once been an NHL referee himself, to really lower the boom on Toe. (Remember Blake had been socked for two grand after slugging referee Dalton McArthur.)

Instead Campbell assessed Toe $200 for what he had said. Powers complained that the fine was "inadequate" and that Campbell "hasn't backed the referees in general during the past years in a strong enough manner."

Powers resigned on the spot. Dalton McArthur had gotten less and less work and Red Storey was long gone. Three referees involved in controversial Canadiens' games and look what happened!

But that wasn't the end of it, I would see to that.

It was March 5, 1962 and we were at Olympia Stadium. Gordie Howe had scored putting Detroit ahead by one. Late in the period referee Vern Buffey hit Plante with a two-minute penalty. As he returned from the penalty timekeeper I got up on our bench and laced into him. Buffey hit me with an unsportsmanlike conduct penalty.

That did it. I flipped out and tossed my stick like a spear right at Buffey and then my hockey gloves. Buffey deflected the stick with his hands but the gloves caught him right in the chest.

My wonderful aim not only got me thrown out of the game but also got me an invitation to visit Campbell's office. He gave me the usual lecture about how there was "no possible excuse" for what I had done and hit me with a five-game suspension. I was stunned.

Considering that we still were in a tight race for first place with Toronto and Chicago this was an extremely severe punishment. But four days later something happened that made me realize that my suspension was small potatoes in the scheme of things. My team-mate Leapin' Louie had his career ended right on Forum ice in front of the eyes of some 14,000 people.

We were home against the Rangers on March 9, 1963. New York had a pretty ordinary team by now. A year earlier when Doug Harvey went down as player-coach they caught fire and actually made the play-offs. But Doug and Muzz Patrick, the Rangers' general manager, had a falling out and Harvey left. Without him New York was nothing, buried in fifth place.

Still there was a bit of a spark in the visitors. They had a big, young, left winger named Vic Hadfield who loved to hit people and was beginning to make a name for himself. In one game Hadfield and Henri Richard had a fight in the penalty box that was so intense the NHL finally decided to set up separate boxes for each team.

Hadfield was the kind of guy who you had to be aware of on the ice and the same could be said for Fontinato for just about the same reasons — except that Louie was older and had been around the NHL for a long time.

Along the end boards in the south end of The Forum Louie and Vic were trying to get hold of the loose puck. Hadfield was charging in pursuit and Lou saw him coming. Fontinato seemed to be trying the "submarine" check ducking his head so that Hadfield would go flying over him.

Maybe Louie didn't go down low enough, I don't know. What I do know is that Hadfield caught him in the neck and the force of the collision sent Louie's head right into the boards and he crumpled in a heap. In seconds all the players realized that Fontinato was in deep trouble.

It's a curious scene on the ice when a player gets hurt. There are always a couple of players who stand right around him leaning over to be sure he's okay or to see how badly he's hurt and then there are the others who distance themselves. To the crowd they appear to be unconcerned when actually they are just as worried but know there's not much they can do by leaning over. (When I had the ruptured bowel Doug Harvey leaned over and told me to stop fooling around!) In Louie's case there was no fooling around.

Dr. Doug Kinnear, the Canadiens' house physician, came right out on to the ice and before he even touched Louie, he knew there was a major, major problem. The big defenseman couldn't move any part of his body and he even warned Doc Kinnear not to touch him.

It was the worst possible news — a broken neck. Lou's condition deteriorated and he underwent a seven-hour operation. There was no visible damage to the nerve roots of the arms and doctors were hopeful of a satisfactory recovery.

Fontinato never played hockey again and retired to his farm near Guelph, Ontario. Lou's accident made us all stop and think. His career was over at age 31 all because of a relatively ordinary check. He and Hadfield hadn't meant to hurt each other. It was just one of those things but I knew full well that it also could have been me. At age 30 I still had plenty of good hockey left in me.

The loss of Louie could have hurt us but our sensational farm system came through again. Blake was breaking in a stringbean defenseman named Jacques Laperriere and he was preparing a tough but awkward kid named Terry Harper who loved to fight, never won but always came back for more. You had to like his enthusiasm.

We stayed in the race for first right down to the wire. Three teams — Montreal, Toronto and Chicago — were neck and neck into the final week of the season. Then the Leafs knocked off Chicago and we went into Toronto for the decisive game. Punch Imlach's team had been hot down the stretch and this time they came from behind to tie us 3-3 and clinch first. At the end we were in third place. Toronto finished ahead of us by three and Chicago ahead by two. A good play-off could make up for all of the season's hardship.

Ever since he had taken over the Leafs in the late 1950s Imlach would razz us and especially Toe Blake every chance he got. He had been saying that his ambition in 1962-63 was to finish first and beat the Canadiens in The Stanley Cup final.

Punch was put out because he wasn't going to get his wish, but final or semifinal, he was determined to beat us. We met Toronto in the first round of the play-offs and Imlach got over his unhappiness very quickly. The Leafs scored three straight goals against Plante before Big Jean put in a power play score and they easily won 3-1.

As if that weren't bad enough Plante's Toronto allergies were acting up and so was his mouth. Right after Game One our goalie sat down with the media and began to carve up our club. His big complaint was that we didn't have a leader which I thought was unfair to our captain Big Jean. Here's what Jacques told them:

> *Not long ago when we were winning easily we always had some fellow who was the sparkplug of the team. First it was Butch Bouchard, then The Rocket who was always a leader, Bert Olmstead, Doug Harvey and a couple of other fellows.*
>
> *They told you off if you were not playing well and the rest of the guys listened to them. A team needs a guy who will give the players a whack in the pants once in awhile.*
>
> *Now we don't have anyone like that. Lou Fontinato helped a bit that way during the season and we certainly miss him in the play-offs. He was no superstar but he was always hollering and helped to give the team a lift.*

Jacques didn't even mention Béliveau but did say that our one possible leader was Dickie Moore. "There's a fellow (Moore) who might be a leader — but he's playing on one leg. It's pretty hard for him to tell guys what to do when he can hardly do things himself."

The brass, especially Blake, Selke and Reardon heard everything Jacques said and were all suitably ticked off but what could they do at this stage of the play-offs? Nothing but bite their tongues and hope for the best. They would take care of the goaltender when the season was over.

But the best was never to come and Imlach got his revenge in spades. Toronto won the next two in a row including a 2-0 decision in Game Three at The Forum that really hurt. Gilles Tremblay spared us the embarrassment of a sweep with a two-goal effort in Game Four but it was just delaying the inevitable. Johnny Bower shut us out 5-0 and we were finished.

After a series loss it usually takes a while for the general staff to react but Toe wasted no time. First he barred the dressing room to reporters and just about everyone else after the humiliating setback. Then he lit into us, his main theme being that a change of attitude was needed by many of us if we hoped to stay with the team.

Blake also made it clear that this time he was seriously thinking of putting an end to his coaching career. He promised an announcement in a week or two after he had time to gather his thoughts.

"I couldn't get through to my players," he said. "When that happens it may be time to get out. We weren't the same team as we used to be and I'm partly to blame. I couldn't get my message across the way I used to."

"I don't blame the players. Most of them gave it everything they had but two or three of them didn't have the right attitude. It wasn't the same as in the `old' days."

Rudy Pilous, coach of the Blackhawks, had Toe pegged perfectly when he said, "Blake has been used to winning and he feels frustrated now when he loses. That happens to everybody who stays in this game long enough."

Who were the "two or three" players lacking the right attitude? Who would be back for 1963-64? We were all guessing. Jacques Plante would probably be traded. Dickie Moore's legs were so bad he was almost a sure thing to pack it in. The others who figured to be on Toe's trade list were Tom Johnson, Phil Goyette and Donnie Marshall for various reasons ranging from injuries to lack of production.

Not that I had anything to brag about. My performance in the final weeks and the play-offs was a disaster and the rumors started that Selke might trade me as well. I had only 23 goals for the season after the 50-goal year. Even so Chicago, New York and Detroit each went public with its interest in me. Imlach went a step further and said he would give up three players for me.

I loved Montreal but was ready to play for any NHL club because I still had another goal to reach. I wanted to become the third-highest goal-getter in history. Ted Lindsay, who finished with 365 goals, was only 15 ahead of me. If I hadn't been hurt I might have passed him in 1962-63.

Jacques Beauchamp, one of my favorite hockey writers asked me how I felt about the trade rumors and I simply laid it on the line with him in *Montréal Matin*: "If Canadiens decide to trade me, I'll prove that I'm still able to hold my own in the NHL."

In a sense I was daring Selke to move me.

Would he take the dare? And if not who would be gone?

CHAPTER 16

Au Revoir, Montreal

It had now been three years since we last won The Stanley Cup and the natives not only were becoming restless, they were downright depressed. For the first time since I arrived with the Canadiens there were mumblings that Frank Selke might be in trouble as managing director.

This was huge news: Selke had run the team since the end of World War II when he left the Maple Leafs and Conn Smythe to reorganize the Habs. The results show that he did a fabulous job with the five consecutive Cups from 1956 through 1960. But that was ancient history as far as the fans were concerned and to a certain extent the Molsons who now owned the team.

1963-64 would be such an important season for the Canadiens, Selke and me. In the meantime we watched axes fall all over the NHL, some in our own backyard.

The biggest surprise was in Chicago where the Blackhawks dumped coach Rudy Pilous, who brought them their first Stanley Cup (1961) in 23 years. Rudy's problem was that he forgot to win the Cup the next two seasons.

Pilous didn't whine and mewl about it. He told it like it is in this business. "Coaches have been hired and fired since the first day they tied a dollar bill to a puck," was the way Rudy put it and that's exactly why Toe Blake was now coaching from year to year.

To say that Toe was unhappy with the way things were going would be an understatement. Not winning the Cup would have been bad enough but there were other major problems. One was the loss of Dickie Moore after 1962-63 which was a tremendous blow. If I said it once I said it a thousand times, Dickie Moore is one of the most underrated superstars in the history of hockey. Dickie's knees had been killing him and when his name was linked to trade rumors he told The Boss not to bother trading him; he would quit — and he did.

As tough as it was losing Dickie, it was just as hard knowing that Tom Johnson no longer would be a teammate. During 1962-63 Tommy had suffered a fractured cheekbone and an eye injury during a practice when Bobby Rousseau's skate jammed him in the face as they fell into the boards. Tommy's vision was impaired and Selke decided that he was no longer useful to us. When Selke put Tom on waivers the Bruins were tickled to pick him up. Toe was saddened to lose someone who had done so much for our hockey club. On the other hand there was a player on the club who no matter how valuable he was often got under Toe's skin. That was Jacques Plante. It had gotten to the point where either the goaltender went or the coach did, and since both Selke and Reardon were also unhappy with Jacques, it was just a matter of time. One shoe had already dropped, so what about the other?

The other shoe fell on June 4, 1963. You could feel the reverberations all the way from Montreal to Manhattan. Plante was shipped out along with Don Marshall and Phil Goyette. In turn the Rangers sent us my favorite goaltending target Gump Worsley along with left wingers Dave Balon, Len Ronson and Leon Rochefort.

Most NHL "experts" thought that New York got the better of the deal. They mentioned that the Rangers picked up the guy who supposedly was "the best goalie in the business" and more talented players up front. Selke disagreed. "The players we acquired give us a total of 11 years in youth. The wingers are a little more muscular which is what we need."

True enough but everyone connected with Canadiens knew that the key was Plante. Toe was fed up with him and that was that. The two other guys we gave up — Marshall and Goyette — were the best penalty killers in the NHL. As far as I was concerned it was a toss-up between Plante and Worsley. I always respected Gump even though I had scored some of my best goals against him. His problem in New York for many years was the team in front of him.

There were years when Gump had a tissue-paper defense and forwards who couldn't even spell the word backcheck. Once when

Gump was having one of his toughest years a reporter asked him which NHL club gave him the most trouble. "Are you kidding?" he said. "The Rangers!"

Worsley had a restaurant in Montreal. While he was still playing in New York he hung a sign in the bistro: Ranger Special — Chicken Salad.

Who would I have rather had at that point — Gump or Jacques?

No question, Gump. Unlike Plante, Worsley came to play every game. He never squawked, never said anything that would cause trouble. His attitude was "I get paid to be in the net. I don't care how many shots I'm going to have thrown at me and I'm not going to wear a mask. Period!"

Gump was a team player. Jacques was a loner, rarely mixed with the fellows off the ice. When it came to pure ability Plante had the edge because he was more agile. I must tell you though that every time I mention Worsley it is with a special affection.

You have to remember that Gump and I had played together since we were teenagers: he was with Verdun and I was with Nationale. I always recall how I would tease him. I'd pump a goal past him and say, "Gump you'll never make the NHL."

He would get mad, throw his stick, his gloves, you name it. I was only kidding; I knew he'd make it because he had all the talent in the world. And now after all those years we were teammates and buddies.

Our dressing room had some other new faces. One was John Ferguson. A lot of people dismissed Fergie as nothing more than a fighter. He had that reputation in the American League. But at training camp I began watching him more carefully and talked to people about him.

Jack Gordon, his coach in Cleveland, put it this way, "When he came to Cleveland he couldn't skate and he couldn't shoot. But he sure could work hard. That's why he eventually got to be a good player."

In his last AHL year he played 72 games for Cleveland and had 38 goals and 40 assists for 78 points. He was an assistant captain and an AHL All-Star. He was good enough for us to send Toe Blake himself to personally scout the guy.

When Fergie came to camp in September 1963 the first thing he did in scrimmages was to run as many opponents as possible. That pleased Toe no end and lo and behold he survived every cut and made the big club. Blake put him on left wing alongside Big Jean and me.

Let me tell you, John Ferguson was something else. First of all he had hands the size of Virginia hams and he knew how to use them. He demonstrated this on the night of October 8, 1963. Before getting into the game itself there is something you should know about our team and the league at that time.

Even though Selke had promised to toughen up Canadiens after we got pushed out of the play-offs by Chicago in 1961 he really didn't do much. Meanwhile other teams were getting bigger and stronger. Imlach's Maple Leafs didn't win Stanley Cups in 1962 and 1963 on skating and stickhandling skill alone. They had big players like Frank Mahovlich and tough ones like Tim Horton, Bobby Baun and Eddie Shack.

Players like Shack and Chicago's Reggie Fleming ran all over the place hitting people and if they weren't neutralized they could make life miserable for the opposition. That's why John Ferguson was so welcome in Montreal and he proved it in the season opener at Boston Garden.

Not that the Bruins were a powerhouse, far from it. But they had a couple of ornery critters who could strike fear in the hearts of the opposition. The meanest of all was a defenseman named Ted Green who had once belonged to Canadiens. As a matter of fact he came to our training camp when he was only 18 and tried to beat up on all three Richard Brothers — Rocket, Pocket and Claude, "The Vest Pocket Rocket."

If you'll excuse the expression Green was a bit too green for Canadiens when we were winning those five straight Cups so Selke finally put him on waivers and Boston claimed him. From his rookie year he fought everyone in sight and never stopped fighting. And he very rarely lost.

Fergie knew this while he was standing next to me and Big Jean during the pregame opening ceremonies. I imagine that Greenie had heard about the way John had handled his dukes in the American League.

Faster than you could say "Where's the referee?" the two went at it right off the opening face-off. Big Jean and I watched with the kind of fascination people have when they see a car wreck on the side of the highway. Both of us instinctively knew that this fight in the opening minute on opening night could have far-reaching significance for our hockey club.

And it did.

Fergie destroyed Green in record time. *Bam! Bam! Bam!* Three straight right crosses and the fight was over. Ted Green was dead meat and for the first time since I became a Canadien I could say that we had a full-time enforcer on our line.

What I loved about Fergie was that he was more than just a fighter. He also could put the puck in the net. He scored two goals in that game and also set me up for one in what turned out to be a 4-4 tie. It didn't take long for me to figure out that John would be a welcome addition. In no time at all I led Canadiens in scoring with Big Jean and Fergie in second and third spots.

The addition of Ferguson made us forget about the loss of good players like Goyette and Marshall. Nobody missed Plante. As soon as he became a Ranger he started to badmouth Montreal and he wasn't too kind to Mister Geoffrion either.

Imagine the nerve of this guy. He told New York reporters that Boom Boom's slap shot had lost its power. When I heard that I said, "Oh boy, wait till we play those Rangers. I'll show Mister Plante how weak my shot is." And I did. As a matter of fact, our whole team got revenge on Plante that night. We blitzed him with 51 shots.

The first time we met I got hold of the puck close to the crease and put everything I had behind the shot. Plante still hasn't seen the puck. It went like a bullet right between his legs and into the net. But I wasn't through with him. As soon as the red light went on I skated up to the crease and gave him a little dig: "Hey Jacques, if my shot is so weak how come you can't see it anymore?"

Toe had a smile on his face. Blake was feeling good behind the bench again. Sam Pollock was sending him great young players like Jacques Laperriere and Claude Larose plus we had another sweetheart of a right winger who had wings on his feet.

Yvan Cournoyer graduated from the Junior Canadiens and when he was 20 the big club called him up for a five-game tryout. This little guy could fly! They didn't call him The Roadrunner for nothing. He popped four goals and looked good enough to stick.

Toe still ran a tight ship. Our practices were very intense because we practiced the way we played. It was just like a game. We really hit and we had real fights in our scrimmages not just fooling around. But after the practice was over we would laugh about it in the dressing room.

It promised to be a very competitive season. We moved right to the head of the pack and stayed in the running in large part because our young guys like Jacques Laperriere and Terry Harper were coming through but especially the one on left wing with me and Big Jean — Fergie.

The club kept its head above water even though others thought we would sink. Our young defense was a pleasant surprise. Bryan "Bugsy" Watson was like a miniature Ferguson behind the blue line and J.C. Tremblay was turning into a star. When Gump pulled a hamstring early in the season he was replaced by little Charlie Hodge. Charlie was nervous and would spend time between games stewing over shots that he might have played differently and would lose sleep over games. His roommate Terry Harper would try to relax him. But when Hodge moved into Worsley's slot in November 1963 he was more relaxed than I had ever seen him before.

The more relaxed Charlie was the more tense Gump became. After recovering from his injury Worsley was sent to Quebec of the American League and told to work himself into shape. He spent a year and a half there "getting himself in shape."

I felt sorry for Gump but we were playing good hockey. Fergie was beating up anyone who would fight him and scoring enough points to be a top candidate for rookie of the year. With Bugsy and Terry Harper on defense we had as much toughness as any of our competitors. By Christmas 1963 we were in second place only six points behind Chicago and Toe said he expected a good second half from me.

It depends on what you mean by "good." After 30 games I had ten goals and was just under a point a game which meant that if I kept that average going I would have a 20-goal season. Not bad for a 33-year-old.

Each season I could look at a single game and tell you without fear of contradiction that *that* contest defined the year for our hockey club. There is something about these games in question that portray the team for better or worse. In terms of Canadiens no game said more about us than the match on January 12, 1964 at Chicago Stadium.

There are certain facts to keep in mind about that game. At the time the Blackhawks were ruling the league and we were on their ice which was never easy. In fact until then we hadn't won a game there and had been shaky every time we faced-off against them.

On this night we were confident. We went up 1-0 in the first, saw them tie us 1-1 in the second and remained tied into the third. Charlie Hodge was first-rate for us in goal. Toe threw our line on and with Fergie leading the way I beat Glenn Hall at 10:04. The goal gave us a 2-1 win and as Toe would later say it was the turning point of our season. "That win," said the coach, "gave us tremendous confidence."

Because we were doing a lot better than the experts had expected Toe was usually in a good mood but every once in a while he would explode. I remember one night when the Leafs beat us 6-0 at The Forum. What a humiliation!

As it happened a magazine writer had come up from New York to do a profile of Bobby Rousseau, who was our second-leading scorer after Big Jean, and Bobby had arranged to meet him in our room after the game. Nobody could have figured we'd get blown out by six. Somehow the writer didn't see all the media waiting outside the room and strolled right in heading for Rousseau's stall.

All of a sudden Toe came along, saw the writer — who really had no business being in there since Blake hadn't opened the room yet — and blew him out with a typhoon of curses. I don't think the poor fellow knew what hit him.

We did. Just about everyone on the team had felt Toe's wrath at one time or another. One of his favorite targets was Ralph Backstrom who had a pretty good sense of humor when the coach wasn't on his case.

One night Blake really chewed Ralph out and then slammed the door behind him. Backstrom was so furious that he grabbed one of his skates, pretended it was a harpoon and pitched it so hard that it stuck in the wooden door!

Speaking of hard pitches any goalie would tell you that by 1964 shots were coming at them at greater speeds than ever before. The reason was as obvious as a slap shot. Half the league was copying the style that I introduced in the early 1950s but some of them were overdoing it taking wild slap shots. My slap shot was a controlled one because I didn't take too big a swing at the puck before I hit it. The players who took the big backswing lost control and telegraphed their shots. The slap shot requires a lot of practice and I practiced for a long time.

Canadiens were neck and neck with Chicago in the run for first place. With only five weeks remaining in the schedule I returned from an injury and made my first appearance in The Forum in a month on February 12, 1964.

We were playing the Maple Leafs and nobody scored in the first period. Up until then Toe had not used me at all and I began to wonder whether I would ever get on the ice.

I got the answer in the second period when he finally put me on with Fergie and Backstrom. There was still no score with less than three minutes left in the period when my linemates set me up and I beat Johnny Bower giving us a 1-0 lead. I needed one more goal for my career three hundred and sixty-fifth which would tie me with Ted Lindsay as the third-highest goal getter in NHL history.

Early in the third period Ron Stewart of the Leafs took a two-minute penalty. Toe sent me out on the power play and on passes from Pocket and Rousseau I got the puck right where I wanted it. My slap shot whistled past Johnny Bower to give us a 2-0 lead. I had done it — number 365!

Blake used me steadily and at one point I thought I had Bower beat but he made a spectacular save and robbed me of my hat trick. Charlie Hodge wound up with a 4-0 shutout and we remained locked in the first place struggle with Chicago. Two weeks later we blanked Toronto 1-0 and I got the lone goal in that game. I had passed Ted Lindsay and was cooking with gas. So was the team.

Not many people knew it at the time but another struggle was going on right inside The Forum. The Molsons who owned the club were exercising more and more control while Selke who had been The Boss as long as most people could remember appeared to be losing ground.

Even though he was 72 years old The Boss loved his work and was not ready to be pushed aside. After Yvan Cournoyer had played so well for us in his five-game trial Selke wanted to sign him to a contract. In other years he would have done that as easy as snapping his fingers but not this time. David Molson had quietly become the Canadiens' power broker and thought Yvan needed more time to mature. He figured it wouldn't be smart to bring Cournoyer in as a regular in 1963-64 and the word was passed down to Selke. He didn't like it but what could he do? The Molsons were now running the team not The Boss.

In other words the handwriting was on the wall for Selke and he knew it long before the playoffs began. Everyone was so distracted by the race hardly anyone was aware of Selke's predicament. On March 3, 1964 Canadiens and Chicago each had 77 points but we had two games in hand.

The Hawks beat us 4-3 on March 1 at Chicago on a late Ken Wharram goal and began moving ahead of us in the standings. Then we caught them and the seesaw kept swinging right down to the final night of the season Sunday March 22, 1964.

Now picture this: we were leading Chicago by one point with just one game left to play. The Blackhawks were in Boston and we

were in New York. Chicago held off a late Bruins' rally to win 4-3.
We had no choice but to beat the Rangers whose goalie just happened to be Jacques Plante.

In the middle of the first period Ron Ingram of the Rangers went off for two minutes. I went out to the right point and Jacques Laperriere was on my left. We won the face-off. The puck went from Jacques to me to Big Jean who popped it in at 10:59. The score stayed that way until 10:59 of the second when Bob Nevin beat Hodge and we headed into the third tied at one.

All I wanted was one more chance to beat Plante and I finally got it before the third period was five minutes old. A rookie, André Boudrias, was on a line with Big Jean and me. They set me up and I whipped the shot past Plante, the last goal of the game, the winner and the first-place clincher.

I wanted one more crack at The Stanley Cup before I retired and this was it. I was 33-years-old and had heard too many rumors about trades and such. My one and only general manager appeared to be losing his power and no one knew how much longer Toe would hang in there as coach.

Before we opened the semifinals against Toronto all the pieces seemed to be in place. I had never seen Toe so relaxed.

As usual Blake took the team to a resort in the Laurentians north of Montreal. It was a hideaway designed to loosen us up before we entered the play-off pressure cooker. It certainly loosened up our coach.

The Maple Leafs who were going for their third straight Stanley Cup were a different team at play-off time. Back in February Punch Imlach had made a blockbuster deal sending five skaters to New York for Andy Bathgate. His slap shot from the right point gave Toronto a power play that was almost as good as ours.

But in Game One the Leafs' power play did nothing. I beat Johnny Bower early in the first and that goal was enough for the win behind Charlie's shutout goaltending. Backstrom gave us insurance in the second. We won 2-0.

Our line got one in Game Two but it wasn't enough. Toronto tied the series with a 2-1 win and the series that was rough to begin with got wilder and wilder and penalty records were broken left and right. *The Hockey News* put it best when it observed, "The penalty bench is the most popular seat in the house for the Hab-Leafs play-offs."

Often when an opening game is riotous the teams will settle down to hockey. In Game Two *only* a dozen penalties were called and 14 in the third. But in the fourth 30 penalties were dished out including six majors and three misconducts. By the time the fifth game was over even the NHL president had to admit that matters were of concern to him.

Although we had Toronto on the ropes we never did get to the jugular. They blanked us 3-0 in Game Six and took a two-zip lead in the finale at The Forum. Ralphie finally got one for us early in the third with about a dozen minutes left to tie the game.

Instead of playing it cozy the Leafs opened up and both teams roared up and down the ice out of control. I thought for sure that on one of those rushes we would tie the score but we never did. And that was it, it was Toronto 2-1. We were out in the first round again.

In seven games I had only one goal and one assist. Big Jean only had two goals while Fergie went through the entire round with just one assist. Pretty dismal. Our first-place finish was now ancient history and I could almost hear the moaning in The Forum boardroom. It was now four years since we had won The Stanley Cup.

I finished with 21 goals in 55 games which was nothing to cry about but I could hear noises from upstairs. There were changes in the wind and the biggest hit like a bombshell. The Boss, Frank Selke, the only general manager I had ever known, was out (along with Ken Reardon) and Sam Pollock was in.

"I'm disappointed," Selke said after he stepped down. "I'd have liked at least one more year to finish reconstructing the team. We're almost there but not quite."

Frankly I didn't know what to do: retire, keep playing, try coaching. I spent weeks thinking about it. I felt that I had at least one more good year in me maybe even two. Hockey was my life but I had to think about my family and our future.

I finally decided that the best thing would be to talk face-to-face with the Canadiens' new boss David Molson. He was a smallish, soft-spoken young man who was running the team for his family.

He was nice enough when we finally met. He pointed out that our American League farm team in Quebec City was due for a coaching change. My old buddy Busher Curry had been behind the bench but there was one problem — Busher couldn't speak French. That was a rather large handicap in a city where 99.9% of the people were francophones!

"You go coach in the American League for two years," said Molson, "get the experience and then you'll be ready for the NHL."

That made sense. Coaching was getting on Toe's nerves and I figured that by 1966 he might just be ready to pack it in. If I did well in Quebec I could move right into The Forum. I went home and explained the situation to Marlene. "He said if I do well, I'd have a crack at the big team after two years."

My wife knew me better than anyone. She understood my passion to play.

"Boom," Marlene asked, "are you sure you don't want to play anymore?"

That sure rubbed a nerve. Of course I wanted to play.

Plus I knew that Marlene wasn't crazy about moving to Quebec. It meant removing the kids from school, packing and moving up to an entirely new environment. That was an agonizing decision. We had all been born and lived our entire lives in Montreal. But at the same time a move to coaching and Quebec also made sense. Canadiens were loaded with talent. And they were bringing in Yvan Cournoyer who was being groomed to take my place. Sure I could hang on for a couple more years as a player but it would only postpone the inevitable.

I was off to Quebec — and a very disturbing episode in my career.

CHAPTER 17

From Quebec to New York

I second-guessed myself all the way along the autoroute from Montreal to Quebec City on that August afternoon in 1964. I kept asking myself did I make the right move? I went over all the possibilities and came to the conclusion that maybe I should have stayed; maybe I should have played as long as I could in the NHL; maybe I should have gone for my four-hundredth NHL goal and maybe even my five-hundredth! Maybe I was getting carried away! I realized that I might have made a mistake but it was too late. Quebec, here I come!

My former linemate and roommate Jean Béliveau owned a house in Quebec City which Marlene and I rented. It was right on the St. Lawrence River, several miles out of the city, a beautiful spot and we loved it there. Linda entered St. Agnes Academy and the boys both attended local Catholic schools.

What was coaching like? I have to tell you I loved it.

First of all I had a neat team. Who wouldn't want Gump Worsley in goal and Doug Harvey on defense? I had them both. Plus I had some other fellows from the Canadiens: Bugsy Watson, Guy Gendron, Red Berenson and Terry Gray all played for me. These were experienced guys and so was John Hanna, the tough defenseman who once played for the Rangers.

When we opened training camp I told them that I wanted one offensive line, one defensive line and two tough guys on my team.

Those were my primary priorities. If we had them we could go anywhere.

And we did.

We went right up to first place in the Eastern Division and stayed there. If I needed goals I had scorers like Wayne Hicks, Ed Hoekstra and a real character named Cleland "Keke" Mortson. One night we were playing Hershey and Mortson got stuck in our end with the puck. He was being chased by one of the Hershey players and Keke knew he was going to lose the puck so he grabbed it with one hand and threw it into the stands!

The referee gave him a five-minute penalty for that and they scored three goals against us. When the penalty was finally over Keke skated across the ice to our bench. As he came in I opened the door and called him an idiot.

When he wasn't doing ridiculous things like that Keke could play the game. So could Terry Gray, Don Blackburn and Bill Sutherland. They could put the puck in the net.

A year after Kenny Reardon had promised to recall him to Montreal "in a couple of weeks" Gump Worsley was still in Quebec. Even though he was down in the minors he loved it. If you sent him to Alaska he would go as long as you put him in front of a net.

One day we were talking and Worsley said to me, "Boom, do you know why some of the players can't score against me? Because they can't find where the corner is. You see I don't move."

I said, "What are you talking about?"

"When you see me in the net do you see me move? I never move. The guys always shoot at me. That's why I've lasted so long. Ask Ted Lindsay how many goals he scored on me. None, because he used to shoot at my belly."

The funny thing about Gump's career is that he wound up getting a nice bit of revenge on Jacques Plante while still in Quebec. Here's what happened.

By the 1964-65 season Plante had worn out his welcome with the Rangers and was shipped to the American League playing for Baltimore. The paths of Jacques and Gump crossed in Quebec City when the Aces hosted the Clippers. This was a major event at Le Colisée and the papers were running headlines like, "Two Old Rivals Meet in the Minors."

Worsley beat Plante in that game and was the happiest guy in the province for the next week. Gump didn't last the whole season with me. Charlie Hodge had begun to slip and Toe Blake decided to give Worsley another shot with Canadiens.

Gump was happy to leave. He had had enough of the "iron lung," which is what the American Leaguers called the buses we rode from city to city. After a career of luxury travel in the NHL we had to get used to the minor league way.

From Quebec City we would get on the bus and ride as far as Hershey, Pennsylvania for a game. That trip took two days. If we went all the way from Quebec to Hershey the bus would stop halfway and we'd sleep at a motel and then move on the next morning.

Even though the trips could be a pain the guys made the best of it. On some of the buses you could turn the seats so the players faced each other and that made it easier to play cards, usually hearts and bridge. Gump told a story about the time he was playing bridge with a sportswriter against Harvey and another guy. Worsley opened with "One no trump." Harvey passed. Then Worsley's partner the reporter bid "two no spades."

Harvey and Worsley looked at each other blankly. They had never heard of such a bid. "Doug threw down his cards," Worsley remembered, " and said, `Aw, let's play hearts!'"

I can't begin to tell you what it was like to coach Doug Harvey. He was really getting on at least in player's years by this time but he could still control a hockey game. I'd play him for 20 sometimes even 30 minutes a game and he never complained.

Doug was an enormous help to me off the ice too. If I made a mistake he'd take me aside just as he used to do when we were playing together — he'd never embarrass you in front of someone else — and quietly say, "You should have done this. You probably shouldn't do that again. . . ." That kind of thing. So even though I was now coaching him I'd occasionally ask his advice.

As I look back I think that Doug Harvey was really important to the success I had coaching in Quebec. He showed me tricks about killing penalties and changing lines more quickly, all of those tremendous skills he had as a player and as a coach he gave generously to me. I remember one time I really gave it to him in the dressing room in front of the other guys. I said, "Doug, if you're going to drag your feet like you just did, you may as well take your equipment and go home because you're not going to play."

Doug knew exactly what I was doing and approved! If I could talk that way to the great Doug Harvey then I could talk that way to anyone in the room. He came up to me afterward and said,

"Boom, I know just why you did that . . . to get respect from the other players. You don't have to be a genius to coach when you have the talent. All you have to do is mold them together and if you want to use me sometimes, that's fine."

Even though this wasn't the National Hockey League the American League at that time was very competitive, full of NHL veterans and youngsters who were on their way to becoming NHL stars. At times I took things too seriously and Doug would help me out then too. "Boom," he'd say, "don't come in the room and throw a fit every game because it gets old and it won't work after a while.

"The guys here are 25, 30, 35 years old, a lot of them and they know the game. Just correct their mistakes. That's all you have to do. You can't do anything else; you can't score goals and you can't help them prevent scoring."

Doug Harvey was the best and I still miss him.

After I lost Gump to Montreal in midseason I replaced him with Gil Banville who played so well we stayed in first place and finished on top 14 points ahead of second-place Hershey. The trouble was we had to play a very tough and very good Rochester team in the first round of the play-offs. At the time the Amerks belonged to the Maple Leafs and were stocked with former NHL players like Bronco Horvath, Eddie Litzenberger and Gerry Ehman. They beat us four games to one and that was the end of my first coaching season. One try, one first-place finish. That's not bad for a rookie eh!

Marlene can tell you what it was like:

Mind you coaching wasn't the only thing at which the Geoffrion family were rookies. Boom's coaching the Quebec team was the first time we had ever lived outside of Montreal, the first time we were without our extended family, and the first time I was a coach's wife instead of a player's.

In all of the years Boom played and then coached I would go to games. But in all of those years there had also never been a "wives' room" as all teams have today. This meant that when we Canadiens' wives got to The Forum we had to sit around in the regular public ladies' room for a couple of hours waiting until we could go to our seats. It wasn't much fun but at least we had each other.

But in Quebec I was the coach's wife and that meant I no longer could hang out with the players' wives. Unfortunately I couldn't really sit or socialize with the management because they were the owners and after all my husband was an employee.

So despite the fact that we were living in the Béliveau's lovely house I was very lonely. When Boom was playing he'd come home from practice and we'd do things together. But now that he was coaching he'd be gone longer. It also meant that I had to get to the games on my own since Boom had our car in town all day now. If I ran out of something that meant that dinner didn't get finished until Boom got back with the car. It also meant whole new strategies for shopping, etc.

Then for Boom's second season we couldn't rent the house again because it was up for sale so we moved to an apartment. That was slightly closer to town but we still had all of the same problems with the car, the long days and shopping. To make things much, much worse there was construction going on next to our building and the most terrible noises screamed out at me from seven in the morning until dark.

By December of that second season I had given up. I couldn't take the noise and the loneliness any longer. So we placed Linda in the boarding school of St. Agnes Convent and I arranged to move back home to Montreal before the first of the year so that the boys could start the semester back in their old Montreal schools. The whole experience had placed a lot of stress on the family and on our marriage. Giving up and moving back to Montreal at least put me back in familiar surroundings with family and friends. But I missed Boom and Linda horribly and I worried about whether I would ever adapt and learn to be a coach's wife.

In my second year of coaching, 1965-66, I had a terrific record for the season — 47-21-4 — good for first place in the Eastern Division 19 points ahead of runner-up Hershey. It was an eight-point improvement over the previous season even though I didn't have Gump goaltending for me anymore. This time I had a kid named Gary Bauman who finished with a 2.94 goals-against average. Keke Mortson was the AHL's second-leading scorer.

I felt great about my coaching and figured that I could do this for another ten years. Then came the play-offs and we met Rochester again in the first round. The Amerks had finished first in the Western Division one point less than our total and had the AHL's leading scorer Dickie Gamble. On top of that Imlach had loaded them with other aces. Gerry Ehman was third-leading scorer, Jim Pappin was fourth and Mike Walton sixth. Gary "Suitcase" Smith, who would make it in the NHL, was their goalie.

What can I tell you? They were just too much for us again but this time it took them six games instead of five. I was upset because I wanted to win The Calder Cup for the American League play-off championship but I still had two first-place seasons in a row. The owner of the team Gerald Martineau seemed pleased and also appeared to understand the accomplishment.

Shortly after the play-offs, Martineau, who had always been nice to Marlene and me, invited us to dinner at his house. It felt great when he congratulated me for the great job I had done with his team. "You don't have to worry about your job," he said. That was good to hear from the owner. I was prepared to go back to Quebec City for a third season. That's how good I felt about the Aces.

Marlene and I said goodnight to Mister Martineau after a lovely evening and went home to prepare to return to Montreal for the summer. I had an entire summer to plan my future, or so I thought.

The next day we had all our belongings together and began our drive. About 75 miles from Montreal we decided to stop at a restaurant. While Marlene and the children went back to the car I picked up a paper to get the morning news and couldn't believe my eyes. Blaring across the sports page was the headline: "Phil Watson Hired as Coach of Quebec Aces."

You could have knocked me over with a feather. I was crushed but I wanted desperately to shield Marlene and the kids from the news at least until we got home. So I composed myself, folded up the paper and put it in my pocket to keep it from Marlene.

She thought I was being absentminded because normally I would have given her the paper to read while I was driving. When she gently eased it out and looked at the headline she was flabbergasted. I looked at her and she looked at me but no words were spoken. We didn't want to upset the children so we both kept the bad news to ourselves. I can never remember ever being so hurt or so angry before. I felt betrayed.

First thing the next day I phoned Martineau but he was "out." I sat in the living room staring at the phone.

I thought about all the hurts I had suffered in hockey. I remembered the booing I got after topping Rocket for the scoring championship in 1955. That hurt a lot but this was worse. Two regular-season championships and all of a sudden I had no job. It didn't make any sense.

That was the most brutal summer of my life. For three months I was a hermit. I didn't want to see anybody, I didn't want to play golf, I didn't want to do any of the things that I usually enjoyed. All I did was sit in the backyard and think gloomy thoughts. I was 34 years old and washed up.

Finally I had brooded long enough and started to think. Toe Blake had maybe another year behind Canadiens' bench and that would be it for him. I said to myself, "After Toe, I've got the big job. I'll come back." Remembering David Molson's words I called him and arranged a meeting. After all he was the one who told me to go to Quebec and get the experience so I could coach in the NHL.

I was in for yet another shock. At our meeting Molson said, "Boom, at the moment the only job we have for you is coaching Junior Canadiens."

It was a step backward. I had won two championships in Quebec and the best offer they had was a junior club at $6,000 a year!

I told him right to his face: "If that's the only job you want to give me I'm coming out of retirement. David, I'm going to make a comeback as a player. I don't know if you can protect me or not but I'm comin' back."

I was very angry at the way Molson treated me and I was upset over wasting those two years in Quebec when I could have been playing. I knew I could still play. But the way I saw it Canadiens wouldn't protect me in the draft because they had replaced me with Yvan Cournoyer so I would be available to other clubs.

Word spread quickly on the hockey grapevine and soon Harold Ballard phoned and asked me to play for Toronto. The Leafs were a good team. Punch Imlach was still running the club and I felt that I could fit in with them especially since Punch always liked to use veterans.

"Mister Ballard," I said, "I'll be glad to skate for the Leafs but I want a four-year contract."

"Boomer," he shot back, "you can have ten if you want. I'll sign you tonight."

Boom Boom Geoffrion as a Toronto Maple Leaf sounded good to me especially since I would be making three times the money I had as a Canadien. But there was a catch. Rangers had finished in last place and had the first draft pick ahead of Ballard. I mentioned this to Harold and he said that he would talk to their general manager Emile "The Cat" Francis.

I wanted to go to Toronto so I called Francis and told him not to pick me. "Emile," I said, "I'll be honest with you. My knees are shot and my back is finished. I can't help your hockey club."

Emile was small, wily and as stubborn as they come. He didn't care about Ballard or the Leafs. He had his heart set on getting me in a Rangers uniform. "I don't care if you come to New York in a wheelchair," he said. "We're not going to pass on you. I'm going to make you a Ranger."

And he did.

For the first time in my professional hockey-playing career I would not be wearing the *bleu, blanc et rouge* of the Canadiens. After 14 years with the Habs I now was a Hab-not. As I thought about it I couldn't help but conclude that mine was an up-and-down career that sometimes seemed to have more downs than ups.

Once Francis drafted me I called him and said, "Okay I changed my mind and I will come to New York. And I guarantee you Emile your team will make the play-offs. I'll change their attitude."

Now the question was whether or not I could get back into playing shape and whether or not I could keep up with the younger guys on the team. I worked my butt off during the summer of 1966 and then reported to training camp. There were times when I thought I was going to die. Those first days of camp were brutal.

But I had come through difficult times before. Six weeks after the emergency surgery on my ruptured bowel I returned to the lineup and scored. I had played with cracked bones and torn muscles and even though they may have left scars I regarded them as an example of my invulnerability.

Still I felt that it was not right for a hockey player to dress for a game when he wasn't healthy although I had done it and after I did I would ask myself why? I did not know why but maybe it was because when it came to hockey The Boomer was not a normal man.

At the age of 35 and after two years of not playing it was no surprise that training camp was so excruciatingly painful. I kept reminding myself of what Bill Head, the Canadiens' physiotherapist, once said about me, "Of all the hockey players I have treated none was willing to play with injuries as often as Boom Boom. His pain level is too high for his own good."

When Emile Francis offered to sign me I begged off. "First," I told him, "let me try out for the team and then if I make it, I'll sign."

But Emile wanted me to sign right away. "What happens," I asked, "if I don't make the club after I've signed?"

Francis laughed. "We'll still have to pay you."

Now I laughed. "OK. Where do I sign?"

You have to understand that on the one hand I knew that I could play but on the other hand I was also worried about looking bad. I survived the training camp but still I had not made the team. I knew that I had to be ready for the possibility that I no longer was good enough for the NHL. I didn't want pity.

The more I studied them the more I was convinced this club could be a winner. One guy in particular fascinated me, their young right winger Rod Gilbert. I liked him because we had a lot in common. We were both from Montreal. Rod grew up near me, our families knew each other and I had even met him when he was a tiny, aspiring hockey player who idolized me in my heyday with Canadiens.

Like myself Rod had come to the NHL directly from junior hockey and we were now both Rangers' stars. I used to sit next to him in the New York dressing room and one day I surprised him. "Guess what Rod?" I mentioned. "I'm going to get more goals this season than you."

He looked at me and laughed. I had said that to him because I knew he could score but I wanted him to have more incentive. That's what I did with any guy I thought I could help.

Vic Hadfield was a big left winger who had developed a hard shot with his banana-blade stick. The trouble was he used to shoot the puck into the stands as often as he kept it inside the rink. He had a good sense of humor. "Have you ever seen a stadium that has the nets in the third balcony?" I kidded him. "Are you blind or what?" His eyesight must have improved, because in 1971-72 he would score 50 goals!

I still hadn't played my first game for New York and I was already getting publicity as if I were a local hero. *New York Post* columnist Maury Allen wrote about me: "He is Mickey Mantle and Y.A. Tittle, Bob Cousy and Stan Musial."

One day I walked into our training camp dressing room and there was a photographer shoving his camera in my face. "I haven't done anything," I shouted. "Why are you taking my picture? Wait till I do something. Maybe I won't make the team." He backed off and then I poked my gloved hand into his ribs. "See you downstairs," I said very softly this time. "You want some locker room pictures?"

The more time I spent with him the more I wanted to do well for Emile. And the more I analyzed our lineup the more I realized something good could come out of that roster. I told The Cat, "With the power we have here there's no doubt in my mind that this team can make the play-offs. You look from the goaltender (Ed Giacomin) to the last guy on the bench, you have quality."

Gradually I got over the hump in training camp and part of the reason was motivation. I had it in spades. Not only was the reputation of Boom Boom Geoffrion at stake but there was my family to think about. When there are three kids and a wife to take care of a man finds more determination than you might think.

Marlene can tell you:

I had tons to prove too. I had to prove that Quebec was just a fluke, that I could survive and provide a good home outside of Montreal. That first season in New York Boom and I rented an apartment in Glen Oaks in Queens. I'll never forget it. Jeanette Goyette and I were sitting in the kitchen and I looked up and cockroaches were crawling all over the kitchen walls! Jeanette and I scrubbed the whole place and called the fumigator.

When we were at games the wives were just one big happy family. In all the years Boom played in Montreal I had never just visited at other wives' houses. I had been very close to Lucille Richard and Marie-Claire Bouchard but it was different here. The Ranger wives visited back and forth all the time because most of them lived right next to each other on Long Island. So the next year Boom and I rented a place down there and I became good friends with several of the other wives.

The Rangers' wives were only allocated six parking places at the Garden so we would take turns car pooling to the games. Finally one day Marilyn Howell called me and said, "Okay Marlene it's your turn." I swear this was worse than trying out for an NHL team! I was having a lot of trouble getting around New York, something which had never happened to me before. I'd start off taking Boom to LaGuardia Airport, and somehow end up at JFK. Once I almost ended up in Connecticut and only got back home thanks to a state trooper who took pity on me.

In fact my problems just getting around Long Island or taking the boys, who were now playing hockey, up to their rink in Yonkers became legendary. As a backup I taught Linda, who was around 13 when we moved to New York, how to make French toast. Then if I wasn't home from taking Boom to the airport in time to make dinner she'd make French toast for herself and her two brothers. Let's just say that Linda made a lot of French toast!

So here was my big night — I was to drive into the city. I picked everybody up and we took off and we made it. I forgot to put on my lights in the midtown tunnel but other than that it was fine. But I had been so nervous that after parking I ran into the Garden, headed right for the ladies room and threw up my whole dinner!

When I made the team I made it on merit but I was still shaky both in the head and in the legs. In my first period as a Ranger I didn't have all my confidence but as the game went on I felt better. It took about a dozen games for me to get my playing head screwed on straight. By that time I had my second wind and my confidence back. Fortunately the fans were patient and supported me right from the very start. In my first game at the old Madison Square Garden as a Ranger I set up a power play goal from the point and the fans fell in love with me. So did my teammates.

It's amazing the difference in attitude between a team like Canadiens which won five straight Stanley Cups and one like Rangers which hadn't won since 1940. I found that I had to give the New York guys pep talks all the time but they knew I was dead serious. In my comeback I didn't want to play for a loser.

One of my better monologues came after we had finished a practice and were sitting in the room. My eyes went from player to player — Jean Ratelle, Rod Gilbert, Bob Nevin, Red Berenson, Orland Kurtenbach, Camille Henry, Jim Neilson, Rod Seiling, Arnie Brown — and then I got up:

I can't believe that you guys can't make the play-offs. I understand that after a while you lose and lose and you get that losing feeling in your mind. But I'll tell you this, I didn't come here to play for a losing team. I came here to prove a point that the Rangers are good enough to make the play-offs.

My speeches meant that I also had to produce. I couldn't be all talk and no action. In road games I scored for the Rangers throughout October 1966 but I couldn't seem to score at home. On November 6 we had a home game against Toronto. It was about time I did something. Late in the second period I had finished serving a two-minute penalty. I stepped out of the penalty box and the puck was on my stick. I had a breakaway from center ice to the goal.

My legs pumped away like in the good, old Montreal days. I said to myself, "You've gotta make this one look good."

Bruce Gamble was the Toronto goalie. I had played against him often enough to know what to do and I did it. I gave him a head feint, he went one way, then another head feint and he was twisted like a pretzel. With one more deke for good measure I swept the puck into the net.

What followed is something that I will never forget and never quite understand. I got the greatest ovation that I ever received. The fans got to their feet and cheered and cheered. It was better than when I had scored my 50 goals. I looked around the Garden at all the people standing and still they wouldn't stop. It went on and on and on. After five minutes I went back onto the ice and took a bow. That just made them cheer harder.

Now what I'm going to tell you may sound like an exaggeration to make a point but it isn't. The ovation I got after scoring my first goal as a Ranger in the Garden was the biggest thrill that I ever had. Furthermore the reception I got from New York fans and the media was better than I could have even dreamed. It was like I owned the town.

Granted I didn't have Big Jean at center or Bert Olmstead on left wing but Cat Francis put together a pretty good line. My center was veteran Earl Ingarfield who had worked with Andy Bathgate and Dean Prentice and who knew what he was doing. My left wing was Reggie Fleming of all people, the same guy who had terrorized Canadiens in the 1961 play-offs when he was a young whippersnapper with Chicago.

Now Reggie was a Stanley Cup veteran who could play hard and make a good play too. Reggie was something like Eddie "Clear The Track" Shack in that you never quite knew what to expect the way he bounced all over the ice.

Once I got into gear the guys began believing in me and in themselves. Rod Gilbert was one of them. One day he said to me, "Boom, if you can give that little extra after all these years so can I." Rod led the team in goals with 28 in 64 games.

Francis was happy he had talked me into coming to New York and I was tickled that we agreed. "Boomer has that winning attitude," Cat told the media. "It's something he could never lose like his great shot. It's part of him. And it infects everybody."

Whatever it was my presence was a catalyst. A year earlier the team had finished dead last with only 47 points. With me in the lineup they made the play-offs and had 25 more points than the previous season. I played in 58 games and scored 17 goals and 25 assists. Forty-two points in 58 games was not bad for an "old" man.

We wound up in fourth place but Canadiens who finished second were only five points head of us. When I went back to The Forum as a Ranger the Montreal fans were fair to me. The real fans, the ones who understood the situation, were behind me a hundred percent. But some of them had never forgiven me for 1955 when I won the scoring championship over Rocket Richard.

Even before I stepped on Forum ice wearing the Rangers uniform I knew I would get a mixed reaction. I warned Marlene, "Fifty to 75 percent of the fans are going to boo me."

There was plenty to smile about especially after our defenseman Jim Nielson gave me a pass and away I went to bang it past Charlie Hodge. If they weren't mad at me before, after I stuck my hand into the net to retrieve the puck they were livid.

I got two goals that night with John Ferguson checking me. Before a face-off I razzed Fergie, "Toe is making his biggest mistake ever. You can't check me." And I showed him. He was on the ice when I scored both my goals and he didn't speak to me for the rest of the year.

The best thing was that we beat them 6-3, 4-3 and 5-0 and I scored three goals and eight assists. I led the whole Rangers team with 11 points against Canadiens.

I really liked playing for Emile Francis. He was a ball of fire who really knew the game of hockey and I give him a lot of credit for our success that year, 1966-67. He knew when to make moves and he worked hard to turn a losing team into a winner.

As luck would have it we played Canadiens in the first round of the play-offs. Montreal swept us in four games but it was not as one-sided as the statistics suggest. We were in every single game but we couldn't get the breaks.

They beat us 6-4 and 3-1 in Montreal. At Madison Square Garden it was 3-2 in Game Three and the killer in Game Four tells you all about our luck. The score was tied one-up and we went into sudden death. Red Berenson, who was now with the Rangers came down left wing and put a beautiful slap shot on the right corner.

It had Rogie Vachon beaten cleanly but it clanged right off the far post and the rebound went to Canadiens. The next thing I knew John Ferguson was lumbering around our defenseman Arnie Brown and put the puck past Ed Giacomin. The time was 6:28 and after that I was officially on vacation.

Some holiday! It took me a couple of months to recuperate. My back was sore, my legs were sore, my whole body was sore. Let's face it my health was not that great but I told Marlene not to say anything to anybody. I didn't want to complain because if it got out that I wasn't feeling well management might have an excuse not to invite me back.

My wife and I had a good talk. This was my conclusion: "Marlene I got a lot of goals. I'm gonna try one more year."

Why did I put my health in jeopardy?

For one thing. You have to know the heart of a professional athlete. My adrenalin was pumping and I was loving the adulation I received in New York. I loved everything about the Big Apple and not just the hockey games.

More than anything I loved the way the team had come together and the way I felt appreciated. Donnie Marshall said, "If I had to pinpoint one specific thing that turned around the Rangers it was Boom Boom Geoffrion. He's a champion."

I was enjoying myself. New York was a great city, the Rangers were a great team to play for and Madison Square Garden was a great arena to play in. The Garden fans knew the game as well as any. If you worked hard you had no problem with them but if you didn't push they would let you know right away. I found that the fans in New York were all so friendly, so were the people on Long Island where we lived.

We were like a big family. If Marlene or I went to the corner store people would recognize us and the kids. If something went wrong someone would call to help. Neighbors would drop by our house just to make us feel at home.

Even though New York looked like it was going to be a temporary home for us we made a lot of good friends there. So many things made me want to come back to New York for a second season.

CHAPTER 18

Give My Regards to Broadway

This was typically Boom Boom. On the one hand I was happy as a lark because I couldn't wait for training camp to begin. I started ahead of time on the first of August 1967 and was almost overtrained by the time camp started.

On the other hand my ulcers were bothering me again. I had suffered from them since my Montreal playing days but nobody knew. When the fans said I was a "moody player" they didn't really know why. I was sick!

One day my ulcer would be fine but the next day it would gnaw away at me. I wouldn't wish a bleeding ulcer on anybody. If you want to know how I was feeling in that 1967 training camp it was as if I had swallowed a red-hot poker. My teammates kept trying to get me to joke around but I couldn't be funny when I was hurting so much I could cry.

I didn't want to tell Emile about my health problems and I hoped it wouldn't affect my play during 1967-68. In case you have forgotten that was the first year of NHL expansion when the league jumped from six to 12 teams. Now we were traveling to six new cities — Philly, St. Louis, Oakland, L.A., Pittsburgh and Bloomington — and it was a whole new ball game.

I didn't have the same spark I had had in my first year in New York but I did what I could to help the team or at least not hurt them. We finished second in the Eastern (Original Six) Division only four points behind Canadiens. I played in 59 games and had five goals and 16 assists.

In the first play-off round we went up against fourth-place Chicago. The opening game was April 4, 1968, a fateful date in my life because it would mark the last time I skated on NHL ice.

It started out a wonderful evening. We knew we were a better team than the Blackhawks and went about the business of proving it with a 3-1 win. I set up the winning goal with a rush down the right side and then a perfect pass to my buddy Harry Howell who beat goalie Denis DeJordy.

That was the good news. The bad news was that Chicago defenseman Doug Jarrett, who was 24 and weighed about 200 pounds, pounded me and I crumpled to the ice.

All of a sudden I felt sick to my stomach and got up slowly. By the time I reached the bench I was spitting blood.

Cat Francis looked at me and said, "Boom you're turning blue. That's it; you've gotta quit this game!"

I looked at him in disbelief. This was the play-offs; maybe my last. "Cat," I said, "let's wait till I finish this game."

I was just going on guts alone but I had my reasons for doing this. I wanted to show the rest of the players that I wouldn't quit on the team. After the game, in the locker room, I felt better and started clowning again. When a reporter interviewed Ron Stewart I stuck my nose in and joked around. But later my stomach hurt and I didn't need a doctor to tell me what it was. I could feel that ulcer hole.

The next day I reluctantly went to the Cat's office. "I didn't want to admit this but I'm in pretty bad shape. I might be through for the play-offs."

"I thought so," said Francis. "We'll get you the best specialists in New York to get your stomach straightened out."

I smiled. "If we do that," I said, "I think I can play another season." Cat shook his head. "Forget that. Next year you'll be our coach." The doctors told me I had a duodenal ulcer which was bleeding. "If you have any more heavy internal bleeding," they said, "you could be in big trouble."

Before Game Two I went to the team's practice rink at New Hyde Park and everyone was telling me how good I looked. "Inside," I told them, "it doesn't look as good."

I was hoping the club could stay on track without me but they didn't. After taking a two games to none lead in the series the

Rangers blew it by losing the next four in a row. When it was over a reporter asked if I would play again. I didn't want to close the door. Even the thought of retirement was still too painful to take. "Next year," I told him, "I don't know what will be. We'll have to wait and see."

I didn't have to wait too long. Major surgery removed a good hunk of my stomach and I knew that I couldn't play anymore. My career ended then and there. I didn't want to aggravate the condition and didn't want my wife and kids to worry about me.

I became Rangers coach in June 1968. I played the game so long I knew how a man should be treated. But I also knew how much it took to win.

I told the Cat we could win with this club. "With the guys you have here we can make the play-offs. Emile you will be surprised how far we could go if the guys make the push. And I can get them to push."

"Your problem" said Cat, "is finding a leader on the team to succeed you."

"Rod Gilbert can be the leader," I said. "And he can score 50 goals just like I did."

Before training camp I heard a lot of negative talk about my coaching potential but I ignored it. I knew I could coach — Quebec proved that. I had learned from experience that when you're the coach you can't try to be the most popular person in the room. My philosophy was not to change the players' style but to give them the kind of confidence in themselves that they never had before. It worked when I was playing with them and I was certain that it would work with me coaching. If a guy didn't want to play for me he was not going to stay very long with the hockey club.

Our camp opened in Kitchener, Ontario early in September 1968. The players were scheduled to take their first practice skates along with members of the Buffalo and Omaha farm teams at the Memorial Auditorium. I was as excited as a kid on his first day of school. You would be too if you were coaching an NHL club for the first time.

The players were sprinting up and down the rink. One of them was Wayne Larkin, a 29-year-old journeyman who had played against me when I coached Quebec. He was a good American Leaguer who like a lot of guys his age was making one last attempt to make it to the NHL. It was a long shot but you always give a guy like that credit for trying.

Larkin skated the length of the ice and suddenly crumpled in the corner. For a split second it reminded me of the time I ruptured my bowel in the collision with André Pronovost on The Forum ice. At the time my teammates at first thought I was joking.

It didn't take long for the players to realize that Larkin was not joking. Screams filled the air. "Get a doctor!"

I climbed over the wooden boards and skidded across the rink. Before I even got there one of the trainers had pushed some smelling salts under Larkin's nostrils.

There was no response. I knew something had to be done right away so I climbed on top of him, straddling his chest and — up-and-down, up-and-down — pumped over his heart.

Long ago I learned that when something like this happens you go for the heart. I had done this once in Florida after I had pulled a guy from the water. I was too late with the Florida swimmer. Now I was only hoping I wasn't too late with Wayne.

I was.

The doctors later called it a "massive coronary thrombosis." In the first hour of my first day of coaching the Rangers a player died in my arms. I had hoped this was not an omen for the coming season.

After a sleepless night I went to the rink and gathered my players. The memory of Larkin collided with my knowledge that I had to put my men through a severe drill. Just like me all of these players were still thinking of Larkin. I don't have to tell you how that shook up the training camp. It was awful but at the same time I knew that I had to pump life into this Rangers team. More than 28 years had passed since they had won The Stanley Cup. Ranger fans were getting impatient. And after the team blew a two-game lead to Chicago in the 1968 play-offs I knew that the players had lost their confidence. I had to teach them not to be afraid of any other hockey club but first I had to get them in shape.

After a few days I could tell that the players were responding to me. They liked the fact that I wasn't messing with their styles. All I did was tell the guys with great shots to shoot more instead of waiting for the perfect play. I was very happy. My health was good again and so was my sense of humor. The guys liked that, even when I put them through a heavy drill. One day I had them doing an end-to-end skate and Vic Hadfield who was a terrific golfer asked me how long I would keep them practicing.

"Vic," I said, "when you play golf do you ask the pro how many holes you're going to play?"

Hadfield laughed but minutes later I whistled play to a stop and explained in French to center Jean Ratelle that his feet had been improperly placed for a face-off. "English please," chirped Hadfield, "so we all can learn."

One of the reporters heard our exchange and pulled me aside later."Does that mean it will be a bilingual dressing room?" he asked.

I answered him so quickly I nearly blew his head off. "Strictly in English!"

The team returned to New York City on September 29, 1968 for two exhibition games against Canadiens and Toronto. I went home for dinner but Marlene knew she was wasting her time. I couldn't eat and I couldn't sleep. I was more nervous than when I played.

One of the reporters asked me what was wrong. "If this team doesn't go well," I said, "who do you think will go first? It will be me." That afternoon I drove to Madison Square Garden and met Toe Blake who had just retired as coach of Canadiens. (The job I had wanted so badly was given to Claude Ruel who had been a defense prospect until he lost an eye and then coached Montreal's junior teams.) I couldn't believe my eyes. Toe was like a kid. I had never seen him like that before. When he was coaching in those last years he was sad and upset. I asked myself, "Is that what coaching in the NHL does to you guys?"

We beat Canadiens and lost to Toronto which left me with my first big coaching decision. Francis had a defenseman named Al Hamilton who had gotten the big build up but really had been a huge letdown. He showed me very little in camp while a kid nobody had ever heard of, Brad Park, was among my best defensemen.

I knew Cat wanted to keep Hamilton but I also knew that Park was better. We decided to go with the older guy and let Park get a little experience with our minor-league team in Buffalo. Hamilton was on defense for us when we opened the season in Chicago on October 13, 1968.

To say my Rangers' coaching debut was a disaster would be an exaggeration but it sure wasn't a rousing success. We got beaten 5-2 and nothing went right. For two days before the game we had practiced shooting the puck but once the real game started they didn't shoot the puck. And they weren't skating or backchecking either.

Not that it was a total disaster. Bob Nevin, a solid up and down right winger, got our two goals and Harry Howell was first-rate on defense. Reggie Fleming was the best. He was good on the ice and he was good off the ice — with the children, the public and the players. He was funny and tough. I'll tell you how tough he was. We had a game against Canadiens at the Garden and you know that John Ferguson never lost a fight to anybody. Well he did on this night. They went punch for punch and Reggie just stood there taking Fergie's best shots. Reggie not only outpointed Johnny but by the time he got through with him Fergie's nose was bleeding. That was a once in a lifetime fight.

Fleming was not a natural but he came to play game after game. During a practice I once kidded him. "Reggie," I said, "your shot is so weak if there was no net the puck wouldn't even reach the end boards!"

Here was a guy who had a neck like a football player, who was tough as nails and when he got mad watch out! But he had a high-pitched voice which didn't suit his gruff exterior.

Orland Kurtenbach, a big center, had a very long fuse. It took him a long, long time to get mad but when he fought he was like a professional. Kurt was a smooth skater with long range but he was another guy who couldn't shoot the puck. I'd say, "I'll go in the net, Kurt, and I'll stop your shot with my bare hand."

I went between the pipes. Kurt took a shot and missed the net.

I had no complaints with him. Kurt gave me what he had but there were other players who drove me nuts because they didn't use the ability they had. Jimmy Neilson was a perfect example.

They called him The Chief because he was a Canadian Indian who grew up in Saskatchewan. He was a strong rusher and a good puck-carrier and he was big — something like six-two and 200 pounds. To me he had the potential to be as great as Ray Bourque because he had more pure talent for his size than anyone I had ever seen. He could shoot the puck and make the big play.

My goalie was great too. I knew Eddie Giacomin from the American League. When I was still playing for Canadiens we once had an exhibition game against the Providence Reds. Giacomin was their goalie but I didn't know him then.

They played in an old building called Rhode Island Arena that had very poor lighting. I remember before the game telling our guys, "Let's shoot from center ice because their goalie will never see the puck!"

We drilled the puck at him but Giacomin kept seeing it so well that we just barely beat them, a minor league club. After the game I went over to Emile Francis and said, "What are you doing with this guy here? Bring him up."

Actually the Rangers didn't own him then but Cat traded four guys — Marcel Paille, Aldo Guidolin, Sandy McGregor and Jim Mikol — for Giacomin in May 1965 so he was a Ranger before I was. As a goalie he was a terrific skater. He liked to come out of his net like Jacques Plante. He was good.

So was Phil Goyette who played with me in Montreal but was playing better hockey for me as a Ranger than he ever did for Toe as a Canadien. Frank Selke made a big mistake letting him go and every time he went out on the ice for me I knew I was right about that. Phil could score — he got 25 goals in 1967-68 — and he could make plays — he made 40 assists that same year. Goyette was the kind of stickhandler who could go right around any defenseman for the goal.

We had our share of jokers. Hadfield was right up at the top. You never knew what to expect from him. Once he even played a trick on my wife Marlene.

One day she approached Hadfield. "I don't want to ask Boomer," she said, "but could you bring me some tape for my boys' sticks?"

"No problem, Marlene," said Hadfield. "When I come back to Long Island you'll see all the tape."

So after practice all the guys ripped the tape off their pads and crunched it into a ball and threw it into the garbage. Vic hung around and gathered all this old tape into a gigantic ball and put it in a bag.

He brought it to our house and with a serious face gave it to Marlene. "Here," he said, "you can have all the tape."

She believed him until she looked in the bag. "I can't do anything with this," Marlene shouted.

Meanwhile Vic was rushing to his car laughing.

Marlene can tell you:

That ridiculous tape story with Vic Hadfield reminded me about those days in New York. Both Robert and Danny were playing organized hockey at a rink all the way up in Yonkers. Emma and Emile Francis' boy was playing there too so Em and I often took turns taking the kids up there. Or we'd sit together while they played. We were both very careful to cheer but tried hard not to second-guess the officials or the coaches. If we lost it and started yelling the boys would immediately remind us that the only coach was behind the bench. Besides I didn't want to make a fool of myself in front of the general manager's wife!

Of course because he was so busy coaching the Rangers Boom had almost no time to come see the boys play. The only coaching they ever got from their Dad was when they'd ask him questions at home. They would wonder about deking a goalie or taking face offs and Boom would tell them. But those precious times were few. When Boom was finally able to make it to one of their games they'd be so nervous they'd try too hard because he was there. Naturally they'd have one of their worst games of the season.

Even though Boom knew better than to interfere in the boys' hockey he did take it upon himself to interfere with his daughter's high-school graduation, and when he interfered he interfered royally!

Linda was well on her way to taking care of all the details of her graduation including her own date. But when Boom realized that this meant she would be out nearly all night with some young man he'd probably never met in his life before he said, "Oh no, you're not going out all night with anybody I don't know."

Right away Linda said, "Come on Dad, fathers don't get girls prom dates. I'll take care of it myself." I tried to explain to Boom that he was just going to have to catch up to the times and let Linda go to the prom with the boy of her choosing, and that included letting them go to after-prom parties and whatnot. But he had a look in his eyes that I knew only too well.

The Bruins were in town for a game against the Rangers and Boom was having a chat with their superstar defenseman Bobby Orr. "Bob did you ever go to a senior prom?" Bobby answered immediately that because of his junior hockey schedule and all he hadn't had time to go to his own senior prom. "Well," said Boom, "then I have a great proposition for you. How'd you like to take my daughter Linda to her senior prom?"

Bobby said he would love to do it and even though this was weeks before the event he promised Boom he'd be in New York City on the right date no matter what. Boom even called Bobby a couple of weeks beforehand to make sure, and Orr reassured him that not only was he coming but he'd ordered a special tuxedo just for that occasion.

At first Linda was mortified and embarrassed but as the weeks went by she started to get really excited. And when prom night arrived there was Bobby Orr all decked out. They had a wonderful time and then just before dawn they came back to our place and we all had breakfast together along with a lot of laughs.

As for my coaching I was laughing for the first two months of the season. The guys were responding to me and we climbed right into first place at the start of December 1968. On a trip to Montreal I sat down with Red Fisher, one of the Canadiens' best writers whom I knew from my playing days.

"In a way," I said, "I am the luckiest guy in the world right now. I have a team that is winning hockey games. I don't think that it's good enough to finish in first place so all I am thinking about is making the play-offs. But I am the luckiest man in the world because everybody has been good to me.

"Only one thing worries me: my health. When I had my ulcer operation last year I thought all of that was behind me. But sometimes I get up in the morning and I am so sick I think I am going to die. Sometimes my color is so bad it scares me."

What scared me just as much as my health was the hockey club. It stopped winning and began falling in the standings. Soon we were looking at last place instead of first and management was looking at me. All this pressure wasn't doing my health any good.

Even though the club was five wins over .500 (18-13-3) at Christmas 1968 we had dropped to last place. I felt we could play better. In mid-January 1969 we headed west for games in Los Angeles and then Oakland. I could feel the pressure from up above.

At that time Irving Mitchell Felt ran Madison Square Garden and Bill Jennings was president of the Rangers. Neither liked anything but a winner. When we were beaten 3-1 by the Kings we were still three wins over .500 (21-18-3) but I could feel the screws being tightened. So could the reporters.

They told me that Jennings was "reevaluating" my situation. One of them said that I had to win in Oakland or I was history. He asked me for a comment. I told him, "I'm not listening to that nonsense. I won't believe any of it until I hear from Emile and he hasn't said anything to me. As far as I'm concerned I'm still the coach and this is still my team."

We flew from L.A. to Oakland for a game against the Seals on January 17, 1969 and I could tell that I was losing my energy although I wasn't sure why. Meanwhile I was hearing that all sorts of bad things were appearing in the papers back east. One of them said that Francis had lost confidence in my ability to run the team and that he was unhappy with my handling of the young players.

That was ridiculous. Brad Park was playing defense for us and everyone in the league was saying that he looked like he could be a great one. There was nothing wrong with the way I was handling him.

It was a Friday night when we played the Seals. I felt lousy before the game and mentioned it to our trainer Frank Paice. During the game I felt worse. Between the second and third periods I asked to see Dr. Robert Aldo, who was the doctor on call at Oakland Arena. He gave me some sugar because he said my blood sugar was low. I got woozy because ever since they had removed part of my stomach my system didn't react normally to food.

I worked the game the way I normally would behind the bench for the entire two and a half hours. On the ice we didn't look at all bad. In fact we beat Oakland 3-1. I wish I could have said the victory made me feel better but it didn't, not physically anyway.

The reporters were waiting for me in the corridor outside the dressing room and I started answering their questions. All of a sudden the entire building seemed to be spinning and I turned pale. I asked the guys if we could continue the interview inside the dressing room on one of the benches. I was feeling weaker by the second.

As soon as I sat down I collapsed against the dressing-room wall. That's the last I remember. Later I found out that I was unconscious for several seconds. Meanwhile some of the players ran to get the doctor.

Dr. Aldo came, quickly gave me some more sugar and that revived me. I was still unsteady and the doctor said I should stay down. He called for an ambulance and the next thing I knew I was bouncing along enroute to Peralta Hospital.

"I think it's your ulcers," the doctor said after he examined me. "I am still sure that's what it is."

The Cat, who was in Memphis on a scouting trip, grabbed a plane and met the club in St. Louis where we were to play the Blues on Sunday night (January 19, 1969). After a couple of days in the hospital I learned that the problem was twofold; I was suffering from a bad case of nerves compounded by my partial stomach, which refused to digest the food I put into it.

When I got out of the hospital Emile told me to take the family down to Florida. "As long as I'm president of this team," he said, "you will have a job in this organization."

That ended my coaching career in New York. The Cat gave me a new title, assistant general manager. In the Rangers' press guide it said, Boom Boom will be "One of the right-hand men of General

Manager-Coach Emile Francis." Maybe the trouble was that The Cat was a lefty.

I was no more an assistant general manager than I was King Farouk of Egypt. What Francis did was make me a scout with a glorified title, that's what. I had to hit the road going to drafty arenas in places I had never heard of. I was alone and very depressed.

I had to report to a guy named Denis Ball, who was The Cat's farm system director. One night I watched a kid prospect in London, Ontario and the next day Ball asked me what I had seen: "Denis," I said, "there's nothing there for the New York Rangers."

"Never mind," he said, "I want you to go back and watch this kid again."

I shook my head. "This kid will never make it."

I was right but I wasn't enjoying myself at all. I wasn't going to quit just yet but I knew that the time was coming for me to give my regards to Broadway!

CHAPTER 19

Boom Boom with a Southern Drawl

If you had told me when I was still working for New York Rangers that one day I would be a bigger hit in Atlanta than I ever was in Montreal or on Broadway I would have recommended that you see 400 psychiatrists one at a time. That's how ridiculous a statement it would have been in 1971.

"Georgia On My Mind" once was a great song hit but the Peachtree State was about as far from my mind in those days as Tahiti.

That is until I got a strange phone call from Cliff Fletcher.

Just so you know a little NHL history, at that time Fletcher was only known to hockey insiders. He had been one of the behind-the-scenes guys with the St. Louis Blues when they entered the NHL in 1967 and he gradually came to be very well respected among people who knew hockey administration.

First he was a Blues' scout and then assistant general manager under Scotty Bowman. It was no coincidence that every year the Blues made the play-offs, but in 1970 the St. Louis owner Sid Salomon Jr. had a falling out with Scotty and both Bowman and Fletcher were canned.

Meanwhile the NHL was thinking about expanding again. It had grown from six to 12 teams in 1967 and then added Buffalo and Vancouver in 1970. Now Long Island and Atlanta were to begin operating for the 1972-73 season.

Tom Cousins and Bill Putnam, who were running the new Atlanta franchise, brought Fletcher in as their first general manager. Since Cliff had grown up with the Canadiens organization and managed the Junior Habs he had been around Montreal long enough to know me and what I could do.

One day in 1971 I was in Montreal still scouting for Rangers when I got a call from Fletcher. "Boom," he said, "how would you like to coach again?"

I said, "What are you talking about?"

His voice got very serious and I knew there was no more kidding around. "There's going to be a new NHL franchise in Atlanta and I'm going to be the general manager. I want you to coach."

I still couldn't believe my ears. "You've gotta be kidding me," I said. "You want me to go to Atlanta, Georgia. What do they know about a puck, a stick and ice?"

Fletcher told me not to worry about that. What he needed to know was whether I was interested. After the miserable time I was having as a Ranger scout of course I was interested. But I told Cliff he had to clear it with Emile Francis.

"If Boomer wants to go," Cat told Cliff, "I'll let him go to Atlanta."

I later found out that I wasn't the only candidate for the job. Red Kelly, Hal Laycoe, Bobby Kromm and even Harry Sinden were some of the names discussed by the media.

But somebody had told Fletcher that to bring in the crowds he needed someone who could talk to the public and the media, who can go on TV and promote the game down South.

When Fletcher decided on me I had to consult with Marlene first. "Boom," she said, "maybe this could be like the light at the end of the tunnel."

She was right.

I phoned Fletcher and told him, "I'm gonna go, no problem. What's my salary?" He said it would be $27,000 a year for three years. With that we had the beginnings of a deal. I still had to fly down to Atlanta and talk to Putnam and work out the details.

Marlene remembers what it was like:

> While I was happy for Boom I was almost certain there was no way the kids and I would move down to Atlanta. I figured I'd go down with him to finish ironing out the contract and then go back to Montreal and that would be it. The kids loved it up north and had now been in schools for a couple of years.

But I changed my mind almost immediately. We met some lovely local people who took us around to some beautiful neighborhoods and the next thing I knew we had both fallen in love with Atlanta. In fact we never left again!

Nobody was supposed to know about me and the Flames until all the details were worked out. In January 1972 Putnam invited me down for a meeting and I did something I don't normally do very well — I kept my mouth shut.

I asked Putnam if I should use a phony name when I checked into the Atlanta Marriott. Bill thought that was a riot. After all, how many Georgians knew what a hockey puck was let alone who Boom Boom Geoffrion was.

Once we dotted the *i*'s and crossed the *t*'s Putnam and Fletcher called a press conference on May 22, 1972 to announce that I was coach. There was a huge turnout and I told them straight-out what was what. "Atlanta is a major-league city. The South likes action and hockey is action. Oh it's gonna take some time and the people are gonna need some patience. But we will have a championship here some day, I guarantee that."

Right off the bat they loved me because I didn't put on any airs. Boom Boom was Boom Boom and that was that. Take it or leave it. My first job was to sell some hockey tickets. Our new arena, The Omni, wasn't open yet so they set me up in a makeshift trailer.

It was hot! The temperature was 105 degrees, my shirt was soaking wet and I remembered Clarence Campbell saying that you can only sell hockey in cold weather cities. I said to myself, "There is no way people are going to want to come to hockey games where it's this hot."

But I could tell from the press conference that there was interest. Big-time writers like Furman Bisher were intrigued by the idea of hockey in the South. I told him, "I am the most surprised guy in the world that you have an NHL franchise here. It's over a hundred degrees outside."

They all laughed. The idea of a French Canadian taking over the South amused them. "Y'all come to see us now, ya'hear," is what I would tell them and they'd crack up.

At first I figured all I had to do was work the bench the way I did in Quebec and New York but Atlanta was different. I said to Fletcher, "Am I the coach or am I promoting this team?"

He said, "Boom, if you want to see people in this building you gotta promote." I got the message and started talking to everyone I could. They even had me do a TV commercial where I came skating out on the ice in a tuxedo and carrying a big bouquet of flowers.

"To all you people in the South," I said, "I offer you these beautiful roses. Now come and see our game. You are going to see something unbelievable — action, fights, whatever you want. It's better than football or basketball. Come to the hockey game."

Pretty soon we began to sell tickets and more tickets. I became a character. The Georgians liked my sense of humor and my accent.

Pretty soon I was getting all sorts of invitations to do commercials for cars, clothes and whatnot. But the best invitation of all came that June when the Hockey Hall of Fame invited me to a luncheon in Toronto. This was for the new inductees and naturally I figured that I was one of them.

I was sitting at the reception, and the emcee called out "Jean Béliveau" and then "Gordie Howe." There I was thinking, "Hey, what about me?"

While the crowd applauded Big Jean and Gordie there was a momentary pause. The emcee fumbled for a few seconds then he grabbed the microphone again and said, "Sorry, there's one more name here — Boom Boom . . . ."

The poor guy never got to my last name because everyone in the joint got to his feet and gave me a standing ovation. By the time Bill Putnam came over I was crying like a baby. This was what they call tears of happiness and I stayed in that frame of mind until August 24, 1972 when I was formally inducted into The Hall of Fame at ceremonies in Toronto.

"Tonight I love everyone in this room because you honor me," I told the audience. "But remember this: when October comes and the season starts, I hate your guts!"

That got a laugh along with my newly acquired Southern accent. "Thank you very much," I shouted as we left the ceremonies, "y'all!"

Once the cheering stopped it was time to go about the business of coaching this brand-new expansion hockey club. There had been raids from the World Hockey Association which was starting its first season at the very same time we were due to open.

Fletcher gave me a pretty decent roster for a first-year team. Everybody knows that goaltending can make or break a club. Cliff got me Phil Myre and Dan Bouchard, two good, young French Canadians from Canadiens and Bruins respectively. It was as good as I could have expected.

There wasn't much available among veterans in the draft but we did pretty well when you think about the castoffs we could get. My defense was Pat Quinn who was tough and had a good head but not much speed; Ron Harris, one of the strongest guys you'll ever meet; Randy Manery, who had a cup of coffee with the Red Wings; Billy Plager, whose brothers Bob and Barclay were with St. Louis; and Noel Price, who had a lot of NHL experience with Pittsburgh, Canadiens, Rangers and Toronto.

Up front there were no 50-goal men. As a matter of fact there weren't even any 30-goal scorers. But all things considered we did okay.

From Pittsburgh Cliff picked up a balding center named Bobby Leiter who had a steel plate in one arm and never scored more than 14 goals in any one of six NHL seasons. With me he would score 26 goals and 34 assists for 60 points in 78 games. Not bad.

They say strength down the middle is what every team needs. We got another center from Canadiens, Rey Comeau, who had played a grand total of four NHL games for Montreal the previous season but hadn't scored a point. With me he would score 21 goals and 21 assists.

Then there was Larry Romanchych — pronounced Roman Chuck in Atlanta — a center from Chicago. He once played ten games for Blackhawks and scrounged only two assists, no goals. He would be my second-leading scorer with 18 goals and 30 assists.

Everyone made a big deal out of who we would get in the amateur draft. After we lost the coin toss Islanders had first pick. They took Billy Harris, a right winger who had played for Toronto Marlboros. We picked next and went for a French Canadian kid out of Quebec City named Jacques Richard. Despite his name he was not related to the Canadiens hockey dynasty but he had potential.

I knew a lot about this kid since he played junior for Quebec Remparts which had been Guy Lafleur's team. But Quebec was going to have a WHA team and they were after Richard as hard as we were. I spent a lot of afternoons playing golf with Jacques that summer until Cliff finally signed him.

Now it was September 1972 and time for training camp in Drummondville, Quebec where we got a royal welcome. The city fathers hung a banner at the entrance to town: Welcome Atlanta Flames!

Once we started playing exhibition games people thought we'd collapse but after six games we had four wins and a tie! Not bad.

Down in Atlanta the fans were starting to get a little excited about our opening. We managed to sell a little more than 7,000 season tickets and were hoping to average about 13,000 per game. The NHL gave us a break putting the Flames in the West Division — Chicago, St. Louis, Minnesota, Philadelphia, L.A., Pittsburgh and California — which wasn't as strong as the East.

My hope was that we would at least be better than the Islanders who we opened the season with at Nassau Coliseum on October 7, 1972. Just to stir things up I told the media that I "guaranteed" a victory over New York. "We've got a better team," I said, "that's why."

The game wasn't exactly a classic but we came out on top 3-2 with Phil Myre outstanding in goal. We were tied for first place with Pittsburgh and Chicago. Next stop was the Windy City.

Even before we played the Blackhawks my guys got maimed. One of the hockey "experts" wrote that the Flames were "the worst assemblage of rejects and has-beens ever in the history of hockey." Then he twisted the knife a little harder and added that we were "totally unworthy" of even playing at Chicago Stadium.

I would have loved to get my hands on that smart aleck but he never showed up at our dressing room. We lost 4-1 but put up a good show. By the time we finished our four-game road trip we were one-and-three and ready to make our world premiere at home.

Marlene can tell you about that:

I will never forget that night. Talk about luxury! No longer did I have to sneak into the ladies' room and wait for the right time to go sit in my seat, there was a whole room just for the wives. Furthermore the first time I walked in there I noticed some sort of covered containers sitting on a table and when I walked over and lifted a lid, there was warm food. For the first time in all the years (and it was now two decades) I had been coming to NHL hockey games to watch my husband play and coach I was going to be given a hot meal courtesy of the team's management.

It was understood right away that the coach's wife was entitled to use the wives' room too and nothing was ever said or done to make

*me feel out of place. In fact I found I could be of some little help to
Boom sometimes.*

*When the Leiters had a new baby I heard in the wives' room that
nobody was getting any sleep at night. Then after the game as we
drove home Boom might say, "Boy, Bobby Leiter sure had a rough
time of it on the ice tonight." Well obviously poor Bobby couldn't
walk up to Boom and say, "Gee coach, sorry I played bad out there
tonight but I haven't slept for a week because of the new baby."*

*But I could tell Boom what was happening at home and why Bob
was so exhausted even though the men would never use this kind of
information as an excuse for the way they played.*

The date was October 14, 1972. We played Buffalo that night and
at the pregame meeting I laid it on the line. "Listen fellas," I said,
"I've got to tell you this. I'm not the greatest coach in the world.
But if you look around this room you'll see that I don't have the
greatest players either." They had a good laugh at that but then I
got serious. "If you go out there and prove to the people that you
want to play this game they will appreciate you."

A few minutes later I walked behind the bench and looked up
at the stands. I got goose bumps. The place was packed top to bottom end to end. Marlene said, "I don't believe this. It's amazing."

The fans looked like they were attending a society ball not a
hockey game. Women were well-dressed while all the men wore
shirts with ties. Obviously I didn't know what to expect from the
fans and the fans didn't know what to expect from a hockey game.
They didn't know a slap shot from a cross-check and I found that
out soon enough.

Not long after the opening face-off the Sabres defenseman Tim
Horton got the puck in his zone and started up the ice. When he
got to center he decided to flip it deep into our end. He sent a high,
soft one that landed a few feet in front of our goalie Phil Myre. It
was as easy a save as Phil had ever made but as he cleared the puck
to the corner Myre got a standing ovation.

It was unbelievable. They were standing up applauding for two
or three minutes just for that! I was watching the crowd so much I
was distracted from coaching. What I saw of the game wasn't great
but wasn't bad either. Ernie Hicke scored for us and Jim Lorenz
scored for them and it ended in a 1-1 tie.

A couple of days later Minnesota came to town and the North
Stars killed us 6-0. I can't tell you how mad I was but the players

found out when we flew to Bloomington to play Minny again. I was still steaming when our bus rolled into the hotel parking lot at 11 p.m.

When the bus driver opened the door I said, "Wait a minute! You guys leave your luggage in the lobby and get over to the rink."

I kept them there past midnight until their tongues were hanging out. On the way back to the rink one of the writers walked over to me and wondered if I had worked them too hard.

"Hey," I said, "when I played for Canadiens and we lost a game like that Toe Blake would work us until we couldn't get up."

My strategy worked. We beat Minnesota 3-2.

Wise guys who said we would be lucky to win five games all season were doing double-takes. Even though we only had two home games out of our first 11 we were 4-6-1. Then we went into Detroit and beat a hot Red Wings team 4-2.

By the middle of November 1972 we were .500, only a point out of first place in the West. These guys were doing everything that I asked them, giving it everything they had.

In any relationship between general manager and coach there are bound to be disagreements over things like who should play and when. I know that even when the Islanders were winning four straight Stanley Cups coach Al Arbour had disagreements with his boss Bill Torrey. For me I couldn't have been luckier with a general manager like Cliff Fletcher. He was the best and I'll be forever grateful to him for bringing me down to Atlanta. What I tried to do was get the most out of the players he gave me.

What really helped us were a couple of deals Cliff made in mid-season. We got big defenseman Noel Picard on waivers from the St. Louis Blues. Then he traded rookie Bill Hogaboam to Detroit for Leon Rochefort, a veteran right winger who had played with me briefly in Montreal.

The Rangers had a huge, young center who had played 16 games for them and had only one assist to show for it. Yet there was something very attractive about Curt Bennett and when Cliff got him for defenseman Ron Harris we were in business.

Curt's father, Harvey Bennett, had been a goalie for the Boston Bruins during World War II so I knew he came from good stock. Plus he was a karate expert and even though he wasn't what you would call a "policeman" he could handle his dukes with the best of them.

And he could score. He went from no goals in New York to 18 goals for me in only 52 games. That was like weaving gold from straw. Curt also could make plays and finished with 17 assists.

The fans loved him. As a matter of fact they loved all of us. When we went to training camp the Flames Fan Club had maybe a dozen members. About two months into the season the Fan Club was so big that when they threw a luncheon for us in the Grand Ballroom of the Marriott Hotel, the place was so packed they had to turn away a hundred people at the door.

One reason they loved us is that we were playing better than anyone had believed. Danny Bouchard and Phil Myre gave us one of the best goaltending combinations in the league, and even though we didn't have a Guy Lafleur we were getting goals. I asked the guys to reach 35 points by Christmas and they delivered. A coach couldn't ask for anything more. Everybody was putting out for me.

I was lucky. I had a terrific captain in Keith McCreary. He wasn't a hot-shot scorer but he had been the leader on Pittsburgh and he was a good guy. "Keith," I told him, "I need your help to mold these guys together." He gave me all the help I could ask for. So did Pat Quinn who told the young fellows what they should expect.

Noel Price was a veteran when he came to us but he had the heart of a 17-year-old kid. I had so much confidence in him that I would think nothing of putting him on the ice for 20 or 25 minutes a game, the way Toe Blake used to play Doug Harvey. He would come to the bench after a shift and I'd say, "Noel get back out there, I need you!" Without ever blinking an eye he would go. If there was a problem I expected them to tell me because I never was afraid to sit down and talk about ways to improve the team.

The guys helped any way they could and one way was to have laughs. One of our funniest players was one of our best, Bobby Leiter. Even though he was still young Bobby was losing his hair so fast I figured that he would look like a billiard ball in a couple of years.

Bobby wished he had a mane like mine and was always reading hair improvement ads. Finally he gave up and bought himself a wig.

Well that did it. The guys never let poor Bobby alone over his new hairpiece, bugging him every chance they could get. After we had stunk up the joint with a bad loss one night, one of the players got hold of Leiter's wig and a pair of scissors and snipped it in half! After getting over the initial shock Bobby joined the clowns and wound up thinking it was as funny as the next fellow. That was Bobby Leiter. But in between laughs he got plenty of big goals for me too.

Unfortunately we couldn't keep it going and in the homestretch we ran out of gas, winning only five out of 29 games. But the fans were great. They loved the Flames in Atlanta and they loved Boom Boom in the state of Georgia. Wherever I went The Boom was a hero and it didn't matter, rich or poor, white or black.

My main job was to sell hockey where it never had been sold before. There were two ways of doing that: winning games which I did pretty well for a first-year expansion team; and being colorful which I did just by being myself. I had no trouble sleeping at night.

As a matter of fact I had no trouble sleeping all during the summer of 1973. Why should I? We had achieved our objective. NHL hockey was a big hit in the South. More than 400,000 fans had come to our games which gave us the third-best gate among the ten expansion teams.

While relaxing on my beach chair in August I asked myself what do you do for an encore? The answer was easy; make the play-offs.

And we did.

To make the play-offs we beat out Pittsburgh, St. Louis, Minnesota and California (Oakland). Our final record was 30-34-14 for 74 points. The Islanders, who were coached by the great Al Arbour, were 19-41-18 for only 56 points. That put us up against first-place Philadelphia in the opening play-off round.

A lot of people were feeling sorry for us. The Flyers weren't called The Broad Street Bullies for nothing. They had tough guys like Dave "Hammer" Schultz, Moose Dupont, Hound Kelly and a few other enforcers. But we had guys who could handle themselves. Big kids like Tommy Lysiak, Eric Vail and Curt Bennett could use their dukes and the first two games at Philly were pretty mild. Our trouble was getting the puck past Bernie Parent. He beat us 4-1 and 5-1 sending us home to Atlanta down two games.

That didn't bother our fans. When we showed up for Game Three The Omni was packed to the rafters with 15,141 people who wanted to see us beat the stuffing out of the Flyers. We did — but not on the scoreboard.

A day before the game Fletcher got into the act. "Philadelphia has been getting away with too much bluff intimidation by guys who can't back it up," he told the media. "I guarantee we'll come out hitting at home."

That put my players on the spot but they came through. The war to end all hockey wars happened in the middle of the second period. And when I tell you it was one of the biggest hockey brawls of all time remember I've seen plenty as a player and as a coach. This one lasted 25 minutes and when it was over the fans were as exhausted as the players.

How does a tremendous hockey fight start?

This one began when Philly's captain Bobby Clarke — a guy who liked to cause trouble but didn't care to fight very much — began messing with Curt Bennett. Next thing you know my guy threw down his gloves and slugged Clarke. That was a sin to Philly players. They treated their captain like a god and anyone who laid a hand on him had to pay the price.

Flyers' forward Bill Flett was close by and jumped Bennett from behind. Then my defenseman Arnie Brown played leapfrog with Flett and it was mayhem. Bennett pounded Flett so hard that the Flyer needed three stitches to close the cut on his cheek.

Finally the referee Dave Newell calmed things down for a bit and threw Bennett and Flett out of the game. As Curt left the ice he was given a huge ovation from the crowd and that must have really bugged the Flyers who never liked to lose a fight.

Meanwhile Schultz had come onto the ice looking for a fight. He skated over to our bench and started yapping. "Any of you guys wanna fight?"

Butch Deadmarsh, who wasn't a very big fellow but had an immense heart, accepted the invitation. Butchie went right over the wall and started pounding away at Schultz. Unfortunately Deadmarsh's geography wasn't too good. He went after Hammer right in front of the Flyers' bench and right then and there Ed Van Impe, Schultz's teammate, conveniently tripped Butchie. By the time Deadmarsh got to his feet a couple of Flyers began smacking him around.

But Butchie gave it right back and some of my other guys — John Stewart and Jacques Richard — got into the act. So did the fans. They wanted Hammer's head and nearly got it before referee Dave Newell finally tossed Schultz out of the game.

When the dust had cleared Newell had handed out a total of 90 penalty minutes and we were still very much in the hockey game. But then in the next minute we got shafted. Rick MacLeish took a shot that hit the crossbar but didn't go in and Dan Bouchard fell on the puck. The goal judge and the linesmen said it was no goal but Newell claimed that it was. Five TV replays showed that the puck never got past the crossbar.

My goalie was so furious he came storming out of his crease after Newell as if he was going to belt the referee with his stick. Deadmarsh was so scared that Bouchard would kill Newell that Butchie ran out of the penalty box and tackled Danny before he could get to the ref.

Newell made a terrible call and probably deserved to get belted but there was no changing the decision. After that we lost all our momentum and they beat us 4-1. I told the players I was very proud of them. Then I met with the press.

"We're comin' back," I told them, "and we're gonna fight to win Game Four. I think the people of Atlanta understand now that Philadelphia has a great hockey club. (They would win The Stanley Cup in 1974.) If we win Game Four it will be very important to this club next season."

For a while it looked like we would win Game Four. We ran up a 3-0 lead and late in the second period it looked like a win would be a piece of cake. Then Schultz showed what well-timed brawling could do.

My center Bryan Hextall was in front of the Flyers' net when Schultz came in with a high stick. Pretty soon they were swinging like a couple of heavyweights. Hexy was doing a terrific job of tying up Schultz until Hammer did one of his typical Philly moves. He head butted Hextall so badly that Bryan screamed at the linesmen, "When are you guys gonna break this up?"

But the damage was done. By the time the zebras moved in Hexy had a long, ugly gash over his left eye and was bleeding from the nose. When he came over to our bench the trainer handed him a towel that turned bright red.

I don't know whether the sight of Hexy's blood affected our players or not but I do know that we blew the three-goal lead and wound up going into sudden-death overtime. Then disaster struck. Schultz got free on a two-on-one breakaway against Phil Myre. My goalie gave him an opening and Hammer put the puck in the net. That was the end of our season.

Even though we didn't win a play-off game our fans still loved us. I was only sorry we couldn't play the Flyers one more time at The Omni. If we had they could have sold tickets for $2,000 apiece.

By now hockey was big, *big* stuff in Atlanta and the Flames had become big stuff in the NHL. Magazines like *Sports Illustrated* were doing stories about us and even *The Hockey News* declared us a shoo-in to make the play-offs again in 1974-75.

But the NHL added two new teams — Kansas City and Washington — for the next season and that meant the Flames were shifted to the Patrick Division along with the Flyers, Rangers and Islanders.

"Anybody who thinks we're a shoo-in to make the play-offs next year needs his head examined," said Fletcher.

Unfortunately he was right.

CHAPTER 20

Atlanta to Montreal

After our terrific second season I felt like the king of Atlanta. I couldn't walk the streets downtown without being recognized and whenever I could I promoted the team.

"You better come see my Flames, you hear?" I would tell anyone I met. And they listened because our attendance was one of the best in the league. Sportswriters would tell me that I was the first coach in Atlanta's history who brought fans to the games just by my personality. Meanwhile the NHL was so big a hit in the South someone even put a minor-league team in the city of Macon. What do you think they called them? The Macon Whoopees.

But as much fun as I was having as the big, new sports star of Atlanta, I was also suffering. The strain of coaching that got to Toe Blake and Dick Irvin and to me in New York was starting to get to me in Atlanta and I began thinking of retiring. I kept saying that once hockey made me sick I would quit coaching because my health and my wife and children were the most important things to me. Nothing would change that.

I couldn't ignore the physical signs. After my first training camp with Atlanta I lost almost 15 pounds and I still hadn't gained them back a year later. The problem was that I couldn't eat like a normal person and I was smoking two packs of cigarettes on game days.

One reason was my perfectionism. I demanded a lot from my players and they would go through a wall for me. Sometimes I couldn't understand why a couple of them didn't pay attention.

Mostly it was the younger guys with the big money who were spoiled. It was much tougher to coach in 1974 than it was when I was playing for Canadiens. There was a very different attitude among the players.

We would lose a game and instead of being upset the way we used to be in Montreal these players now would get on the bus laughing. I promised myself that I wouldn't lose any sleep over these problems but I still found myself taking the games home with me and losing sleep.

I felt I was losing the players. During a game with the Seals I yelled at a player to come off the ice and he yelled back at me! After that game I felt like quitting. I didn't and we came back and beat Chicago, a tough team. We'd be up and down like a seesaw. We'd be great at home and terrible on the road. We'd have a big winning streak and then a big losing streak.

By February 1975 we seemed to be okay but Cliff and I had begun to disagree on some things. We didn't see eye to eye on goaltending. Goalies are peculiar and when you have two equally talented guys like Phil Myre and Dan Bouchard it's sometimes hard to make a decision. But at this critical point in midseason I knew what I wanted.

We had been beaten at home 4-2 on January 31 with Bouchard in goal and this was after we had tied a very weak Kansas City team 4-4. I figured after the game that I had to do something with the lineup so in the next game — February 2 at Minnesota — I put Myre in goal. When Cliff found out he came running down to the dressing room area. We met in a little room near the bench.

He said, "Boom, what are you doing?"

"What do you mean?" I asked.

"Why are you putting in Phil Myre?"

I said, "Who got knocked off the other night for a bunch of goals? — Bouchard."

"Never mind," Cliff said, "I want Bouchard in the net tonight."

I shook my head. "No way. Phil Myre is staying in there."

He did and we won the game 5-3.

This was our first major misunderstanding and today, more than two decades later, I can honestly say I would have been better off had I listened to Cliff. After all he was the boss. But I didn't and the rest is history. After the game I approached him.

"Cliff," I said, "you better call (minor league coach) Fred Creighton because I'm resigning. I don't think I have it anymore."

The real reason was that I didn't want Cliff interfering with my decisions. It was my team. I was the coach, not him. What I should have understood then was that Cliff was the general manager and in the end the general manager runs the team.

Sure I had threatened to quit before, even in the second season I had talked to Cliff about it, but he talked me out of leaving. This time there was no turning back and Fletcher knew it. When we got back from Minnesota on Monday February 3, 1975 Cliff called a press conference for later in the afternoon.

Fletcher didn't tip his hand about what it was about and since the Flames were still a good play-off contender nobody would think that the coach would leave. But by the time all the media gathered at The Omni word had leaked out and when I arrived with Marlene it was no secret anymore.

Cliff made it official when he got up on the podium and told the crowd, "Bernie Geoffrion has announced his retirement. As of today he will be my assistant and the coaching duties will be turned over to Fred Creighton."

Now it was my turn. This was going to be tough especially since I could see Marlene in the back crying.

When the reporters pressed me I just said, "I don't have it anymore."

One of the newspaper reporters came right back at me and said, "What do you mean you don't have it anymore? You just beat Minnesota 5-3."

I said, "I don't have it no more. I'm losing it." And that was it. I left.

After Cliff made me his assistant the owners wanted to cut my pay so I said, "No thank you!" and returned to Montreal.

I got a job as president of a company that represented 200 athletes but I wasn't crazy about the sports agency business. One day Fletcher was in Montreal with the Flames and he met with Marlene and me. This was just after Christmas 1975 and Cliff offered me a job as vice president in charge of season-ticket sales and promotion, as well as color commentator on the telecasts with Jiggs McDonald.

As soon as Fletcher finished Marlene said, "We're already packed!"

Atlanta was just as much fun the second time around and a lot more relaxing. Cliff brought me back because attendance had dropped after I left. Now they wanted me to make personal appearances and sell ads for the broadcasts. This was great because I was still in demand but I didn't have to worry about winning and losing.

Boom Boom \ **237**

Visiting broadcasters would always invite me to appear on their shows. Once the Rangers were in town and their interviewer was Bill Chadwick who had been a tough referee when I was still playing. Chadwick had me on between periods and when he got through with his questions I turned to him. "Hey, Bill," I said, "how come you understand what I say now? When I was playing you never understood anything I said when I questioned one of your calls."

One thing the fans understood was that the Flames weren't the same without Boom Boom behind the bench. They didn't make the play-offs in 1974-75 after Freddie Creighton took over and they missed again in the next two years. Atlanta finally made it in 1977-78 but Detroit knocked them out in four straight and Toronto did the same to them in the spring of 1979.

They were awful in that last game at Maple Leaf Gardens losing 7-4 and I ripped into them on the air as hard as a hometown broadcaster can be. Some people didn't like what I said but when I got questioned by a few writers I told them straight out: "If you think I was going to say the Flames put on a good show after giving up three goals in 28 seconds, no way! I just told it like it was. I couldn't do anything but give it to them. They deserved it."

That was the spring when Canadiens won their fourth straight Stanley Cup with Scotty Bowman behind the bench. Montreal was in the midst of a big front office shakeup with Sam Pollock leaving as general manager. Scotty had been waiting to move in as general manager and when he didn't get the job — it went to Irving Grundman — Bowman quit and became general manager-coach of Buffalo.

When Scotty left Canadiens needed a coach and sure enough Grundman called and said, "How would you like to coach the Montreal Canadiens?"

I didn't hesitate. "It would be a dream come true. The only thing I could ever want is to win a Stanley Cup coaching Les Canadiens."

My old buddy Jean Béliveau was working for Canadiens as a vice president at the time. He was always thinking about my well-being. In his book Béliveau confesses that he told Grundman not to hire me because of my health problems in New York and Atlanta and he thought the pressure would get to me. Fair enough. But once I was hired Big Jean didn't hesitate to help.

"Boom," he said, "I am telling you. You are going to have a lot of work to do especially with the media in Montreal. You know how they are. And if you don't win you know what's going to happen."

I appreciated his advice. "Jean," I said, "I know and I'm not afraid."

The press conference announcing my position came right after Labor Day 1979. A minute after the reporters started asking questions I knew Big Jean was right about the media. Almost immediately they began questioning me about my health until I finally interrupted them.

"I'm sick and tired of answering questions about my health," I said. "A month ago I went into the hospital for five days for a check-up. My health is a thousand percent better than it was when I was playing."

"I don't want you guys coming to me in the middle of the year and asking me how my health is."

"People talk about pressure," I said, "but I don't care about pressure. The more pressure I've got the better I like it. I love the competition."

Then there was the question of my son Danny who had played for Quebec in the WHA during the 1978-79 season. Like his older brother Robert, Danny played for the junior team in Cornwall, Ontario. Starting at age 14 Danny played five seasons in Cornwall. In his last two years there he became the team leader both as a scorer and fighter.

By the 1977-78 season Danny was ready for the pros and Canadiens had drafted him. But the war between the WHA and the NHL was still hot and Quebec Nordiques made him a much better offer. Canadiens were furious when Danny signed with Quebec but I knew he had done the right thing.

When the NHL and WHA merged before the 1979-80 season Danny was taken by Canadiens in the reclaiming draft so naturally a reporter asked what it would be like coaching with my son on the team. They wanted to know about possible favoritism.

"I can't see any difficulty," I said. "Off the ice he's still my son. On the ice he's a player just like any other player. If he doesn't do things the way I like them he will be benched just like any other player."

When Grundman signed me he had already announced that Toe Blake had a new title — vice president, hockey. Not only would I have to report directly to Grundman but Blake would be on the road with the hockey club all season. On top of that they also had another former coach Claude Ruel as a coaching advisor.

I should have sensed then and there that that would be trouble.

But I couldn't see anything but victories once I took over the club in training camp. The players were responding; they were in shape and working hard. In our first exhibition game at The Forum we played Scotty Bowman's new team, the Sabres, but he didn't even show up. Roger Neilson and Jimmy Roberts handled the coaching and we beat them 5-2.

Remember this was not the same Canadiens that had won four straight Stanley Cups. Two great players had retired. Ken Dryden, one of the best goalies of all time, had packed it in and so had Jacques Lemaire, a brilliant center who had helped turn Guy, Lafleur into a star. We had three goalies, Bunny Larocque, Denis Herron and Richard Sevigny but none could come close to Dryden. There simply was no replacing a talent like Lemaire.

Still we did well quickly climbing over the .500 mark and taking over first place in the Norris Division. But there always seemed to be a problem in one form or another.

In mid-November 1979 we came from behind to tie Pittsburgh 3-3. After the game Lafleur complained to the press that Ruel was interfering too much in the operation of the team. "Bernard (Geoffrion) should do the same thing with Claude that (Scotty) Bowman did," said Lafleur. "Geoffrion is getting advice from here and there and he doesn't know where to turn. If Claude wants to coach let him go behind the bench."

I was livid when the story appeared and threatened to ban all reporters from the team charters. The press had gotten on my case for a few moves I had made. For example they beefed about my benching Rod Langway and Brian Engblom, and when I moved Larry Robinson up to left wing for a short time they questioned that.

When the reporters quizzed me I didn't hide. I admitted that I had decided to put Larry Robinson up front. "It was me who decided not to dress Engblom against Pittsburgh. I'm the guy who makes the lineup."

I was also the guy in the eye of the hurricane and the storm was taking its toll on me. By the first week of December 1979 I had lost 15 pounds since taking over behind the Habs' bench.

There were a lot of reasons for this. One of them was the attitude of the fans. One false move and they were all over the team. On December 9, 1979 we played the lowly Colorado Rockies at The Forum. Larocque had an awful time in goal and we got plastered

7-5 giving up five goals in the third period. They really booed us that night.

Another problem was having my son Danny on the team. Not that Danny couldn't play on the NHL level; he could. And I knew it but the organization didn't want him to play. One night I planned to dress him but I got word from Claude Ruel that I couldn't put him in the lineup.

That really hurt. I had to go tell my son that he was not playing even though I knew that he was good enough. Why Ruel didn't want me to play him I'll never know. It was as if they were determined that I should play guys who were not as good as Danny.

Then there was the interference. Toe Blake was following the team around and Ruel was doing the practices with me. I had three or four guys telling me what to do. Who could coach like that?

One of the opposition coaches came up to me one day and said, "Hey Boom, when are you gonna play Danny? He's as good as anyone else on your team?"

I managed to get him in once against Atlanta and put him on a line with Guy Lafleur. Danny got two assists that night and we beat the Flames. Then when we went back to Montreal they forced me to dress someone else who wasn't as good. Every time I wanted to dress him I'd get the "No, no, no" from upstairs even though Danny gave 125 percent every time he was on the ice.

One day Serge Savard, who was one of the senior defensemen on the club, said to me, "Boom, I know why you are hurting. You are hurting because you can't dress Danny."

I said, "You got that right. This is what hurts me the most. They are boycotting him."

By now I was seriously thinking of resigning. I told Savard and Blake. Both tried to talk me out of it. Nobody could give me a good explanation why I couldn't play Danny. I could never find the answer.

On the whole I was getting a fair shake from the Montreal media. My theory on the press is this: you could say anything about my team when we played badly as long as they got the same treatment when they played well.

Even though we had a slump early in December 1979 the club still had a fine record. After 30 games I had 15 wins and only nine losses plus six ties. We were in first place. Superficially everything seemed great. I had a three-year contract, I was making big money, I was driving a Cadillac and we lived free in a penthouse apartment. Yet if you looked at me at that time I looked older than I do today 20 years later! When we returned from our road trip Marlene couldn't believe how bad I looked.

"Boom," she said, "Are you happy as coach of the Canadiens?"

I said to her, "Marlene, I hate it. I hate it. I don't know if I can make it until the month of April." It wasn't the pressure. It was my broken heart over not being able to play my son Danny.

Marlene was very logical. "You need to do something. I'm afraid of what this is doing to your health. Go see Irving Grundman and tell him that you won't coach anymore."

Once we talked this through and my mind was made up the relief was enormous. The world had been lifted off my shoulders; I had just been concerned that Marlene wouldn't want to give up all the perks we had, but they were unimportant if I was going to go crazy. I had coached my last game in the NHL. Ruel replaced me and Canadiens got knocked out of the play-offs by an inferior Minnesota team in the second play-off round. The four-year run of Stanley Cups was over.

I had done everything in Montreal. I won rookie of the year, the Hart Trophy (MVP), the scoring title twice and scored 50 goals in a season. The only dream I had never accomplished with Montreal Canadiens was winning The Stanley Cup as coach. It was now clear that this would never happen.

My dream had turned into a nightmare.

CHAPTER 21

On to a New Career

When someone like me has been in hockey all his life — first as a player, then as a coach — it's hard to imagine doing a job away from the rink.

I had a taste of nonhockey work twice; one experience was just awful and the other was great.

The terrible job happened after I left my Atlanta coaching spot and returned to Montreal. This was at a time when the WHA was still around and players were making more and more money. It also was at a time when agents were trying to get a piece of the pie.

I hooked up with some Montreal lawyers who had moved into the business of representing hockey players. They wanted me to be their frontman on the theory that the name Boom Boom Geoffrion would get young players to sign with them instead of with other agents. Mind you these kids weren't even in the NHL yet.

Being an agent is like being a beggar and I hated it. Don't ask me why I ever took this job. Every night when I came home I felt more uptight than I ever felt coaching a hockey club. I hated the job so much I told one of the bosses, "I don't know how long I can do this job before I kill somebody."

After a year and a half I finally told Marlene, "Forget this job. It's not for me." I had been traveling all over the place trying to get clients for this outfit and all the time realizing that it was the biggest mistake of all. If it wasn't hockey work, I couldn't be happy.

That's when Cliff Fletcher rescued me with the job promoting the Flames and more important, to my career as a hockey broadcaster. Now when I say broadcaster I don't want you to think I was the second coming of Foster Hewitt, René Lecavalier or Danny Gallivan.

What I became was a color commentator or, as they say in the business, an analyst.

They partnered me with one of the best play-by-play men anywhere, Jiggs McDonald and we had a million laughs. For me the great thing was that I could go to all the hockey games but have none of the worries that I had as a player and a coach.

At first I don't think Jiggs was prepared for the way I handled my new job because he was accustomed to working with people who spent hours and hours going over statistics. In retrospect I should have listened to Jiggs and studied some stats, because after a while I realized that being a color commentator was a hard job although some of the pros made it look easy.

I knew the game inside out so when Jiggs would ask me at the pregame meeting, "Boom, did you do your work?" I would say, "What work? What are you talking about?"

Jiggs would get upset and tell me that I had to look up all the records and stuff in the media guides.

"Jiggs," I would say, "that's *your* job. You look at the record and you ask me any kind of questions you want and I'll answer you. I know the game Jiggs."

Sometimes Jiggs would try to pull a fast one on me. He wouldn't tell me that I had to do an interview between the first and second periods then all of a sudden near the end of the first period he'd say, "Boom, in about 30 seconds you've got to interview this guy."

He thought he was going to make me nervous but I told him, "No problem. Where do I have to go?" I already knew that talking hockey was a lot easier than coaching.

He told me there was a studio down below so I jumped over the fence and went downstairs. Next thing I knew a floor manager was counting down, "Five, four, three, two, one," and I was sitting there with a hockey player.

I said, "How're ya doin' big guy? How are you enjoying the game so far?"

I loved it. All I had to do was ask all kinds of hockey questions and when the interview was over I said, "Good luck in the game."

Naturally I wanted to look good on camera so I told Marlene to tell me if I made any mistakes. "Teach me," I said, "and my English will improve."

I should have known better. The Georgians loved the way I fractured the language. Mail poured in and the letters went something like this: "Oh Boom, we just think you are so great on camera and interviewing and all that stuff. Sometimes we don't understand what you're talking about but we love you just the same."

Marlene got the message and after the third broadcast she told me, "Boom, you were perfect. I didn't spot an error."

That gave me confidence and I didn't have to worry that Marlene would find any "mistakes." I was being myself and that's what the public wanted.

Jiggs knew that he couldn't put me on the spot. I didn't care if the president of the United States came on — as long as he talked hockey — nothing would bother me when I was on camera. And it didn't bother me if the players were upset with what I said.

I knew that lots of other broadcasters were afraid to say that such and such a player made a mistake. But the people watching at home would see the mistake and they couldn't be fooled. They'd say, "Hey why didn't that analyst say something?"

And they were right. I would go on the air and say, "Jiggs, this kid made a mistake. He should never have been where he was on the ice. After the game go ask him and he'll tell you he made a mistake."

I didn't say these things to hurt anybody; all I wanted to do was explain the way the game should be played. The right way. But I didn't care about the details anybody could find in the media guides.

One night Jiggs and I were out eating before a game. Between courses Jiggs pulled out the visiting team's lineup. We discussed most of the players until he came to the name of a guy up from the minors neither of us knew. I saw a glint in McDonald's eyes and I knew that the rascal wanted to pull a fast one on me during the game so I warned him in advance. "Jiggs," I said, "don't you ask me to find out where this guy comes from." He wasn't even in *The Hockey News*!

Some announcers get too serious. They come out with words that the average fan doesn't understand. Me, I was simple. The fans loved it, I enjoyed it and we all had a ball.

I didn't miss coaching at all. My popularity was as great behind a mike as it had been behind the bench. A lot of people wanted me to coach again. They saw that attendance was falling and it wasn't the same as in 1972, 1973 and 1974. But I was having too much fun and every game fans would come over to my broadcast position and ask for autographs.

But by the 1979-80 season the team had been losing money and Tom Cousins, the owner, was worried. I saw the handwriting on the wall and told my partner, "Jiggs you better start lookin' for another job." He didn't want to believe me.

I was convinced that Cousins couldn't keep losing so much money and I was right. Calgary was looking for an NHL team and sure enough Cousins wound up selling the Flames at the end of 1979-80. Atlanta was suddenly without its big-league hockey club.

They asked me to go west with them but I said, "That's it for me. I am not moving. Good-bye! And thank you very much. I am staying here in Atlanta." I loved Georgia. We had a nice house, a swimming pool and in the winter there was no snow. And I had still another new profession — star of TV commercials.

This bit of good luck started in the late 1970s when New York sportsmarketer Marty Blackman phoned and asked me if I would like to do a Miller Lite Beer commercial. It turned out that Miller had been using top pro athletes for several years and the campaign was very successful.

"Boom," said Blackman, "when can you come to New York?"

"Right now," I said. "Now! Not tomorrow. I'm ready now!"

Then Blackman told me he had a confession to make. "I cannot believe I'm calling you Boomer because I was a Ranger fan when you played for Montreal and I hated you with a passion. I booed you all the time."

We both had a good laugh about that one, especially after I told him about the times I was so nervous going into the Garden and how I wondered who that guy was who always booed me! From that point on Blackman and I got along famously.

As a matter of fact it marked the start of a 13-year gig for me as the star of Miller Beer commercials. One minute I was out of a job and the next minute Miller was flying me first-class all across the country and putting me in hotel suites fit for a king.

I was floating on air. I didn't walk to my room, I flew. I got a phone call telling me that the first shoot for the commercial would be at four in the afternoon. I said, "I'll be there. Just direct me to the studio."

They gave me a release to sign and I barely read it because I wanted to do the commercial so much. I didn't even ask how much money I was being paid. They gave me a script and then I was doing a solo for 30 seconds.

Instantly the ham in Boom Boom Geoffrion came out and I was loving this acting with a passion. I memorized the script in 20 minutes and we did the rehearsal. When it was over the producer said, "We shoot tomorrow morning at nine."

I said, "What do you mean we will shoot tomorrow? Why don't we shoot now?"

They weren't in as big a hurry as Boom so I was gracious enough to wait until the next morning. Since I had some spare time I looked more closely at my contract and saw that they were paying me $20,000. Twenty thousand dollars for 30 seconds of work!

I couldn't believe my eyes so I reread it over and over again to make sure the numbers didn't change. In 16 years playing in the National Hockey League I never made more than $27,000 for a whole season. Here I was in New York and they were going to pay me $20,000 for 30 seconds. That was my idea of a good time.

When I say good time I don't mean just the money. I was loving the camaraderie because I was working with other great athletes from different sports. I would walk into a room with guys like Billy Martin of the Yankees and other sports immortals like football commentator John Madden, Bubba Smith of the Oakland Raiders and Dick Butkus of the Chicago Bears. I looked around and said to myself, "What am I doing here?"

For the first two commercials I was quieter than usual because I was awed by these American sports legends. As I got more acquainted with them I began to loosen up. I began socializing with them. One day I approached Billy Martin, who was known for his toughness and willingness to fight anyone, including his own players even though he was such a small, slim guy.

"Billy," I said, "you're lucky if you weigh 140 pounds and you're gonna tell me that you could fight anybody. How come you didn't fight Reggie Jackson?"

He laughed. Actually Martin was one of the nicest guys I've ever met. As a matter of fact most of them were. Bubba Smith was something else. Once he did a dinner commercial and I swear he must have eaten 28 steaks at one sitting.

Comedian Rodney Dangerfield worked with us for a while and I have to tell you he was so funny he could make a dog laugh. But he was never on time and it got to the other guys. One day we got even.

We were doing a commercial at a beach in Florida and everybody was ready to go but Rodney was late again. When he finally showed up we grabbed him and threw him right into the ocean.

Nobody knew that Rodney couldn't swim. There he was yelling for help, choking and sputtering and all the guys are yelling, "The sharks are coming! The sharks are coming!"

Eventually we pulled him out but after that he didn't go near the water. And he started showing up on time.

Dick Butkus was the biggest disturber. He was always playing jokes, always trying to get someone mad at someone else so he could have a good laugh when they almost came to blows.

When we were in New York one time shooting a new commercial, the Miller people had us staying at the Grand Marquee Hotel on 42nd Street. I went up to Butkus' room and there he was sitting with Bubba Smith. Dick was pretending to read the paper when he looked up at Smith and says, "Hey Bubba, do you know what they're sayin' about you?"

Bubba didn't know what to make of it. Then Butkus continued, "They're saying, `How come Bubba is making commercials when he ain't even in The Hall of Fame?'"

Now Bubba was fuming. He stood up and glared at Butkus. "Who's sayin' that? Are you sayin' that because I'm not in The Hall of Fame I shouldn't be doin' these commercials?"

Really I thought the two of them were going to slug it out right in front of me. All of a sudden Butkus exploded in laughter and Bubba knew he'd been had. Then again just about everyone who worked those Miller commercials was "had" by Butkus at one time or another — me included.

He got me while we were shooting a commercial in California. During a break Butkus nonchalantly walked over to me and said, "Boom, you have a nice watch that the Miller people gave you. But how come you don't have the one with the diamonds?"

I said, "Dick, what are you talking about? What diamonds?"

Still very serious he added, "You'd better call Marty Blackman. Every one of us doing the Miller ads has a watch with diamonds except you! And I don't think that's fair."

I'm wondering. "Why did I get left out?"

After the shoot I went up to my room and phoned Blackman. "Hey Marty," I shouted. "What's going on here? I've been with you guys for five years and you give me a cheap watch and the other guys get watches with diamonds?"

"Boom," Marty replied rapidly figuring out where it came from, "have you been talking to Dick Butkus?"

I admitted that I had and Blackman explained that Butkus had pulled that line on seven guys before me and they all called Marty complaining. Butkus had struck again.

Bob Uecker was another funny guy. After a shoot in California a bunch of us went golfing and at one point we looked around for Uecker. There he was in the pond up to his knees, trying to hit the ball out with a six-iron. Incredibly he whacked it and the ball took off like a rocket. The next thing you know the ball bounced off a weather vane on top of a barn next to the course and back onto the fairway!

The Miller deal went on and on and got better and better. What a life! We would finish a shoot, come back to the hotel suite, pick up the phone and order food fit for kings from room service. We drove around in limos, traveled first class, had the best hotel suites, vacations in Hawaii and cruises to the Virgin Islands. What a life! It lasted 14 years. It was work but you couldn't believe the good times!

When Miller introduced Lite in Canada they asked me to do the commercials in French. I was thrilled. I toured all across Canada and was greeted everywhere by hockey fans. When I left Canadiens I felt rejected, now I felt accepted again. And I was making great money on top of it all! It all came to an end in 1989 when I retired from "show business" and a new phase of my life began.

EPILOGUE

There's Life After Hockey

If Hollywood were writing "The Geoffrion Saga" I am sure the writers would have extended our family's hockey connection from Howie Morenz to Boom Boom Geoffrion and on down to my two sons Danny and Bobby, inserting them into the Hall of Fame along with Howie and me.

But Hollywood deals with fantasy and hockey reality is something entirely different. My sons never became stars on the ice the way I did but they did suffer a lot of heartache and so did their father.

Both kids had terrific potential.

Bobby, otherwise known as Robert George, was born December 6, 1954 the season I won my first scoring championship, beating out Rocket and getting half the population of Montreal mad at me. His talent showed from the very beginning.

But he also found out what it was like to be the son of a star like Howie Morenz Jr. or any one of Rocket Richard's kids. They are always reminded that they are supposed to be a chip off the old block.

When Bobby would miss a breakaway people would say, "Oh he'll never be like his old man." (I always liked Bobby's comeback. He would say, "You won't find *anyone* like my old man!")

What made me feel good about Bobby was that he dedicated himself to hockey the way I did when I was his age. He lifted weights and trained in the off-season and disciplined himself. And when he played I could tell that he had a big heart even though he wasn't that big physically.

What the junior team Montreal Nationales was to me in 1949 when I was a teenager the Cornwall Royals was to Bobby in the early 1970s. As a left winger he became a key member of the team that beat a very strong Peterborough club to win the 1972 Memorial Cup.

In 1974 he was drafted by the Buffalo Sabres (twelfth choice, 196th overall) and gradually moved up the minor-league ladder. I was luckier in the sense that I jumped straight from Nationales to Canadiens. Bobby had to pay his dues in the minors in cities all over the continent. One year he went to Winston-Salem, North Carolina where he was making $100 a week and living out of a van because he couldn't afford an apartment.

He also played in Des Moines, Iowa and Toledo, Ohio and then in 1975-76 I thought he got a break. Salt Lake City of the Central League signed him and he wound up winning the team's Mister Hustle Award.

Whenever I could I tried to encourage Bobby and I was hopeful that after playing two years in Salt Lake City he would get a break. Of all things my onetime opponent Ted Lindsay had become general manager of the Detroit Red Wings, and Bobby got invited to their training camp in Kalamazoo, Michigan.

Just as we had hoped he had a terrific camp, came away with one of the best records there and fully expected to get a contract with the Wings. But when the camp ended Bobby Kromm, Detroit's head coach, pulled him aside and began apologizing.

"Bobby," he said, "if it was up to me you would be with the club but the unfortunate thing is that they don't have any more contract spots!"

The kid was crushed. What kind of excuse was that?

He had tears in his eyes when he told me about it.

"Dad," he said, "I'm burned out."

"Are you sure?" I asked him.

"I'm done," he said. And that was that.

Bobby left hockey and went to work for Eastern Airlines where he remained for ten years. Now he works for Plymart, a lumber company in Atlanta where he has become its number one salesman. We see each other all the time and are closer now than we ever have been in our lives.

Danny's personality is a bit different from Bobby's. Both are very funny kids but Bobby always was the kind of guy who could walk into a room and immediately take it over. (Maybe he got that from me.) Whereas Danny is like his sister Linda. They like to stand back and observe. (Maybe they got that from Marlene.) Danny and Linda can look at a room full of people, then at each other, and know precisely who they like and don't like. But at family dinners all Geoffrions are equal. There it's a case of who can talk loudest.

Danny always was a very caring individual and that's why his horrible experience with Canadiens was so difficult for me to endure.

Danny was born on January 24, 1958 right in the midst of our great run of Stanley Cup championships in Montreal after we had won two in a row with three more straight to come.

Like his brother Bobby he wanted to be a hockey player in the worst way and naturally I encouraged him as much as I could. Danny made it clear that he wanted to follow in my footsteps. Not many fathers can say that they were their son's idol but that was the way Danny looked up to me.

As a matter of fact Danny followed his older brother to Cornwall. He was all of 14-years-old at the time, just a kid. One good thing was that Danny's older brother Bobby was already playing for the Royals so Danny automatically had a roommate he knew and loved as well as a teammate. For a short time, they would make beautiful music together. And at least one very clever headline. It happened one night when Danny scored on the night when Bobby was out nursing a sprained ankle. The next day the headline in the Cornwall paper was, "Boom And Boom = Dynamite."

Danny played there six years which meant he was away from home all through the hockey season and didn't come back to us until July and August. So really he spent only two months out of the year with his mother and father during his formative teenage years.

Unlike many father and son relationships we didn't go fishing or hunting together, and we really didn't get to know one another with the kind of bonding we would have liked. What reassured me though as a parent, was the fact that Danny was progressing smoothly in the amateur hockey ranks.

Then came the big event, the 1978 Amateur Draft. Danny's first choice was to be drafted by Cliff Fletcher in Atlanta. His second choice was any team but one — he did *not* want to play for

Canadiens. "I don't want to go to Montreal," he said, "because I don't need all that pressure of being Boom Boom Geoffrion's son and Howie Morenz's grandson." I could understand that.

For a while it looked like Atlanta might pick him. Then at the last second Fletcher and Irving Grundman of Montreal swapped picks and Canadiens made him their first choice (eighth overall). But the World Hockey Association offered a wonderful alternative, Les Nordiques in nearby Quebec City.

So Danny opted to play for Quebec. He felt he had more of a chance with Nordiques and didn't want people thinking he made the team because of his father. Besides, we loved the way Les Nordiques did business. They flew us up to the old capital in a Learjet and treated us like royalty. Danny and I couldn't have been happier.

For a rookie he had a good year and a good play-off and was looking forward to his second season with Nordiques but there was a problem — the NHL-WHA merger. That gave Canadiens first pick on any number one they had selected in the draft. Danny had no choice but go back to Montreal. Then Irving Grundman offered me the Canadiens' coaching job.

Hollywood would have loved the circumstances: Hall of Famer Boom Boom Geoffrion signs to coach Canadiens. Son Danny signs to play for his dad on his father's and grandfather's team. On paper it looked so wonderful but as usual reality was different.

I could see the pitfalls before I even put my signature on a Montreal contract. Having his father as a coach could do Danny more harm than good and I told him so. "If you don't want me to take the job," I said, "I won't and I'll understand your feelings completely."

Good kid that he is Danny insisted that I fulfill my ambition and take the job. With 20-20 hindsight I now can say it was the worst decision of my life. The rest was the terrible situation I mentioned earlier. And what made it so much more difficult was the inability of my son and me to really communicate about all the problems that we were going through. When all was said and done, because we had been apart for so many years, Danny really didn't know me and I didn't really know him.

As soon as Danny put on the *bleu, blanc et rouge* of Les Canadiens he was acutely aware that he was the coach's son and this affected him in every way. He paid more attention to getting his Canadiens teammates to like him than concentrating on being a major league hockey player. Plus he wanted to be sure that his teammates did-n't view him as a tattletale — the guy who would go running to the coach behind their backs telling him (me) what was going on in the dressing room. Danny wanted to be accepted by all the players which was natural.

It was a terrible situation especially since management, as I said earlier, made it clear to me they didn't want me to use him. This baf-fled Danny because the chief culprit was Claude Ruel, the very same guy who had scouted Danny and recommended him to be drafted.

One incident was a real killer. On this particular night Danny was sitting at the end of the bench with Gilles Lupien, the big defenseman who also got little ice time. We had a power play and I went over and tapped Danny on the back to go out there. I was going against Ruel's wishes but I didn't care.

Danny was shocked because it was a miracle if he got on the ice for a normal shift let alone the power play. So when he went over the boards I could see that he thought the whole world was staring at him and you could hear a pin drop in The Forum. The face-off took place in the other team's end of the rink and the next thing I knew Danny was skating to the boards and climbed over back onto our bench.

"What are you doing here?" I asked him.

"I'm tired," he said.

What he really was tired of was being jerked around and not get-ting the ice time he deserved. And my problem was that I was being the good organization man listening to what the general staff — especially Ruel — was telling me to do and not doing what I knew was the right thing. It was an awful battle that I was fight-ing with myself and my conscience about what to do with my son on my team. Aggravating the situation was the fact that I was never able to fully express my feelings to him at the time. We sim-ply did not have a close enough father-son relationship then for me to convey to Danny all the mental anguish I was feeling for him. I wanted very badly to give him the break he needed and to tell him that, but we simply weren't communicating.

The front office just wouldn't give me the reins and my players knew it just by seeing what was going on from game to game. One night Bob Gainey asked me in front of the whole team, "Who's run-ning this club, you or Ruel?"

That hurt me as much as being forced to keep Danny off the ice. It's difficult to say, even in retrospect, but Gainey's question may have been the straw that broke The Boomer's back as head coach.

The interesting thing is that after I resigned as coach Danny didn't dress for a single game after that. His misery in Montreal ended on October 8, 1980 when the Winnipeg Jets obtained his rights. He was tickled to go to Winnipeg and his new coach Tommy McVie was terrific. He just let him do his thing and Danny finished with 20 goals and 26 assists for 46 points — not bad for a kid who had no goals in Montreal.

But then Tom Watt took over as coach, brought in his own players and Danny was gone. He had one last shot at an NHL job. One of my former Atlanta players Billy MacMillan had become general manager-coach of the New Jersey Devils and invited Danny to training camp.

He did well and New Jersey was ready to give him a contract but Danny still belonged to Winnipeg. My former left wing, John Ferguson, was general manager of the Jets now and he knew the Devils were interested in my boy. You would figure that Fergie would give him a break, right?

Wrong. Fergie wanted compensation for Danny — even though the Jets had long ago given up on him — and New Jersey just wouldn't go for that. That was his last shot at the NHL. "I take 90 percent of the blame," Danny told me, "and the other 10 percent was that I just didn't get the breaks."

He had a great year with Sherbrooke (AHL) in 1982-83, then played a season in Japan. After that he gave up hockey altogether.

"I just didn't bloom in the NHL but the experience made a better man out of me," Danny said. "It was a challenge everyday I was on the ice but now I've put it all behind me."

He meant it too. Danny eventually got into the financial business, as marketing manager for Insurers Premium Finance Company, and moved to Nashville. Maybe he didn't become a Hockey Hall of Famer like his father or grandfather but what he has become is a Hall of Fame son, just like his brother.

"The experiences I had then have made us so close today," said Danny. And he's right. Our family is tighter knit now than it has ever been and that includes my daughter Linda who did what I never thought possible — she married a hockey player just like her mother did! But I'll get to that in a minute.

Linda had me figured out even when she was a kid. She would say that I was, "a lion on the outside and a lamb on the inside." What she meant was that I was a disciplinarian with my children because my father was with me. I never spanked them but I could shape them up just with a stare or eight little words: "I want to talk to you after dinner." When I said that they knew it was trouble and suddenly they weren't hungry anymore.

They were taught discipline and manners and they learned to do the right thing. Maybe it was because I always trusted them, I don't know but they chose not to do stupid things although I wasn't so sure about that when I discovered that Linda was in love with a hockey player!

This is a funny story. I was back in Montreal scouting for the New York Rangers at the start of the 1970s. Watching the juniors was one of my main assignments but naturally I couldn't see every single game. On this night Linda told me that she was going to see the Junior Canadiens play at The Forum.

A couple of fellows from the team, Glenn Griggs and Rob Fee, lived in our neighborhood and were friends of Linda's. They had invited her to the game and when I heard about it I had an idea. "Do me a favor," I said. "Take a pad and a pen and write some notes on the players who look good. I might be able to use them."

Linda did exactly as I told her. When she returned Linda told me about a forward named Hartland Monahan who had scored two goals and was on his way to a hat trick when he broke his wrist. The idea was that I should keep an eye on this kid. (Little did I know that someday he would be my son-in-law!) I said I would.

A week later Linda went to another Junior Canadiens game. After it was over Griggs and Fee introduced her to their teammate with the cast on his wrist. Hartland Monahan asked Linda for her phone number and since he seemed like a gentleman, she gave it to him. Then like a typical 17-year-old she forgot about it.

Two days later the phone rang and she picked it up.

"Linda," the voice said, "you'll never guess who this is?"

"Who?" she said.

"It's number 17 on Montreal Canadiens."

She started to guess who was 17 on the NHL club. "You mean Phil Roberto?" she asked.

"Ah no," the other shot back, "try a lower league; like juniors."

My daughter started thinking. "Oh yeah, you're the guy with that funny name."

That's how their romance began. But the funny thing is that Hartland Monahan had no idea who Linda Geoffrion's father was. Geoffrion is a common name in Montreal and he didn't know that I was *the* Bernard Geoffrion. Linda never wanted her dates to know because she figured that it would either scare them off or that they would want to talk hockey all night.

But a couple of evenings later Hartland had another date with Linda and this time he picked her up at our house. When he rang the bell *the* Bernard Geoffrion answered the door. Monahan looked at me and turned pale. For a second I thought he was going to faint. He seemed to be thinking, "What am I doing here?"

I had his whole pedigree before he walked into the house. My daughter would only be allowed to date a good kid and I had already learned that Hartland was polite and would not be a problem. What I couldn't guess was what kind of player he would be or how serious Linda felt about him.

It didn't take long to find out on either count. Monahan became one of Junior Canadiens' best right wingers and was drafted by the California Golden Seals in the 1971 Amateur Draft (third choice forty-third overall) and in 1971-72 turned pro with Baltimore in the American League.

He was dead serious about hockey — and my daughter.

When Hartland finally asked Linda to marry him she told him straight out that she was an old-fashioned girl from an old-fashioned family. She accepted on the spot because she loved Monahan but that meant nothing until Boomer gave the seal of approval.

Linda knew that that wouldn't be easy. She told him that he had to obtain my personal approval. "You have to get my father to accept you and bless you before we can tie the knot," she said.

On the fateful day, our conference took place in a little office I had in front of our house. Marlene and Linda were very worried that our talk wouldn't go well. Linda loved Hartland and Marlene liked the young man very much. The two of them paced back and forth outside my office like a couple of expectant fathers.

I was very businesslike with my future son-in-law. I took out a legal-sized pad and a pen. Then I began itemizing things. "You've been in the pros for a year," I said, "and you were not a top pick. How much money do you make?"

Item by item I went over his assets and then I pointed out what his responsibilities would be to my daughter and how much money it would cost him to sustain a family after marriage. Years later Hartland told Dad, "Boom, by the time you were done with me I already was in debt and I wasn't even married yet!"

I just wanted to be sure that's all.

An hour later we walked out of the office and Hartland's face looked ashen as if he had just been through a war. In a similar situation another suitor might just as well have said, "See ya later" to Linda and gone after another girl with a less demanding father.

But I could tell how much Hartland wanted her and she wanted him so I shook his hand and said, "We welcome you into the family!"

Linda has really grown up to be a very special daughter. She is so kind and sensitive to others. Even though she has a hectic schedule, she checks daily on Marlene and me by calling or stopping by. We especially love to share Sunday dinners with her family. Linda is the oldest of three and she looks like her mom but has many of my traits, such as being a perfectionist and a "neat freak." She could have been a professional figure skater, she definitely had all the natural abilities. Unfortunately she had to forfeit her dreams because of Bob and Dan's heavy hockey schedules. Linda works for Schultz and Rowson (a dental insurance company) as secretary to the boss, who else? Her husband, Hartland Monahan, works for UPS in Atlanta as an operations supervisior. Hartland has turned out to be a great son-in-law by the way. I could go on about Linda forever. She is one of my favorite subjects and I just want to be sure the world knows I have a wonderful daughter.

Now I have eight grandchildren — Shane, Mechelle, Joey, Brittney, Nicholas, Blake, Sebastian and Brice — who are very near and dear to Marlene and me. Despite all the obstacles encountered over the years we are a more loving, close family today than we ever were when I was winning all those Stanley Cups and Hart Trophies.

I can say for myself and for Marlene that none of this would have been possible had it not been for our rekindled belief in God. This may sound strange to those who knew me as a pretty wild guy with Canadiens but I am a born-again Christian and so is my wife.

How did it happen?

When I was coaching Atlanta one of my defensemen on the Flames was a fellow named Ed Kea whose wife Jennifer was involved with a Bible class. Marlene had nothing to do one day so she accepted Jennifer's invitation and pretty soon she was going to Bible study on a regular basis.

I couldn't blame her. Our marriage was not in the best of shape at the time. My insecurity was bothering me and there were times when the two of us simply couldn't communicate even though we had been married for a long time. The plain fact was that our marriage was slowly but surely going downhill. Each of us was well aware of it but neither of us would dare mention it.

Marlene saved us. The more she went to the Bible classes the more she learned how to make our marriage work. I had become so consumed with coaching that I really didn't pay close attention to what was happening with her until one day Marlene told me that she had turned her life over to the Lord, making her a born-again Christian. "What is that?" I asked.

Marlene replied, "Before, I was spiritually dead to the things of God. Now it's like a spiritual awakening."

I said nothing, after all who would interfere with God?

Then she told me that Jennifer and Ed Kea ran a Monday night Bible study for couples and would I like to go? Actually I wasn't too crazy about the idea and for weeks I made excuses to get out of it.

Meanwhile I kept noticing what a distinctly different person that Kea was compared to the other players. It began to dawn on me that he really *was* different. There was a certain serenity about him that I noticed in various situations; one of which was on our trips out-of-town. When the other players were carrying on during a road trip he would be sitting in his seat on the plane with the Bible in his hand.

From time to time a few of the wise guys on the team would needle him. "What's happening in the Book, Ed?"

This annoyed me. I didn't like the idea that he was being unfairly bugged by the boys. During one trip I got so angry I stood in the aisle of the plane during our flight and gave it to them good. "Maybe if you'd be more like this man," I told them, "I wouldn't have so many problems with you guys."

Kea's behavior impressed me enough that I finally told Marlene I would go to the Bible study with her. Part of my reason for doing this was that I also could see firsthand how dramatically Marlene's disposition was changing for the better.

Then a big event took place that *really* changed our lives. Ed told Marlene about a seminar in Arizona that he thought would interest us. This coincided with an article I had read about how a professional football player named Ron Pritchard had pulled himself out of a serious alcohol problem and now was on the straight and narrow. Although I was hesitant at first, we went to Arizona and the experience was a big breakthrough for me.

It was the very beginning of my spiritual turnaround. Instead of putting me and my job and my hockey first — as I had done for all of my life — I understood that it was time for a 180 degree spiritual turn for The Boomer. There and then I switched to God and knew in my heart of hearts that my wife and children had to top the list immediately after Him. These were my new priorities and they have remained coupled to me ever since.

Significantly Ron Pritchard was at the seminar and after he completed his talk we took a stroll. He asked me if I wanted to accept Christ and I told him that I wanted to wait a little bit and think it over. But Pritchard told me not to delay and at that precise second I was convinced. I have been a different person ever since. And I can safely say that these experiences with the Lord helped not only save our marriage but made it stronger and more loving than ever before.

Thanks to Jesus Christ I have been able to weather some pretty heavy physical and mental storms and so has Marlene. She has had problems with her heart — her aorta valve was replaced and a pacemaker was inserted a couple of years after — and so have I. Among my ailments were prostate cancer and arteriosclerosis in both legs. An operation was successful in one leg but the surgery on the other was not and I still limp a bit.

So even though parts of my body may be getting old I have a brand-new soul and I am a happy man with a great wife, three wonderful kids and eight grandchildren all of whom I adore.

Once upon a time I used to believe that hockey was everything. It isn't. God and family come first. Being happy with the Lord and my family is a lot better than winning 500 Stanley Cups!

When you are flat on your back the only place to look is up — to God. These words come to my mind: "What does it profit man to gain the whole world and suffer the loss of his soul."

My feelings about life can best be summed up in the following poem *God's Hall of Fame* by Walt Huntley.

Your name may not appear down here
  In this world's Hall of Fame;
In fact, you may be so unknown,
  That no one knows your name.
The Oscars here may pass you by,
  And neon lights of blue;
But if you love and serve the Lord,
  Then, I have news for you!
This Hall of Fame is only good
  As long as time shall be;
But keep in mind, God's Hall of Fame

Is for Eternity!
To have your name inscribed up there
  Is greater, yes, by far,
Than all the Halls of Fame down here,
  And every man made star.
This crowd on earth they soon forget
  The heroes of the past,
They cheer like mad until you fall,
  And that's how long you last!
But God, He never does forget,
  And in His Hall of Fame,
By just believing in His Son,
  Inscribed you'll find your name.
I tell you friend, I wouldn't trade
  My name, however small,
That's written there beyond the stars
  In that celestial Hall
For every famous name on earth
  Or glory that they share:
I'd rather be an unknown here,
  And have my name up there!

PLAYING RECORD
Regular Season

Montreal Canadiens

Season	GP	G	A	Pts	PIM
1950-51	18	8	6	14	9
1951-52	67	30	24	54	66
1952-53	65	22	17	39	37
1953-54	54	29	25	54	87
1954-55	70	38	37	75	57
1955-56	59	29	33	62	66
1956-57	41	19	21	40	18
1957-58	42	27	23	50	51
1958-59	59	22	44	66	30
1959-60	59	30	41	71	36
1960-61	64	50	45	95	29
1961-62	62	23	36	59	36
1962-63	51	23	18	41	73
1963-64	55	21	18	39	41

New York Rangers

Season	GP	G	A	Pts	PIM
1966-67	58	17	25	42	42
1967-68	59	5	16	21	11

Play-offs

Montreal Canadiens

Season	GP	G	A	Pts	PIM
1950-51	11	1	1	2	6
1951-52*	11	3	1	4	6
1952-53	12	6	4	10	12
1953-54	11	6	5	11	18
1954-55	12	8	5	13	8
1955-56*	10	5	9	14	6
1956-57*	10	11	7	18	2
1957-58*	10	6	5	11	2
1958-59*	11	5	8	13	10
1959-60*	8	2	10	12	4
1960-61	4	2	1	3	0
1961-62	5	0	1	1	6
1962-63	5	0	1	1	4
1963-64	7	1	1	2	4

* Won Stanley Cup

New York Rangers

Season	GP	G	A	Pts	PIM
1966-67	4	2	0	2	0
1967-68	1	0	1	1	0

NHL Totals

	GP	G	A	P	PIM
Regular Season	883	393	429	822	689
Play-offs	132	58	60	118	88

Individual Honors

1951-52	Calder Trophy	(League Rookie of the Year)
1954-55	Art Ross Trophy	(League Scoring Title)
1960-61	Art Ross Trophy	
1960-61	Hart Trophy	(League Most Valuable Player)
1972	Inducted into Hockey Hall of Fame	

COACHING RECORD

New York Rangers

Season	P	W	L	T
1968-69	43	22	18	3

Atlanta Flames

	P	W	L	T
1972-73	78	25	38	15
1973-74	78	30	34	14
1974-75	52	22	20	10

Montreal Canadiens

	P	W	L	T
1979-80	30	15	9	6

| **Career** | 281 | 114 | 119 | 48 |

INDEX